BELLAM

European Union

2 New York Street
Manchester
M1 4HJ

LNCH- 1b (comp)

BELLAMY & CHILD

European Union Law of Competition

SUPPLEMENT TO THE SEVENTH EDITION

Monckton Chambers

JON TURNER QC

CONSULTANT EDITOR

Monckton Chambers

OXFORD

UNIVERSITY PRESS

OXFORD
UNIVERSITY PRESS

Great Clarendon Street, Oxford, OX2 6DP,
United Kingdom

Oxford University Press is a department of the University of Oxford.
It furthers the University's objective of excellence in research, scholarship,
and education by publishing worldwide. Oxford is a registered trade mark of
Oxford University Press in the UK and in certain other countries

© Oxford University Press 2014

The moral rights of the authors have been asserted

First Edition published in 2014

Impression: 1

Published in the United States of America by Oxford University Press
198 Madison Avenue, New York, NY 10016, United States of America

British Library Cataloguing in Publication Data
Data available

Library of Congress Control Number: 2013958188

ISBN 978–0–19–870783–7

Printed and bound by
Lightning Source UK Ltd

CONTENTS

PREFACE AND HIGHLIGHTS OF THE SUPPLEMENT TO THE 7TH EDITION

Since the 7th Edition of *Bellamy & Child* was published, OUP has launched the online service, *Oxford Competition Law*. This supplement is available in online format, as well as the traditional paper format, together with the 7th Edition itself and the Materials Volume.

We are particularly indebted to the Editors of the 7th Edition, Vivien Rose (now Mrs Justice Rose, Judge of the Chancery Division of the High Court), and David Bailey, for setting aside their time to guide us through the task of updating this comprehensive work. Sincere thanks also go to Andrew Macnab for his ongoing dedication to ensuring that the materials continue to be comprehensive and user-friendly, and to the contributors who have assisted with updates: Alistair Lindsay (Chapter 4), John Boyce, Claire Jeffs and Ingrid Lauwers (Chapter 8), Oke Odudu (Chapter 9), Brendan McGurk (Chapter 10), Ligia Osepciu (Chapter 12), Julianne Kerr Morrison (Chapter 14), and Alan Bates (Chapter 17); and to Ligia Osepciu for her assistance with the judgments which are only available in French. Thanks also go to Ruth Anderson and Francesca Halstead, and their respective teams at Oxford University Press, for their inextinguishable patience, support, and good humour.

We have endeavoured to ensure the updated text is correct as at 31 October 2013, and where possible we have incorporated subsequent judgments handed down in early November. As the updating will be an ongoing exercise, we would be happy for any reader who notices any errors or omissions to contact us in Chambers and draw them to our attention.

The following paragraphs refer to the main developments affecting each chapter of the 7th Edition.

Chapter 1: EU Competition Law and its Territorial Reach   On 1 July 2013, Croatia joined the EU, bringing the number of Member States to 28.

On the Commission's jurisdiction over undertakings established outside the EEA, the General Court dismissed a complaint that the Commission breached the EU's obligations under the Euro-Mediterranean Agreement establishing an association between the EU and their Member States and the Republic of Tunisia (OJ 1998 L97/2), and the principle of international comity, by addressing a decision to an undertaking established in Tunisia: Case T-406/08 *Industries chimiques du fluor v*

Commission, judgment of 18 June 2013 (on further appeal, Case C-467/13P, not yet decided).

The Court of Justice has confirmed that, although it is not always necessary to define the relevant market in order to determine whether there is an appreciable effect on trade between Member States, in the context of verifying whether market share thresholds have been exceeded it is by definition necessary to define the market: Cases C-429/11P *Portielje and Gosselin v Commission*; and C-439/11P *Ziegler v Commission*, judgments of 11 July 2013.

Chapter 2: Article 101(1)   There have been a number of important judgments on the constituent elements of Article 101(1).

On the concept of an 'undertaking', the Court of Justice confirmed in Case C-440/11P *Commission v Portielje and Gosselin*, judgment of 11 July 2013, that if a company holds all the capital, or almost all the capital, in a subsidiary company, that is sufficient basis for the application of the presumption of decisive influence; it is not necessary to consider whether the parent company is also itself engaged in an economic activity and individually constitutes an undertaking, if it is part of the same undertaking as the subsidiary. The Court upheld the Commission's appeal, and overturned the judgment in Cases T-208&209/08 *Gosselin Group v Commission* [2011] ECR II-03639, [2013] 4 CMLR 671 in which the General Court had held that the Commission had not established that a parent company was itself an undertaking, relying on the Court of Justice's conclusion in Case C-222/04 *Cassa di Risparmio* [2006] ECR I-289, [2008] 1 CMLR 705 that mere holding of shares is not itself an economic activity. The Court of Justice also confirmed, in Cases C-179/12P *Dow Chemical Company v Commission*, and C-172/12P *El du Pont de Nemours v Commission*, judgments of 26 September 2013, that two parent companies, and the joint venture in which they each have a 50 per cent shareholding, can be considered to be a single undertaking for the purposes of establishing liability for participation in an infringement of competition law, provided that the factual evidence demonstrates the actual exercise of decisive influence.

On the concept of 'concerted practices', the General Court's judgments in the appeals against the Commission's decision in COMP/38698 *CISAC Agreements*, decision of 16 July 2008, are particularly significant. The General Court considered that the Commission did not have sufficient evidence to establish a concerted practice, and held that the need for the collecting societies to monitor the use of copyrighted material provided a plausible explanation for their parallel behaviour. The decision was therefore partially annulled: Cases T-392, 398, 401, 410, 411, 413–422, 425, 428, 432–434, 442/08, judgments of 12 April 2013.

The Court of Justice considered further the concept of a single and continuous infringement in Case C-441/11P *Commission v Verhuizingen Coppens*, judgment of 6 December 2012, [2013] 4 CMLR 312, where it held that if an undertaking did not participate in the single and continuous infringement found by the Commission, it must still be held liable for the parts of the infringing behaviour in which it did participate.

The Court of Justice and the General Court have considered several cases on 'object' infringements, including the Court of Justice's judgments in Case C-32/11 *Allianz Hungária Bistozitó*, judgment of 14 March 2013 (vertical agreements that were likely to affect two markets); and Case C-68/12 *Protimonopolný úrad v Slovenská sporitel'ňa*, judgment of 7 February 2013, [2013] 4 CMLR 491 (an agreement intended to exclude a competitor that had been operating illegally on the market); as well as the General Court's judgments in the appeals against the decisions in COMP/39188 *Bananas*, decision of 15 October 2008 (Cases T-587/08 *Fresh Del Monte Produce v Commission*, and T-588/08 *Dole Food Company v Commission*, judgments of 14 March 2013 (on further appeal Cases C-293 & 294/13P *Fresh Del Monte Produce*, and C-286/13P *Dole Food Company*, not yet decided)); and in the appeals against the *CISAC* decision, finding that the membership and exclusivity clauses in the societies' model contract were a restriction by object: for example, Case T-401/08 *Säveltäjäin Tekijänoikeustoimisto Teosto v Commission*, judgment of 12 April 2013, [2013] 5 CMLR 15.

On the concept of 'appreciability', the judgment in Case C-226/11 *Expedia Inc*, judgment of 13 December 2012, [2013] 4 CMLR 439 confirms that, although NCAs may take account of the market share thresholds set by the Commission's *De Minimis* Notice when determining whether an agreement has an appreciable effect on competition, they are not required to do so. The Court also held that an agreement that may affect trade between Member States and that has an anti-competitive object constitutes, by its nature and independently of any concrete effects that it may have, an appreciable restriction of competition. The Commission is currently consulting on a revised *De Minimis* Notice to take account of this judgment.

The Commission decision in COMP/39839 *Telefónica and Portugal Telecom*, decision of 23 January 2013, is of particular interest in respect of ancillary restraints (on appeal, Cases T-208/13 *Portugal Telecom v Commission*, and T-216/13 *Telefonica v Commission*, not yet decided).

Chapter 3: Article 101(3)   The General Court has dismissed a number of appeals against decisions in which the Commission concluded that the criteria of Article 101(3) were not met. The Article 101(3) analysis in the Commission's *CISAC* decision was upheld in Case T-451/08 *Föreningen Svenska Tonsättares Internationella Musikbyrå*, judgment of 12 April 2013 (the only judgment in which the finding of a concerted practice was upheld, and in which the Court therefore went on to consider the application of Article 101(3)); the analysis in the *Bananas* decision was upheld in Cases T-587/08 *Fresh Del Monte Produce v Commission*, and T-588/08 *Dole Food Company v Commission*, judgments of 14 March 2013 (on further appeal Cases C-293 & 294/13P *Fresh Del Monte Produce*, and C-286/13P *Dole Food Company*, not yet decided); and the analysis in COMP/38606 *Cartes*

Bancaires, decision of 17 October 2007 in Case T-491/07 *CB v Commission*, judgment of 29 November 2012.

The Commission has also concluded in COMP/39839 *Telefónica and Portugal Telecom*, decision of 23 January 2013, that the requirement of indispensability is not met (on appeal, Cases T-208/13 *Portugal Telecom v Commission* and T-216/13 *Telefónica v Commission*, not yet decided).

Chapter 4: Market Definition   The Court of Justice's judgment in Case C-457/10P *AstraZeneca v Commission*, judgment of 6 December 2012, [2013] 4 CMLR 233, upholds the General Court's conclusions on market definition in the context of its dominance analysis. In Case C-439/11P *Ziegler v Commission*, judgment of 11 July 2013, the Court has confirmed that it is necessary to define the relevant market in order to apply a market share criterion (in that case, to determine whether there was an appreciable effect on trade between Member States in that market).

In addition, two decisions in the merger field that contain detailed market definition analyses have been published: M.5830 *Olympic/Aegean Airlines* (26 January 2011); and M.6166 *Deutsche Börse/NYSE Euronext* (1 February 2012).

Chapter 5: Cartels   The discussion in the main text of the Commission's decision in *Bananas*—in particular, in section 1(c) of Chapter 5 on arguments typically used to justify cartels, and section 2 on prices and pricing restrictions—should now be read alongside the General Court's judgments in Case T-587/08 *Del Monte Fresh Produce v Commission*, judgment of 14 March 2013; and Case T-588/08 *Dole Food Company v Commission*, judgment of 14 March 2013, which uphold the Commission's analysis on liability (on further appeal Cases C-293 & 294/13P *Fresh Del Monte Produce*, and C-286/13P *Dole Food Company*, not yet decided).

The General Court has confirmed that where an alleged cartel includes an exchange of commercially sensitive information, it is necessary that the recipient of the information be active on the cartelised market, such that there is potential for that recipient to modify its behaviour as a result of receiving the information, in order for the exchange to breach Article 101. It distinguished its judgment in Joined Cases T-456&457/05 *Gütermann and Zwicky v Commission* [2010] ECR II-1443, relied upon by the Commission, which it held would apply to a disclosure of commercially sensitive information with a view to restricting competition in the market on which the recipient of the information is active, by a disclosing party that is not itself active on that market, whereas in the decision under appeal, COMP/39092 *Bathroom Fittings*, decision of 23 June 2010, the Commission had (as the Court held, wrongly) found that the purpose of the disclosure was to restrict competition in a market on which the disclosing party was active but the recipient was not: Case T-380/10 *Wabco Europe v Commission (Bathroom Fittings)*, judgment of 16 September 2013, paras 79 and 98–99; and Joined Cases T-379&381/10

Keramag Keramische Werke and Others (Bathroom Fittings) v Commission, judgment of 16 September 2013, paras 92 and 221.

In the UK, the cartel offence in s 188 of the Enterprise Act 2002 has been amended by the Enterprise and Regulatory Reform Act 2013, which will enter force in April 2014.

Chapter 6: Non-Covert Horizontal Cooperation   The discussion in the main text of the Commission's decision in *Bananas* should be read alongside the General Court's judgments in Case T-587/08 *Del Monte Fresh Produce v Commission*, judgment of 14 March 2013; and Case T-588/08 *Dole Food Company v Commission*, judgment of 14 March 2013 (on further appeal Cases C-293 & 294/13P *Fresh Del Monte Produce*, and C-286/13P *Dole Food Company*, not yet decided). The discussion of the *Cartes Bancaires* decision in section 9(b) of Chapter 6 on agreements in the banking and payments services sector should be read alongside the General Court's judgment in Case T-491/07 *CB v Commission*, judgment 29 November 2012.

On the concept of unlawful 'information exchanges', as noted above in respect of Chapter 5, the General Court held in Case T-380/10 *Wabco Europe v Commission (Bathroom Fittings)*, judgment of 16 September 2013, paras 79 and 98–99; and Joined Cases T-379&381/10 *Keramag Keramische Werke and Others (Bathroom Fittings) v Commission*, judgment of 16 September 2013, paras 92 and 221, that there will only be a breach of Article 101 where the recipient of the information is active on the relevant market.

The UK Competition Appeal Tribunal judgment in *Tesco v OFT* [2012] CAT 31 discusses the state of mind required to satisfy the test laid down by the Court of Appeal in *Argos, Littlewoods v OFT and JJB v OFT* [2006] EWCA Civ 1318, for unlawful 'hub and spoke' arrangements.

There have been a number of developments in the banking and payments services sector, discussed in section 9(b) of Chapter 6. Regulation 260/2012 establishing technical and business requirements for credit transfers and direct debits in euro and amending Regulation 924/2009, OJ 2012 L94/22, was adopted on 12 March 2012 and requires a move to the new Single Euro Payment Area systems established by the European Payments Council. The Commission also adopted on 24 July 2013 a legislative package which includes a proposed revised Directive on payment services in the internal market (COM(2013) 547 final, 2013/0264 (COD)) and a proposed Regulation on interchange fees for card-based payment transactions (COM(2013) 550 final, 2013/0265 (COD)). At the time of writing, a number of investigations are also ongoing in the sector, including into the setting of benchmark interest rates for interest rate derivative trading; COMP/39745 *CDS – Information Market* in which a statement of objections has been issued (Press Release IP/613/630 (1 July 2013)); COMP/39730 *CDS – Clearing*; and

COMP/39398 *Visa MIF* in which the Commission is consulting on proposed commitments (MEMO 13/431 (14 May 2013)). The Court of Justice's eagerly awaited judgment in Case C-382/12 *MasterCard Europe v Commission*, on the lawfulness of MasterCard's cross-border interchange fee arrangements, is pending.

Chapter 7: Vertical Agreements Affecting Distribution or Supply   On the issue of sales by a distributor via the internet, the Irish High Court in *SRI Apparel v Revolution Workwear and others* [2013] IEHC 289 held that the use by a distributor of the website Amazon was active selling rather than passive, and that an agreement to restrict such activity was within the scope of Article 4(b)(i) of the Vertical Block Exemption. The Office of Fair Trading has concluded in its decision in CE/9578-12 'Roma-branded mobility scooters: prohibitions on online sales and online price advertising', decision of 5 August 2013, that an agreement or concerted practice in which a manufacturer prevented the distributors in its selective distribution system from selling its products online, or advertising their prices online, was a restriction of competition by object.

The Commission has accepted commitments in COMP/39847 *E-books*, decision of 12 December 2012 (OJ 2012 C283/7) and of 25 July 2013 (Press Release IP/13/746 (25 July 2013)) from five publishing companies, and Apple, under which they have agreed to terminate their agency agreements, which the Commission considered in its preliminary assessment were entered into on a coordinated basis in order to implement a common strategy in the EEA. Under the commitments, the publishers are required to allow retailers full discretion to set their e-book prices for at least two years, and not to enter into most favoured nation clauses for five years.

Chapter 8: Merger Control   The General Court judgment in Case T-332/09 *Electrabel v Commission*, judgment of 12 December 2012, rules for the first time on a Commission decision to impose a fine for implementing a concentration without prior notification and approval. The judgment in particular considers various arguments said to bear upon the proportionality of the fine, and holds that the Commission was correct to conclude that a failure to notify is a serious infringement of EU merger law.

The Court of Justice has given judgments in the parallel appeals in *Éditions Odile Jacob*, regarding the significance of warehousing arrangements for the clearance of concentrations, and the role of trustees in approving purchasers of divested assets. In Case C-551/10P, judgment of 6 November 2012, [2013] 4 CMLR 11 the Court dismissed the appeal regarding the clearance of the concentration (Case T-279/04 *Éditions Odile Jacob v Commission* [2010] ECR II-0185), and held that even if the General Court had erred in its conclusion that the transaction was within Article 3(5)(a) Merger Regulation, that does not bear upon whether the concentration is compatible with the common market, only upon whether the notification was late or the concentration implemented prematurely. In Cases C-553 & 554/10P *Commission v Éditions Odile Jacob*, judgment of 6 November

2012, [2013] 4 CMLR 55, the Court disagreed with Advocate General Mazák and upheld the General Court judgment regarding the approval of a purchaser of the assets to be divested (Case T-452/04 *Éditions Odile Jacob SAS v Commission* [2010] ECR II-4713). The Court discusses the requirement for trustees to be independent, and confirms that any lack of independence does not need to be shown to have affected a trustee's choice of purchaser for its decision to be annulled.

The Commission has issued two prohibition decisions since the main text was published: M.6570 *UPS/TNT Express* (30 January 2013) (on appeal, Case T-194/13 *United Parcel Service v Commission*, not yet decided); and M.6663 *Ryanair/Aer Lingus III* (27 February 2013) (on appeal, Case T-260/13 *Ryanair v Commission*, not yet decided). It has also accepted a failing firm defence in M.6360 *Nynas/Shell/ Harburg* (2 September 2013); and M.6796 *Aegean /Olympic II* (9 October 2013).

The Commission has published for consultation a set of proposals for simplifying procedures under the Merger Regulation. The proposals include a draft Regulation amending the Implementing Regulation, and draft revised annexes, including a revised Form CO, Short Form, Form RS, and a revised Simplified Procedures Notice. They are discussed in detail in the updates, but the most significant changes proposed include revising the categories of cases in which the simplified procedure is available, and redefining what is considered to be an 'affected market'. The Commission also proposes to encourage parties voluntarily to submit a description of the data that each of the undertakings collects and holds in cases where a quantitative economic analysis of the affected markets is likely to be useful, and voluntarily to submit a list of any non-EEA competition authorities that are also reviewing the concentration and to waive confidentiality to allow the Commission to engage in discussions with those authorities.

Chapter 9: Intellectual Property Rights   The politically charged issue of moving towards harmonisation of the laws governing intellectual property rights took a step forward in Cases C-274 & 295/11 *Spain & Italy v Council*, judgment of 16 April 2013, in which the Court of Justice has upheld the legality of the Council's decision authorising the use of the enhanced cooperation procedure in Article 20 TEU in the area of the creation of a unitary patent (Council Decision 2011/167/ EU of 10 March 2011).

The General Court's judgments in the appeals against the Commission's *CISAC* decision, and the Court of Justice's judgment in Case C-457/10P *AstraZeneca*, judgment of 6 December 2012, [2013] 4 CMLR 233, are particularly significant in respect of the application of competition law to intellectual property rights. In addition, the Court of Justice has given two significant judgments on the interpretation of Article 3(1) of the Copyright Directive: it has clarified that the concept of 'communication to the public' in Article 3(1) is limited to situations where the public is not present at the place where the performance or direct presentation takes place (Case C-283/10 *Circul Globus București*, [2011] ECR I-12031), and it has considered the application of Article 3(1) to a company that captures television broadcasts and retransmits them via the internet in real-time, holding that the original broadcast does not exhaust the right to communicate to the public and retransmission via the internet constitutes a 'communication to the public' within Article 3(1) that the rights holder is entitled to prohibit (Case C-607/11 *ITV Broadcasting and others*, judgment of 7 March 2013, [2013] 3 CMLR 1).

The Commission has continued to monitor patent settlements between originator and generics companies following its pharmaceutical sector inquiry, and it published its Third Report of 25 July 2012, in respect of the period January to December 2011. It has issued a decision in COMP/39226 *Lundbeck* (Press Release IP/13/563 (19 June 2013)). In its ongoing investigation into the enforcement of standard essential patents, statements of objections have been sent in COMP/39939 *Samsung – enforcement of ETSI standards essential patents* (Press Release IP/12/1448 (21 December 2012)); and COMP/39985 *Motorola – enforcement of ETSI standards essential patents* (Press Release IP/13/406 (6 May 2013)).

Chapter 10: Article 102   The Court of Justice has considered a number of issues relating to the interaction between Article 102 and intellectual property rights in Case C-457/10P *AstraZeneca*, judgment of 6 December 2012, [2013] 4 CMLR 233. On the issue of dominance, the Court discusses the arguments raised as to the relevance of a patent holder's first-mover status, its financial resources, and its intellectual property rights, as well as the relevance of the powers of the State as a monopsonist purchaser and as a price regulator. On the issue of abuse, the Court considers the circumstances in which an undertaking abuses its dominant position by making objectively wrong representations to patent offices. While it leaves open the question of where the line should be drawn between abusive and non-abusive behaviour, it confirms that deliberately to mislead patent authorities is abusive, whereas innocently to misrepresent is not, provided that the representations are withdrawn immediately upon the undertaking realising that they are not correct.

In England and Wales, the Competition Appeal Tribunal has considered how to quantify damages caused by margin squeeze in *Albion Water v Dŵr Cymru's Cyfyngedig* [2013] CAT 6. The Tribunal rejected Dŵr Cymru's argument that it had to determine the highest price that could lawfully have been charged, and held that a counterfactual should be constructed using a figure in the middle of the range of potential lawful prices.

On the issue of refusal to satisfy demand for parallel trade, the High Court in *Chemistree Homecare v Abbvie* [2013] EWHC 264 (Ch) considered the test laid down in Cases C-468/06, etc, *Sot Lelos kai Sia v GlaxoSmithKline* [2008] ECR I-7139 of whether orders are 'ordinary'. It held that where a pharmaceutical company organises its business around supplying only to retailers, orders placed by a customer for the undisclosed purpose of reselling the product on the wholesale market are not ordinary (upheld on other grounds by the Court of Appeal,

Chemistree Homecare v Abbvie [2013] EWCA Civ 1338, concluding that dominance could not be established).

Chapter 11: The Competition Rules and the Acts of Member States   The Commission has issued a new Staff Working Document on the interaction between Article 106(2), State aid, and public procurement '*Guide to the application of the European Union rules on state aid, public procurement and the internal market to services of general economic interest, and in particular to social services of general interest*'.

Chapter 12: Sectoral Regimes   In the field of electronic communications, the Court of Justice has confirmed that Member States may lawfully impose spectrum use renewal fees under the Authorisation Directive (Case C-375/11 *Belgacom v Belgium*, judgment of 21 March 2013). The Commission has considered a number of significant mergers, including a full-function JV established by three of the leading UK MNOs (M.6314 *Telefónica UK/Vodafone UK/EE/JV* (4 September 2012), creating a JV to operate in the nascent 'mCommerce' sector), and a merger of two of Austria's four leading MNOs (M.6497 *Hutchinson 3G Austria/Orange Austria* (12 December 2012)). In *Recall Support Services Ltd et al v Secretary of State for Culture, Media and Sport* [2013] EWHC 3091 (Ch) the High Court held that the UK's decision to impose a specific licence requirement, going beyond a general authorisation, on the commercial provision of communications services to multiple users through GSM gateway devices was justified on grounds of public security.

In the energy sector, the Commission has accepted commitments in COMP/39727 *CEZ* that include CEZ divesting itself of generation capacity, and it has initiated a number of investigations into undertakings operating in the sector in Eastern Europe: COMP/39816 *Upstream gas supplies in Central and Eastern Europe*, Press Release IP/12/937 (4 September 2012); COMP/39767 *BEH*, Press Release IP/12/1307 (3 December 2012); and COMP/39984 *Romanian Power Exchange*, Press Release IP/13/486 (30 May 2013). In the postal sector, the Commission has prohibited a proposed merger in M.6570 *UPS/TNT Express* (30 January 2013), and in the transport sector two significant developments are the adoption of Directive 2012/34/EU establishing a single European railway area, and the Commission's confirmation that it will not renew the Maritime Transport Guidelines which expired on 26 September 2013.

Chapter 13: Enforcement and Procedure   The impact of the entry into force of the Charter on Fundamental Rights, following the Lisbon Treaty, has begun to be reflected in the judgments handed down in appeals raising procedural questions. A number of cases have considered the application of Articles 41 and 47 of the Charter in particular: see, for example, Case C-501/11P *Schindler v Commission (Elevators and Escalators)*, judgment of 18 July 2013 (the imposition of fines by the Commission, rather than by a court, is compatible with Article 47); Case C-439/11P *Ziegler v Commission*, judgment of 11 July 2013 (it is the principle of good administration in Article 41 that applies to administrative proceedings before the Commission); and Case C-199/11 *Europese Gemeenschap v Otis*, judgment of 6 November 2012, [2013] 4 CMLR 141 (there is no breach of Article 47 if the Commission brings a civil action in a Member State to seek to recover the damages it has itself suffered as a result of a cartel).

The General Court has considered a number of cases on the Commission's exercise of powers of inspection under Article 20 of Regulation 1/2003, and the reviewability of its exercise of those powers. In Case T-135/09 *Nexans and Nexans France v Commission*, judgment of 14 November 2012, [2013] 4 CMLR 195 it held that Article 20(2) contains powers to take measures to implement inspection decisions, such as copying documents and asking representatives of the investigated undertaking for explanations of facts and documents, and that the exercise of one of these powers does not have binding legal effects, separate from the inspection decision. As such, the exercise of these powers cannot itself be the subject of an annulment application before the General Court, but can only be examined in the context of an appeal against an infringement decision under Article 101, or an appeal against a decision imposing a penalty for refusing to cooperate with the inspection. In Case T-410/09 *Almamet v Commission*, judgment of 12 December 2012, [2013] 4 CMLR 788 the General Court further held that if the Commission has followed the procedures in Article 20 for gathering evidence, it is only the addressee from whom evidence has been gathered who can complain of irregularities in the way in which the process has been carried out. In respect of Article 20(4), the General Court accepted in Joined Cases T-289/11, etc, *Deutsche Bahn and others v Commission*, judgment of 6 September 2013, that the exercise of the Commission's powers of inspection under Article 20(4) is a 'clear interference' with the right to respect for private and family life under Article 8 ECHR / Article 7 Charter of Fundamental Rights, but held that the absence of a requirement for prior judicial authorisation does not render it a disproportionate interference.

On the ability of non-addressees to challenge Commission decisions, the General Court judgment in T-442/08 *International Confederation of Societies of Authors and Composers (CISAC) v Commission*, judgment of 12 April 2013 stands in contrast with the approach taken by the General Court in Case T-358/06 *Wegenbouw-maatschappij J. Heijmans v Commission*, Order of 4 July 2008. Like Heijimans, CISAC was an addressee of the Commission's statement of objections, but not of the decision. Unlike Heijimans, CISAC is a non-profit non-governmental organisation whose principal task is representing the entities that were addressed by the Commission decision, and facilitating cooperation between them. In *CISAC* the General Court considered that the decision was of direct and individual concern to CISAC, as its activities would be relevant to assessing whether the addressees were bringing to an end the concerted practice found in the decision, and as the decision affected its role as a facilitator of cooperation (particularly in mediating between the societies on issues relating to the grant of multi-territorial licences).

On the admissibility of evidence in proceedings before the Courts, the General Court has drawn a distinction between the admissibility of evidence in the context of a review of an infringement decision, and in the context of a review of the amount of a penalty. A document on which the Commission did not rely in its decision is inadmissible for the purposes of the substantive review of legality, but it can be taken into account in the exercise of the Court's unlimited jurisdiction regarding fines: Case T-462/07 *Galp Energía España v Commission*, judgment of 16 September 2013.

The judgment in Case C-441/11P *Commission v Verhuizingen Coppens*, judgment of 6 December 2012, [2013] 4 CMLR 312 considers the question of partial annulment/severance in circumstances where the Commission has found a single and continuous infringement.

The Commission exercised its power under Article 23(2)(c) of Regulation 1/2003 for the first time in COMP/39530 *Microsoft – Tying*, decision of 6 March 2013, for Microsoft's failure to comply with the commitments decision of 16 December 2009. It imposed a fine of €561 million.

Chapter 14: Fines for Substantive Infringements   Significant judgments have been given by the Court of Justice on the procedure for reviewing the Commission's decisions on fines. It has confirmed that the 2006 Fining Guidelines do not impose a more onerous obligation on the Commission to state reasons for its fining decisions than did the 1998 Guidelines (Cases C-444/11P *Team Relocations v Commission* and C-439/11P *Ziegler v Commission*, judgments of 11 July 2013). It has also held that the 'manifest error' test, applied by the General Court to reviewing the exercise of the Commission's discretion to assess an undertaking's cooperation under the Leniency Notice, does not meet the requirements of Article 47 of the Charter. The General Court cannot rely on the Commission's margin of discretion as a basis for not conducting an in-depth review of the law and facts (Case C-510/11P *Kone v Commission*, judgment of 24 October 2013).

The Court of Justice and General Court have considered a substantial number of substantive appeals against the fines imposed by the Commission. Of particular interest are the following:

The General Court has confirmed that an undertaking's value of sales within the EEA can be determined by reference to its sales invoiced in the EEA, rather than sales delivered in the EEA, provided that that reflects the reality of the market: Case T-146/09 *Parker ITR and Parker-Hannifin v Commission (Marine Hoses)*, judgment of 17 May 2013, [2013] 5 CMLR 712.

In Case T-566/08 *Total Raffinage Marketing v Commission (Candle Waxes)*, judgment of 13 September 2013, paras 549 et seq, the General Court held that the Commission must comply with the principle of equal treatment in determining the multiplier for duration, and that a practice of rounding part years to the nearest whole number can breach the principle of equal treatment by treating the different situations of undertakings in the same way.

In Case C-508/11P *Commission v Eni*, judgment of 8 May 2013, [2013] 5 CMLR 607 the Court of Justice considered the requirements which the Commission must meet if it is to impose an uplift for recidivism. The Commission has issued a second statement of objections, providing the explanation of the capacity in which the undertakings concerned were considered to have participated in previous infringements, held by the Courts to have been lacking from its previous decision.

On the issue of parental liability, which continues to be raised in a large proportion of the cases considered by the General Court, the Court of Justice confirmed in Joined Cases C-628/10P & 14/11P *Alliance One v Commission*, judgment of 19 July 2012, [2012] 5 CMLR 738 that there would be a breach of the principle of equal treatment if the Commission relied on evidence of actual exercise of decisive influence in order to attribute responsibility to some parent companies, but sought to rely solely on the presumption of decisive influence as a basis for attribution in respect of others. In Case C-286/11P *Commission v Tomkins*, judgment of 22 January 2013, [2013] 4 CMLR 466, it held that where a parent company's liability is wholly derived from that of its subsidiary, and where both companies have brought actions before the European Courts seeking a reduction in their fines on the same basis (in this case, on the basis of the duration of the infringement), then the fine imposed on the parent company can be recalculated on account of the outcome of the appeal by the subsidiary. It is not necessary for the scope of their actions, or the arguments deployed, to be identical. In Case T-343/06 *Shell Petroleum v Commission*, judgment of 27 September 2012, [2012] 5 CMLR 1064 the General Court upheld the Commission's conclusion that conduct could be attributed to a parent company which held only 40 per cent of the shares in the infringing subsidiary, because at the time of the infringement the subsidiary was owned by two parent companies, both within the Shell undertaking, and the Court agreed that the situation was analogous to that in which a single parent company fully controls the subsidiary.

On the issue of inability to pay, the Court of Justice in Case C-439/11P *Ziegler v Commission*, judgment of 11 July 2013 considered the Commission's powers under paras 35 and 37 of the Fining Guidelines to reduce the amount of the fine. In addition, the General Court considered the issue of inability to pay and the impact of the Commission deciding to reduce the fine imposed on one among several undertakings on that basis, but not the others, in the appeals against the Commission's decision in COMP/39396 *Calcium carbide and magnesium based reagents*, decision of 22 July 2009 (Case T-410/09 *Almamet v Commission*, judgment of 12 December 2012, [2013] 4 CMLR 788; Case T-352/09 *Novácke chemické závody v Commission*, judgment of 12 December 2012, [2013] 4 CMLR 734; and Case T-392/09 *1. garantovaná v Commission*, judgment of 12 December 2012).

The ECN has issued a revised Model Leniency Programme. The main changes are that all undertakings applying to the Commission for leniency in cases concerning more than three Member States will be able to submit a summary application to national competition authorities, where previously only the first applicant, ie the immunity applicant, was entitled to use summary applications under the model leniency programme; and the ECN has agreed on a standard template for summary applications, which can be used in all Member States.

Chapter 15: The Enforcement of the Competition Rules by National Competition Authorities   Litigants have continued to dispute whether, and if so at what point, national proceedings should be stayed pending investigations by the Commission, and appeals to the European courts by the addressees of Commission decisions. On the issue of the impact of pending Commission investigations, the Court in *Secretary of State for Health v Servier* [2012] EWHC 2761 (Ch) granted a stay until after the oral hearing before the Commission in COMP/39612 *Perindopril (Servier)*, but refused to extend the stay until a decision was issued; the Court in *Infederation v Google* [2013] EWHC 2295 (Ch) refused a stay other than on one issue and otherwise ordered disclosure while the Commission investigation in COMP/39740 *Google* is ongoing. On the impact of pending appeals to the European courts, in *WM Morrison Supermarkets v Mastercard & Ors* [2013] EWHC 1071 (Comm) the High Court followed *National Grid* and refused to stay damages proceedings that were brought in reliance on the decision in COMP/34579 *Mastercard I*, decision of 19 December 2007; and in *CDC Project 14 v Shell & Ors*, judgment of 1 May 2013, Case No C/09/414499/HA ZA 12-293, the District Court of the Hague refused to stay proceedings before pleadings had closed in a claim brought in reliance on the decision in COMP/39181 *Candle Wax*, decision of 1 October 2008.

In addition, as part of the ongoing modernisation of the State aid regime, the Commission has been given powers to transmit information, or opinions, to national courts considering State aid cases in the same way as under Article 15 of Regulation 1/2003 in Article 101/102 cases: Regulation 734/2013, amending Regulation 659/99, adopted on 22 July 2013 (OJ 2013 L204/15). This is discussed in the updates to Chapter 17.

Chapter 16: Litigating Infringements in the National Courts   There have been a number of significant legislative developments in the field of private enforcement of competition law. A recast Brussels Regulation ('Brussels II'; Regulation 1215/2012) was adopted on 20 December 2012, and will apply from January 2015. On 16 June 2013 the Commission adopted a proposal for a Directive on certain rules governing actions for damages under national law for infringements of the competition law provisions of the Member States and of the European Union (COM(2013) 404 final, COD 2013/0185) ('Draft Damages Directive'), and alongside it a Communication on quantifying harm in actions for damages based on breaches of Article 101 or 102 TFEU (COM(2013) 3440, OJ 2013 C167/19), and an accompanying Practical Guide on quantifying harm in actions for damages based on breaches of Article 101 and 102 TFEU (SWD(2013) 205). On 11 June 2013, it also adopted a Recommendation on common principles for injunctive and compensatory collective redress mechanisms in the Member States concerning violations of rights granted under Union law, OJ 2013 L201/60. In the United Kingdom, the draft Consumer Rights Bill 2013 was published on 12 June 2013, which includes proposals to confer on the Competition Appeal Tribunal power to grant injunctions, to introduce mechanisms for collective redress, and to align the time limits for bringing damages claims in the Competition Appeal Tribunal with those in the High Court.

Questions have continued to arise on the application of Brussels I to cross-border competition cases. In *Deutsche Bahn v Morgan Crucible* [2013] EWCA Civ 1484 (refusing permission to appeal in a reasoned judgment by two Lord Justices) the Court of Appeal dismissed an argument that damage suffered by indirect purchasers was not capable of founding jurisdiction under Article 5(3). In *Bord Na Mona Horticulture v British Polythene Industries* [2012] EWHC 3346 (Comm) the High Court considers the 'centre of interest' for the purposes of Article 5(3), and the application of Article 6 where the action against an anchor defendant is inadmissible. On the nature of the cause of action, the Court of Appeal in *W H Newson Holding & Ors v IMI and Ors* [2013] EWCA Civ 1377 confirmed that proceedings in England and Wales do not have to be brought as a claim for breach of statutory duty, and that a claim could be available for the tort of unlawful means conspiracy, provided the requisite element of subjective intent to cause loss could be established. That could be problematic in a case brought in the Competition Appeal Tribunal, where the requisite intent would have to be established on the basis of the Commission's decision alone, and also in a case where there is a real possibility of pass-on of any overcharge.

The Competition Appeal Tribunal's judgment in *Albion Water v Dŵr Cymru Cyfyngedig* [2013] CAT 6 is a useful, detailed illustration of the quantification of competition law damages. Following its earlier judgments finding that Dŵr Cymru had engaged in unfair pricing and margin squeeze, the Tribunal determined what non-abusive price would have been charged absent the abusive conduct (a figure in the middle of a range of lawful prices, not the highest that could lawfully have been charged) and fed that price into a detailed counterfactual that looked at what Albion's input costs would have been, and what price it could have charged its customers. The Tribunal also allowed Albion to recover for the loss of a chance to bid successfully on an additional contract, although it rejected the claim for exemplary damages.

Chapter 17: State Aid   The State aid modernisation programme has continued apace. On 22 July 2013, the Council adopted Regulation 733/2013, amending Regulation 994/98 (the Enabling Regulation) and increasing the categories of aid in respect of which the Commission is able to adopt block exemption regulations (OJ 2013 L217/28) and Regulation 734/2013, amending Regulation 659/99 (the Procedural Regulation) (OJ 2013 L204/15). Significant reforms include powers for the Commission to request information from Member States other than the notifying Member State, or from an undertaking or association of undertakings; to conduct sector inquiries in the same way as in Article 101/102 cases; and to transmit information, or opinions, to national courts in the same way as under Article 15 of Regulation 1/2003 in Article 101/102 cases. The Commission has also published for consultation a new general *De Minimis* Regulation, which would introduce a safe harbour provision for loans below €1 million repayable within five years. As to the Commission's guidelines, it adopted on 19 June 2013 new Guidelines on regional State aid for 2014–2020 (OJ2013 C209/1); on 19 December 2012 a new Communication on Short-term Export-credit Insurance (OJ 2012 C392/1); on 26 January 2013 new guidelines on the application of State aid rules in relation to the rapid deployment of broadband networks (OJ 2013 C25/1); and on 13 November 2013 a new Communication on the criteria for assessing State aid for films and other audiovisual works (OJ 2013 C332/1). It has also published for consultation new guidelines on State aid to airports and airlines, and for rescuing and restructuring non-financial undertakings in difficulty.

The Court of Justice has considered several cases on the constituent elements of a State aid, including the application of the market economy investor principle to partial payment of tax debts (Case C-73/11P *Frucona Košice v Commission*, judgment of 24 January 2013); the engagement of state resources where an offer of a shareholder loan is made publicly, to the undertaking's economic advantage, but is never actually taken up (Cases C-399/10P & C-401/10P *Bouygues Télécom v Commission*, judgment of 19 March 2013); the degree of discretion that can be granted to authorities in determining whether to grant the benefit of a tax exemption if that exemption is not to be considered selective (Case C-6/12 *P Oy*, judgment of 18 July 2013); and the provision of support for the construction of infrastructure (Case C-288/11P *Mitteldeutsche Flughafen and Flughafen Leipzig-Halle v Commission*, judgment of 19 December 2012).

On the role of Member States in recovering unlawfully paid aid, the Court of Justice has imposed a fine of €20 million on Spain for its long-standing failure to recover aid that the Court ordered ten years previously it should recover, and a daily fine of €50,000 until it is recovered (Case C-610/10 *Commission v Spain*, judgment of 11 December 2012).

Laura Elizabeth John, Editor

Jon Turner QC, Consultant Editor

15 November 2013

ALPHABETICAL TABLE OF EU CASES AND DECISIONS

TABLE OF EUROPEAN COURT OF HUMAN RIGHTS AND NATIONAL CASES

1

EU COMPETITION LAW AND ITS TERRITORIAL REACH

1. Introduction

Plan of this Chapter. There are now 28 Member States, Croatia having joined **1.002**
the EU on 1 July 2013.

2. The EU Treaties

The Charter of Fundamental Rights. The Court of Justice held that the **1.008**
Commission is bound by Article 41 of the Charter on Fundamental Rights
when conducting investigations into potential breaches of competition law: Case
C-439/11P *Ziegler v Commission*, judgment of 11 July 2013, para 154.

3. EU Competition Law

(c) The interpretation of the EU competition rules

The effectiveness of the competition rules. **1.020**
Fn 70 See also Case C-536/11 *Bundeswettbewerbsbehörde v Donau Chemie*, judgment of 6 June 2013, [2013] 5 CMLR 658.

(d) The EU Competition Rules

Articles 107–109. Regulation 994/98, which enables the Commission to adopt **1.028**
block exemption regulations for State aids, was amended on 22 July 2013 by
Council Regulation 733/2013: OJ 2013 L217/28. On the same day Regulation
659/99 which sets out general procedural rules for State aid notifications was
amended by Regulation 734/2013: OJ 2013 L204/15. The amendments are discussed in detail in the updates to paragraphs 17.070 and 17.075, below.

(e) Other provisions of the TEU and TFEU

1.038 **Other relevant Treaty provisions.** The Commission's decision in COMP/38698 *CISAC Agreements*, decision of 16 July 2008, [2009] 4 CMLR 577, has been partially annulled by the General Court: Cases T-392, 398, 401, 410, 411, 413–422, 425, 428, 432–434, 442/08, judgments of 12 April 2013. Only one appellant contended that the Commission had erred in its conclusions as to the impacts of the territorial restrictions in the licences on cultural diversity, and this appeal was dismissed: Case T-451/08 *Föreningen Svenska Tonsättares Internationella Musikbyrå*, judgment of 12 April 2013, [2013] 5 CMLR 577, paras 73 et seq (this appellant had not pleaded that the Commission had insufficient evidence to establish a concerted practice, which was the argument which succeeded in the other appeals).

4. The Institutional Structure of the EU

(a) The EU institutions

1.041 **The official languages of the EU.** Following Croatia's joining the EU, on 1 July 2013, there are 24 official languages of the EU, Croatian having been added.

1.042 **The European Parliament.** Following Croatia's joining the EU on 1 July 2013, and as at 31 October 2013, membership of the European Parliament stood at 766.

1.044 **The European Commission.** Following Croatia's joining the EU on 1 July 2013, and as at 31 October 2013, there are 28 members of the Commission.

(c) The EU and EFTA Courts

1.050 **The Court of Justice of the European Union.** Following Croatia's joining the EU on 1 July 2013, there are 24 official languages of the EU.

(d) The Directorate-General for Competition

(iii) Enforcement through investigation and decision

1.071 **The European Competition Network.**
Fn 263 In respect of the NCAs applying the procedures and powers provided by national law when applying Articles 101 and 102 TFEU, see also the ECN's Report on Investigative Powers and Report on Decision-Making Powers, both of 31 October 2012, which contain comparative analyses of the enforcement powers conferred on NCAs in different Member States, and identify areas of divergence; available on the ECN section of the DG Comp website.

Fn 264 A revised Model Leniency Programme, available on the ECN section of the DG Comp website, was issued in November 2012, in particular to extend the concept of summary applications to NCAs to all leniency applicants, not just the first to approach the Commission.

Enforcement by national courts.   As well as asking the Commission for informa-   **1.072**
tion or its opinion on questions concerning the application of Articles 101 and 102, national courts may now also ask the Commission for information or its opinion on questions concerning the application of Articles 107 or 108 TFEU: Regulation 734/2013, amending Regulation 659/99 and adding Article 23(a): OJ 2013 L204/15.

(v) Guidelines and guidance

Legal status of Commission notices and guidelines.   **1.076**
Fn 283 The Court of Justice held in Case C-226/11 *Expedia Inc*, judgment of 13 December 2012, [2013] 4 CMLR 439, para 31, that a national competition authority 'may take into account' the Commission's *De Minimis* Notice, but 'it is not required to do so'.

5. Territorial Ambit of EU Competition Rules

(a) The Member States: enlargement

Becoming 27 Member States.   Following Croatia's joining the EU on 1 July   **1.086**
2013, there are now 28 Member States.

Candidate countries.   Croatia joined the EU on 1 July 2013.   **1.087**

(c) EFTA and the EEA

Allocation of jurisdiction under the EEA Agreement.   **1.095**
Fn 351 The Commission's decision in COMP/38698 *CISAC Agreements*, deci-sion of 16 July 2008, [2009] 4 CMLR 577, has been partially annulled by the General Court, on other grounds: Cases T-392, 398, 401, 410, 411, 413–422, 425, 428, 432–434, 442/08, judgments of 12 April 2013.

(d) Agreements between the EU and third countries

Competition cooperation agreements with other States.   The EU has con-   **1.102**
cluded a fifth cooperation agreement on competition matters, with the Swiss Confederation, subject to ratification: see Press Release IP/13/444 (17 May 2013).

Association agreements between the EU and other states.   **1.104**
Fn 405 The General Court dismissed a complaint that the Commission deci-sion in COMP/39180 *Aluminium Fluoride*, decision of 25 June 2008, was issued in breach of the EU's obligations under Article 36 of the Euro-Mediterranean Agreement establishing an association between the European Communities and

3

their Member States, of the one part, and the Republic of Tunisia, of the other part (OJ 1998 L 97/2): see T-406/08 *Industries chimiques du fluor v Commission*, judgment of 18 June 2013 (on further appeal, Case C-467/13P, not yet decided), paras 208 et seq.

6. The Territorial Jurisdiction of the EU Institutions

(c) Jurisdiction over undertakings outside the EU

1.115 **Agreements involving undertakings located in third countries.** The General Court dismissed a complaint that the Commission's decision in COMP/39180 *Aluminium Fluoride*, decision of 25 June 2008, which was addressed to an undertaking established in Tunisia, was issued in breach of the EU's obligations under Article 36 of the Euro-Mediterranean Agreement establishing an association between the European Communities and their Member States, of the one part, and the Republic of Tunisia, of the other part (OJ 1998 L 97/2): see Case T-406/08 *Industries chimiques du fluor v Commission*, judgment of 18 June 2013 (on further appeal, Case C-467/13P, not yet decided), paras 208 et seq.

Fn 447 Two of the appeals against COMP/398181 *Candle Waxes*, decision of 1 October 2008, were largely dismissed: Cases T-548/08 *Total v Commission*, judgment of 13 September 2013; and T-566/08 *Total Raffinage Marketing*, judgment of 13 September 2013 (fine reduced on grounds of duration). The other appeals are still pending.

1.117 **International comity.** The General Court dismissed a complaint that the Commission decision in COMP/39180 *Aluminium Fluoride*, decision of 25 June 2008, which was addressed an to undertaking established in Tunisia, was issued in breach of the EU's obligations under Article 36 of the Euro-Mediterranean Agreement establishing an association between the European Communities and their Member States, of the one part, and the Republic of Tunisia, of the other part (OJ 1998 L 97/2) and of international comity: see Case T-406/08 *Industries chimiques du fluor v Commission*, judgment of 18 June 2013 (on further appeal, Case C-467/13P, not yet decided), paras 208 et seq.

7. Effect on Trade between Member States

(a) Generally

1.123 Trade
Fn 472 The Court of Justice in Case C-440/11P *Commission v Portielje and Gosselin*, judgment of 11 July 2013, upheld the Commission's appeal on

other grounds, and has overturned the General Court judgment in Cases T-208&209/08 *Gosselin Group v Commission* [2011] ECR II-03639, [2013] 4 CMLR 671. The appeal, also on other grounds, in Case C-429/11P *Portielje and Gosselin v Commission*, judgment of 11 July 2013, was dismissed.

Fn 478 The Commission's decision in COMP/38698 *CISAC Agreements*, decision of 16 July 2008, [2009] 4 CMLR 577, has been partially annulled by the General Court, on other grounds: Cases T-392, 398, 401, 410, 411, 413–422, 425, 428, 432–434, 442/08, judgments of 12 April 2013.

Fn 487 See also Case C-1/12 *Ordem dos Técnicos Oficiais de Contas v Autoridade da Concorrência*, judgment of 28 February 2013, [2013] 4 CMLR 651 regarding the professional services of chartered accountants.

Potential effect. 1.128
Fn 520 The Court of Justice has dismissed the appeal on other grounds in Case C-181/11P *Compañía española de tabaco en rama v Commission*, judgment of 12 July 2012.

Indirect effects. 1.129
Fn 533 The Court of Justice has dismissed the appeal on other grounds in Case C-181/11P *Compañía española de tabaco en rama v Commission*, judgment of 12 July 2012.

Application of the 'NAAT-rule'. 1.132
Fn 547 On the requirement to define the relevant market for these purposes, see also Cases C-429/11P *Portielje and Gosselin v Commission*; and C-439/11P *Ziegler v Commission*, judgments of 11 July 2013; in particular see para 65 of *Portielje and Gosselin*, and para 63 of *Ziegler*.

Fn 549 The Court of Justice dismissed the further appeal in Case C-439/11P *Ziegler v Commission*, judgment of 11 July 2013.

Fn 550 The Court of Justice dismissed the further appeal in Case C-439/11P *Ziegler v Commission*, judgment of 11 July 2013. The Commission requested that the Court substitute new grounds for the General Court's judgment insofar as it held that turnover generated as a subcontractor could be excluded for these purposes (para 35) but the Court held there was no need to rule on this request (para 89).

NAAT-rule is a rebuttable presumption. In respect of NCAs and national 1.133
courts not being bound by the Commission's guidance documents, the Court of Justice has confirmed, on the preliminary reference from the French Cour de Cassation, that although NCAs may take account of the market share thresholds set by the Commission's *De Minimis* Notice when determining whether an agreement has an appreciable effect on competition, they are not required to do so: Case C-226/11 *Expedia Inc*, judgment of 13 December 2012, [2013] 4 CMLR 439, para 31.

1.134 **Presumption of appreciable effect in relation to certain agreements.** The Court of Justice in Cases C-429/11P *Portielje and Gosselin v Commission*; and C-439/11P *Ziegler v Commission*, judgments of 11 July 2013, held that the Commission had in fact provided a sufficiently detailed description of the services with which its decision was concerned to constitute a definition of the market for these purposes (paras 67–73 of *Portielje and Gosselin* and paras 71–77 of *Ziegler*), and in any event it considered that there were factors including in particular the geographic scope of the cartel and the cross-border nature of the services affected that supported the conclusion that there was an appreciable effect on trade (para 99).

(b) **Particular aspects of effect on trade**

1.136 Effect of conduct in Article 102 cases.

Fn 562 The Court of Justice in Case C-457/10P *AstraZeneca v Commission*, judgment dated 6 December 2012, [2013] 4 CMLR 233, has upheld the General Court's judgment and dismissed the further appeals.

2

ARTICLE 101(1)

2. Undertakings

(a) Generally

Economic activity.   **2.005**
Fn 13 The Court of Justice confirmed, in Case C-288/11P *Mitteldeutsche Flughafen and Flughafen Leipzig Halle v Commission*, judgment of 19 December 2012, [2013] 2 CMLR 483, the General Court's conclusion in Joined Cases T-443&455/08 *Freistaat Sachsen and Land Sachsen-Anhalt v Commission* [2011] ECR II-1311, that the operation of an airport constitutes an economic activity (such that financial assistance granted to enable the building of an additional runway at the airport could constitute a State aid).

Fn 15 The Court of Justice upheld the Commission's appeal in Case C-440/11P *Commission v Portielje and Gosselin*, judgment of 11 July 2013, paras 41–46, and overturned the General Court judgment in Cases T-208&209/08 *Gosselin Group v Commission* [2011] ECR II-03639, [2013] 4 CMLR 671: see the update to paragraph 2.011, below. The appeal in Case C-429/11P *Portielje and Gosselin v Commission*, judgment of 11 July 2013, was dismissed.

Individuals as undertakings.   Chartered accountants have also been held to be   **2.010**
undertakings, see C-1/12 *Ordem dos Técnicos Oficiais de Contas v Autoridade da Concorrência*, judgment of 28 February 2013, [2013] 4 CMLR 651, para 38.

Shareholders as undertakings.   The Court of Justice upheld the Commission's   **2.011**
appeal in Case C-440/11P *Commission v Portielje and Gosselin*, judgment of 11 July 2013, and overturned the General Court judgment in Cases T-208&209/08 *Gosselin Group v Commission* [2011] ECR II-03639, [2013] 4 CMLR 671. The Court confirmed that if a company holds all the capital, or almost all the capital, in a subsidiary company that is sufficient basis for the application of the presumption of decisive influence (para 41). It is not relevant to consider whether the parent company is also itself engaged in an economic activity and individually constitutes an undertaking, if it is part of the same undertaking as the subsidiary

(paras 42–46). The Court also overturned the General Court's conclusion that Portielje had rebutted the presumption of decisive influence (paras 65–73). The appeal in Case C-429/11P *Portielje and Gosselin v Commission*, judgment of 11 July 2013, was dismissed.

(b) The State as an undertaking

2.020 **Regulatory bodies.** See also Case C-1/12 *Ordem dos Técnicos Oficiais de Contas v Autoridade da Concorrência*, judgment of 28 February 2013, [2013] 4 CMLR 651, paras 46 et seq, regarding the body that regulates chartered accountants in Portugal.

(c) Treatment of economically linked legal entities

2.027 **Parent company and partly-owned subsidiaries.** The General Court in Case T-587/08 *Fresh Del Monte Produce*, judgment of 14 March 2013, [2013] 4 CMLR 1091, upheld the Commission's decision in COMP/39188 *Bananas*, decision of 15 October 2008, discussed in the main text, in which the Commission held Del Monte liable for the conduct of Weichert: paras 50 et seq (although it reduced the fine; see the update to paragraph 14.063, below). On further appeal, Cases C-293 & 294/13P, not yet decided.

2.028 **Parent companies and joint ventures.** The Court of Justice dismissed the further appeals against the Commission's decision in COMP/38629 *Chloroprene Rubber*, decision of 5 December 2007 (at footnote 118 of the main text), in Cases C-179/12P *Dow Chemical Company v Commission*; and C-172/12P *El du Pont de Nemours v Commission*, judgments of 26 September 2013. Provided the factual evidence demonstrates the actual exercise of decisive influence, there is no error of law in holding two parent companies and the joint venture in which they each have a 50 per cent shareholding to be a single undertaking for the purposes (and only for the purposes) of establishing liability for participation in an infringement of competition law: see in particular *Dow*, para 58 and *du Pont*, para 47.

3. Agreements, Decisions and Concerted Practices

(a) Agreements

2.035 **Agreements may be informal.** The General Court upheld the Commission's decision in COMP/38698 *CISAC Agreements*, decision of 16 July 2008, insofar as it found the membership clause in the collecting societies' agreements infringed Article 101: Cases T-392, 401, 422, 432/08, judgments of 12 April 2013, [2013] 5 CMLR 15. It partially annulled the decision on other grounds in Cases T-392, 398, 401, 410, 411, 413–422, 425, 428, 432–434, 442/08, judgments of 12 April 2013.

Agreements may be incomplete. **2.036**
Fn 160 Two of the appeals against COMP/398181 *Candle Waxes*, decision of 1 October 2008, were dismissed: Cases T-548/08 *Total v Commission*, judgment of 13 September 2013, paras 210–214; and T-566/08 *Total Raffinage Marketing*, judgment of 13 September 2013, paras 163 et seq (fine reduced on grounds of duration). The other appeals (Cases T-540/08, etc, not yet decided) are still pending.

Authority to enter into agreements. In Case T-146/09 *Parker ITR and* **2.038** *Parker-Hannifin v Commission (Marine Hoses)*, judgment of 17 May 2013, [2013] 5 CMLR 712, paras 151 et seq, the General Court held that the fact that an individual established a fraudulent scheme to allow him, and the companies which he controlled or to which he was linked, to benefit from the illegal gains of the cartel, did not affect the undertaking's liability for the infringement found in COMP/39406 *Marine Hoses*, decision of 28 January 2009, since the individual was authorised to act on the undertaking's behalf irrespective of whether he was acting with its knowledge (on further appeal, Case C-434/13P *Commission v Parker Hannifin Manufacturing and Parker-Hannifin*, not yet decided).

Fn 166 See also Case C-68/12 *Protimonopolný úrad v Slovenská sporitel'ňa*, judgment of 7 February 2013, [2013] 4 CMLR 491, para 28, where the Court of Justice held 'it is not necessary to demonstrate personal conduct on the part of a representative authorised under the undertaking's constitution or the personal assent, in the form of a mandate, of that representative to the conduct of an employee of the undertaking who has participated in an anti-competitive meeting'.

Fn 168 Two of the appeals against COMP/398181 *Candle Waxes*, decision of 1 October 2008, on other grounds were largely dismissed: Cases T-548/08 *Total v Commission*, judgment of 13 September 2013; and T-566/08 *Total Raffinage Marketing*, judgment of 13 September 2013 (fine reduced on grounds of duration). The other appeals (Cases T-540/08, etc, not yet decided) are still pending.

Incorporation of terms in an agreement. **2.043**
Fn 191 The General Court upheld the Commission's decision in COMP/38698 *CISAC Agreements*, decision of 16 July 2008, insofar as it found the membership clause in the collecting societies' agreements infringed Article 101: Cases T-392, 401, 422, 432/08 judgments of 12 April 2013, [2013] 5 CMLR 15. It partially annulled the decision on other grounds in Cases T-392, 398, 401, 410, 411, 413–422, 425, 428, 432–434, 442/08, judgments of 12 April 2013.

Infringement actions and rights delimitation agreements. On the application **2.047** of Article 101 to agreements settling infringement actions, see the Commission's enforcement action in the pharmaceutical sector following the sector inquiry report (discussed in paragraph 9.061 of the main text). The Commission has initiated enforcement proceedings against several originator companies and the generic companies with which they entered patent settlement agreements: it has issued a decision against Lundbeck and four groups of generics companies for 'reverse' settlement agreements reached in respect of the drug citalopram in COMP/39226 *Lundbeck*: see Press Release IP/13/563 (19 June 2013). The decision is under appeal: Cases T-460/13, etc, not yet decided. Investigations are ongoing in COMP/39612 *Perindopril (Servier)*; and COMP/39685 *Johnson & Johnson and Novartis*. The enforcement action taken by the Commission since the sector inquiry report is summarised in MEMO/12/593 (25 July 2012). Similar concerns regarding patent settlements have arisen in the United States, and the US Supreme Court judgment in *Federal Trade Commission v Actavis and others*, of 17 June 2013, 570 U.S. (2013), has clarified that in the United States a 'rule of reason' approach is to be applied to antitrust scrutiny of such agreements, that is, the courts will consider in the light of all the relevant facts and circumstances whether a particular agreement has overall pro-competitive or anti-competitive effects on the relevant market (see further paragraphs 2.104 et seq of the main text).

On the application of Article 102, see also the Commission's ongoing investigation into alleged abusive conduct in relation to intellectual property rights used in international telecoms standards. The Commission has issued statements of objection to Samsung and Motorola: see Press Release IP/12/1448 (21 December 2012) regarding COMP/39939 *Samsung – enforcement of ETSI standards essential patents*; and Press Release IP/13/406 (6 May 2013) regarding COMP/39985 *Motorola – enforcement of ETSI standards essential patents*. Its preliminary view is that it is an abuse of dominance, contrary to Article 102, for the holder of a standard essential patent to seek injunctions for patent infringement in circumstances where it has given a commitment that it will grant licences on fair, reasonable, and non-discriminatory ('FRAND') terms and where the potential licensee has agreed to accept a binding determination of the terms of a FRAND licence by a third party. At the time of writing, the Commission is consulting on commitments proposed by Samsung under which it would agree, in essence, for a period of five years not to seek an injunction before any court or tribunal in the EEA for infringement of its standard essential patents (including all existing and future patents) implemented in smartphones and tablets against a potential licensee that agrees to, and complies with, a particular framework for determining the terms of a licence: see OJ (2013) C302/11.

The Landgericht of Düsseldorf has referred to the Court of Justice for a preliminary ruling various questions concerning the circumstances in which it is an abuse for an undertaking to seek an injunction for breach of its standard essential patent: Case C-170/13 *Huawei Technologies v ZTE*, not yet decided.

2.049 **Terminated or 'spent' agreements.** The General Court upheld the Commission's decision in COMP/38698 *CISAC Agreements*, decision of 16 July 2008, discussed in the main text, insofar as it found the exclusivity clause in the collecting societies' agreements infringed Article 101: Case T-401/08 *Säveltäjäin Tekijänoikeustoimisto*

Teosto v Commission, judgment of 12 April 2013, [2013] 5 CMLR 15. It partially annulled the decision on other grounds in Cases T-392, 398, 401, 410, 411, 413–422, 425, 428, 432–434, 442/08, judgments of 12 April 2013.

Fn 212 See also Case C-70/12P *Quinn Barlo v Commission* ('*Methacrylates*'), judgment of 30 May 2013, [2013] 5 CMLR 637, para 40, in which the Court of Justice held that an infringement may be found throughout the period in which unlawful prices were applied by an undertaking even though the unlawful contacts formally have come to an end.

Judicial settlements and compromise of litigation. As part of the Commission's **2.050** ongoing enforcement action following the pharmaceutical sector inquiry, it has issued a decision against Lundbeck and four groups of generics companies for 'reverse' settlement agreements reached in respect of the drug Citalopram in COMP/39226 *Lundbeck*: see Press Release IP/13/563 (19 June 2013). The decision is under appeal: Cases T-460/13, etc, not yet decided. Investigations are ongoing in COMP/39612 *Perindopril (Servier)*; and COMP/39685 *Johnson & Johnson and Novartis*.

Agreements made prior to date of accession to the EU. Two of the appeals **2.054** against COMP/398181 *Candle Waxes*, decision of 1 October 2008, on other grounds, were largely dismissed: Cases T-548/08 *Total v Commission*, judgment of 13 September 2013; and T-566/08 *Total Raffinage Marketing*, judgment of 13 September 2013 (fine reduced on grounds of duration). The other appeals (Cases T-540/08, etc, not yet decided) are still pending.

(b) Concerted practices

Generally.   **2.055**
Fn 245 The General Court upheld the Commission's decision in COMP/39188 *Bananas*, decision of 15 October 2008, finding an unlawful concerted practice: Case T-587/08 *Fresh Del Monte Produce v Commission*, judgment of 14 March 2013, [2013] 4 CMLR 1091 (reducing the fine but dismissing the appeal on liability), paras 295 et seq; and Case T-588/08 *Dole Food Company v Commission*, judgment of 14 March 2013, paras 53 et seq. On further appeal, Cases 293&294/13P *Fresh Del Monte Produce v Commission*, not yet decided; and Case 286/13P *Dole Food Company v Commission*, not yet decided.

Concertation or cooperation between undertakings.   **2.058**
Fn 265 The General Court upheld the Commission's decision in COMP/39188 *Bananas*, decision of 15 October 2008, applying the judgment in *British Sugar* discussed in the main text (Case T-202/98, etc, *Tate & Lyle v Commission* [2001] ECR II-2035), in Case T-587/08 *Fresh Del Monte Produce v Commission*, judgment of 14 March 2013, [2013] 4 CMLR 1091 (reducing the fine but dismissing the appeal on liability), para 369; and Case T-588/08 *Dole Food Company v Commission*,

judgment of 14 March 2013, para 403. On further appeal, Cases 293&294/13P *Fresh Del Monte Produce v Commission*, not yet decided; and Case 286/13P *Dole Food Company v Commission*, not yet decided.

2.061 **The presumption may apply to a meeting on a single occasion.**   The General Court has applied the approach set out by the Court of Justice in *T-Mobile* discussed in the main text (Case C-8/08 *T-Mobile Netherlands v Commission* [2009] ECR I-4529, [2009] 5 CMLR 11) in its judgments upholding the Commission's decision in COMP/39188 *Bananas*, decision of 15 October 2008: see Case T-587/08 *Fresh Del Monte Produce v Commission*, judgment of 14 March 2013, [2013] 4 CMLR 1091 (reducing the fine but dismissing the appeal on liability), paras 351–352; and Case T-588/08 *Dole Food Company v Commission*, judgment of 14 March 2013, paras 368 et seq. On further appeal, Cases 293&294/13P *Fresh Del Monte Produce v Commission*, not yet decided; and Case 286/13P *Dole Food Company v Commission*, not yet decided.

2.063 **Proof of a concerted practice.**
Fn 282 See also the General Court's approach in its judgments partially annulling the Commission's decision in COMP/38698 *CISAC Agreements*, decision of 16 July 2008, in which it had found an unlawful concerted practice: for example, Case T-442/08 *CISAC v Commission*, judgment of 12 April 2013, [2013] 5 CMLR 536, paras 92–94.

2.065 **Relying on conduct as evidence of a concerted practice.**   The Commission's decision in COMP/38698 *CISAC Agreements*, decision of 16 July 2008, discussed in the main text has been partially annulled by the General Court: Cases T-392, 398, 401, 410, 411, 413–422, 425, 428, 432–434, 442/08, judgments of 12 April 2013. It held that the Commission did not have sufficient evidence to establish the existence of a concerted practice, and that the need for monitoring the use of copyrighted material did provide a plausible explanation for the parallel behaviour of collecting societies within the EEA.

2.066 **Alternative explanations for parallel behaviour.**   See also the General Court's judgments partially annulling the Commission's decision in COMP/38698 *CISAC Agreements*, decision of 16 July 2008, discussed in the update to paragraph 2.065, above.

2.067 **Disclosure of pricing information from retailers to suppliers.**   The state of mind required to satisfy the test laid down by the Court of Appeal in *Argos & Littlewoods and JJB Sports v Office of Fair Trading* [2006] EWCA Civ 1318, para 140, was discussed at length by the Competition Appeal Tribunal in *Tesco v OFT* [2012] CAT 31. At stage (i) it is not sufficient to show that retailer A knew supplier B 'might' pass on the information (para 78), and the Tribunal expressed doubts as to whether anything short of intention or actual foresight that supplier B will pass on the information will suffice (paras 350–354).

Concerted practices in vertical relationships.   The Commission's decisions in   **2.069**
COMP/39847 *E-Books*, decisions of 12 December 2012 (OJ 2012 C283/7) and
of 25 July 2013 (Press Release IP/13/746 (25 July 2013)), illustrate that as well as
a supplier entering into a concerted practice with one or more of its customers,
a concerted practice can also arise between multiple suppliers and a single distributor. The Commission accepted commitments from five publishing companies
and Apple in respect of their arrangements for the sale of electronically formatted
books. The publishing companies had each entered into agreements with Apple
(having also discussed the arrangements between themselves) under which Apple
acted as their sales agent and the publishers agreed to particular pricing terms.
The Commission's preliminary assessment was that the publishers and Apple had
engaged in a concerted practice of moving from a wholesale arrangement to an
agency arrangement, with a view either to raising the retail price of e-books or to
avoiding the emergence of lower prices (in particular, to eliminate price competition between Apple and Amazon).

(c) Single continuous infringement

Concept of a single continuous infringement.   **2.071**
Fn 330 The Court of Justice has dismissed the appeals in Case C-457/10P
AstraZeneca v Commission, judgment of 6 December 2012, [2013] 4 CMLR 233.

Fn 334 The Court of Justice in Case C-441/11P *Commission v Verhuizingen
Coppens*, judgment of 6 December 2012, [2013] 4 CMLR 312 reversed the
General Court's judgment annulling the Commission's decision in COMP/38543
International Removals Services, decision of 11 March 2008. It held that even though
Coppens did not participate in the single and continuous infringement found by the
Commission, the General Court erred in annulling the decision entirely. It was to
be annulled only in respect of the infringing behaviour in which Coppens had not
engaged, and in respect of the attribution of a single and continous infringement.

Single continuous infringement: requisite elements.   The characterisation of an   **2.073**
infringement as single and continuous does not relieve the Commission of the
obligation to demonstrate that the various agreements and concerted practices
constituting that single and continuous infringement themselves restricted competition: Case T-380/10 *Wabco Europe v Commission (Bathroom Fittings)*, judgment of 16 September 2013, para 92.

Fn 341 The Court of Justice dismissed the further appeal in Case C-444/11P
Team Relocations v Commission, judgment of 11 July 2013.

Overall plan.   The General Court upheld the Commission's conclusion in   **2.074**
COMP/398181 *Candle Waxes*, decision of 1 October 2008, that there was a single and continuous infringement across two different product markets, where
those product markets were vertically related. Slack wax is the raw material used

in the manufacture of paraffin wax, and the anti-competitive agreement in respect of the upstream product was intended to strengthen the agreement in respect of the downstream product: Case T-566/08 *Total Raffinage Marketing*, judgment of 13 September 2013, paras 270–273 (fine reduced on grounds of duration). The appeal, on other grounds, was dismissed in Case T-548/08 *Total v Commission*, judgment of 13 September 2013, and the other appeals against the decision (Cases T-540/08, etc, not yet decided) are still pending.

The General Court has also upheld the Commission's conclusion in COMP/39092 *Bathroom Fittings*, decision of 23 June 2010, that there was a single and continuous infringement across three different product markets where those product markets were for complementary products: Case T-378/10 *Masco and others v Commission*, judgment of 16 September 2013, paras 56 et seq, and 115–116. The General Court noted in particular that the products were sold to a common customer base within the same distribution system, that the undertakings concerned belonged to umbrella associations and cross-product associations, and that the unlawful practices were implemented using the same methods, at the same time, in each of the three markets.

Fn 345 The Court of Justice dismissed the further appeal in Case C-444/11P *Team Relocations v Commission*, judgment of 11 July 2013.

2.075   **Intentional contribution to the overall plan.**
Fn 350 See, however, the General Court's judgments in Case T-380/10 *Wabco Europe v Commission (Bathroom Fittings)*, judgment of 16 September 2013; and Joined Cases T-379&381/10 *Keramag Keramische Werke and Others (Bathroom Fittings) v Commission*, judgment of 16 September 2013. Where the alleged cartel includes an exchange of commercially sensitive information, it is necessary that the recipient of the information be active on the cartelised market, such that there is potential for that recipient to modify its behaviour as a result of receiving the information, in order for the exchange to infringe Article 101. The Court emphasised at para 79 of *Wabco* that:

> 'it cannot be presumed that an agreement or a concerted practice whereby under-takings exchange information which is commercially sensitive but which relates to a product sold on a market on which they are not competitors has an anti-competitive object or effect on that market. A practice whereby an undertaking which is active on two distinct product markets provides to its competitors – which are present on one market – commercially sensitive information which relates to a second market – on which those competitors are not present – is not capable, in principle, of having an impact on competition on the second market.'

The Court held that its judgment in Joined Cases T-456&457/05 *Gütermann and Zwicky v Commission* [2010] ECR II-1443, relied upon by the Commission, would apply to a disclosure of commercially sensitive information with a view to restricting competition in the market on which the recipient of the information is active, by a disclosing party that is not itself active on that market; whereas in the decision under appeal, COMP/39092 *Bathroom Fittings*, decision of 23 June 2010, the Commission had (as the Court held, wrongly) found that the purpose of the disclosure was to restrict competition in a market on which the disclosing party was active but the recipient was not: see paras 98–99. See also Joined Cases T-379&381/10 *Keramag Keramische Werke and Others (Bathroom Fittings) v Commission*, judgment of 16 September 2013, paras 92 and 221.

Fn 351 See also Case C-444/11P *Team Relocations v Commission*, judgment of 11 July 2013, para 52.

Fn 353 The Court of Justice in Case C-441/11P *Commission v Verhuizingen Coppens*, judgment of 6 December 2012, [2013] 4 CMLR 312 reversed the General Court's judgment annulling the Commission's decision in COMP/38543 *International Removals Services*, decision of 11 March 2008. It held that even though Coppens did not participate in the single and continuous infringement found by the Commission, the General Court erred in annulling the decision entirely. It was to be annulled only in respect of the infringing behaviour in which Coppens had not engaged, and in respect of the attribution of a single and continous infringement. In contrast, in Case C-444/11P *Team Relocations v Commission*, judgment of 11 July 2013, the Court of Justice dismissed the appeal against the finding of a single and continuous infringement in the *International Removals Services* decision as against Team Relocations, because the General Court had found on the facts of that case that Team Relocations was aware of the infringing behaviour in which it did not participate.

Fn 354 Two of the appeals against COMP/398181 *Candle Waxes*, decision of 1 October 2008, on other grounds, were largely dismissed: Cases T-548/08 *Total v Commission*, judgment of 13 September 2013; and T-566/08 *Total Raffinage Marketing*, judgment of 13 September 2013 (fine reduced on grounds of duration). The other appeals (Cases T-540/08, etc, not yet decided) are still pending.

Awareness.   In Case T-378/10 *Masco and others v Commission*, judgment **2.076** of 16 September 2013, paras 61–62 and 82, the General Court upheld the Commission's conclusion in COMP/39092 *Bathroom Fittings*, decision of 23 June .2010, that where undertakings are members of umbrella associations, or cross-product associations, they must be considered to have been aware of the infringing behaviour taking place in the product markets in which they were not themselves active.

The General Court upheld the Commission's decision in COMP/39188 *Bananas*, decision of 15 October 2008, in Case T-587/08 *Fresh Del Monte Produce v Commission*, judgment of 14 March 2013, [2013] 4 CMLR 1091 (reducing the fine but dismissing the appeal on liability); and Case T-588/08 *Dole Food Company v Commission*, judgment of 14 March 2013. On further appeal, Cases 293&294/13P *Fresh Del Monte Produce v Commission*, not yet decided; and Case 286/13P *Dole Food Company v Commission*, not yet decided.

Fn 359 The Commission's conclusion at para 252 of the decision in COMP/39188 *Bananas*, decision of 15 October 2008, was upheld on appeal by the General Court in Case T-587/08 *Fresh Del Monte Produce v Commission*, judgment 14 March 2013, [2013] 4 CMLR 1091, paras 586 et seq. On the facts, although the decision found the producer Chiquita was aware of the bilateral discussions between the other producers Dole and Weichert, it had found that there was not sufficient evidence to conclude Weichert was aware of discussions between Chiquita and Dole (Commission decision paras 254–258). The decision could not be interpreted therefore as attributing responsbility to Weichert for the infringement as a whole: para 646. On further appeal, Cases 293&294/13P *Fresh Del Monte Produce v Commission*, not yet decided.

Fn 362 In respect of the cases noted in the footnote, the Court of Justice, disagreeing with Advocate General Mengozzi's Opinion of 28 February 2013, dismissed the Commission's appeal in Case C-287/11P *Aalberts Industries v Commission* ('*Copper Fittings*') judgment of 4 July 2013, [2013] 5 CMLR 867, paras 37–45. It also dismissed the further appeal in Case C-70/12P *Quinn Barlo v Commission* ('*Methacrylates*'), judgment of 30 May 2013, [2013] 5 CMLR 637.

In addition, the Court of Justice in Case C-441/11P *Commission v Verhuizingen Coppens*, judgment of 6 December 2012, [2013] 4 CMLR 312 reversed the General Court's judgment annulling the Commission's decision in COMP/38543 *International Removals Services*, decision of 11 March 2008. It held that even though Coppens did not participate in the single and continuous infringement found by the Commission, the General Court erred in annulling the decision entirely. It was to be annulled only in respect of the infringing behaviour in which Coppens had not engaged, and in respect of the attribution of a single and continous infringement. In contrast, in Case C-444/11P *Team Relocations v Commission*, judgment of 11 July 2013, the Court of Justice dismissed the appeal against the finding of a single and continuous infringement in the *International Removals Services* decision as against Team Relocations, as the General Court had found on the facts of that case that Team Relocations was aware of the infringing behaviour in which it did not participate.

2.077 **Evidence of participation.**
Fn 365 The Court of Justice dismissed the further appeal in Case C-70/12P *Quinn Barlo v Commission* ('*Methacrylates*'), judgment of 30 May 2013, [2013] 5 CMLR 637. See also the update to paragraph 2.075, above, regarding the need to establish that the undertaking's conduct was infringing.

2.078 **Continuity and duration of participation.**
Fn 373 See also the General Court's judgment in T-147&148/09 *Trelleborg v Commission*, judgments of 17 May 2013, [2013] 5 CMLR 754, partially annulling the decision in COMP/39406 *Marine Hoses*, decision of 28 January 2009, as regards the duration of the infringement by two of the participants (see the update to to footnote 374, below).

Fn 374 The appeal against the Commission's decision finding a single and continuous infringement in COMP/39406 *Marine Hoses*, decision of 28 January 2009, was upheld in T-147&148/09 *Trelleborg v Commission (Marine Hoses)*, judgment of 17 May 2013, [2013] 5 CMLR 754. Similarly to, and following, its findings in Case T-18/05 *IMI v Commission* [2010] ECR II-1769 referred to in the main text, the General Court found that the Commission had not demonstrated that Trelleborg's conduct continued uninterrupted. There was no evidence of its ongoing participation during one particular period, or that it was aware of the ongoing contacts between the other underrtakings, and the Commission was not therefore entitled to rely on the fact that it had not publicly distanced itself from the cartel as sufficient basis for establishing its ongoing involvement (paras 66–68). However, as Trelleborg accepted that the cartel it rejoined was the same as that which it had left the infringement was to be treated as a single repeated infringement (paras 72 et seq) and the duration of the infringement was reduced accordingly. The decision was also partially annulled, on other grounds, in Case T-154/09 *Manuli Rubber Industries v Commission (Marine Hoses)*, judgment of May 2013, paras 202 et seq (fine reduced on grounds of cooperation); and Case T-146/09 *Parker ITR and Parker-Hannifin v Commission (Marine Hoses)*, judgment of 17 May 2013, [2013] 5 CMLR 712 (duration of the infringement attributed to the parent reduced) (on further appeal, Case C-434/13P *Commission v Parker Hannifin Manufacturing and Parker-Hannifin*, not yet decided).

(d) Public distancing

Passive participation.   2.079
Fn 376 See also Case T-154/09 *Manuli Rubber Industries v Commission (Marine Hoses)*, judgment of May 2013, paras 182 et seq, in which the General Court rejected a contention that the undertaking maintained contact with the other cartelists in order to give the impression it had an interest in relaunching the cartel, and to protect itself against reprisals.

Publicly distancing oneself from an infringement.   If an infringement is ongo- **2.080** ing, and there is no evidence of an undertaking's actual participation in ongoing contacts or that it was aware of them, the Commission cannot rely on the undertaking's failure to distance itself publicly as a basis for establishing ongoing participation: Case T-147&148/09 *Trelleborg v Commission (Marine Hoses)*, judgment of 17 May 2013, [2013] 5 CMLR 754 (see the update to footnote 374, above). If there is evidence of an undertaking being left off the invitee list for meetings, that may be sufficient to establish that it has publicly distanced itself from the infringement: Case T-566/08 *Total Raffinage Marketing*, judgment of 13 September 2013, para 387 (fine reduced on grounds of duration).

Fn 384 The Court of Justice dismissed the appeal in Case C-286/11P *Commission v Tomkins*, judgment of 22 January 2013, [2013] 4 CMLR 466. It held, disagreeing with Advocate General Mengozzi, that the General Court did not err in law by giving Tomkins the benefit of its subsidiary's appeal. In circumstances where the liability of a parent company is wholly derived from that of its subsidiary, and where both companies have brought actions before the European Courts seeking a reduction in their fines on the same basis (in this case, on the basis of the duration of the infringement), then it is not necessary for the scope of their actions, or the arguments deployed, to be identical in order for the General Court to recalculate the fine imposed on the parent company on account of the outcome of the appeal by the subsidiary.

Fn 388 See also Case T-462/07 *Galp Energía España v Commission*, judgment of 16 September 2013, para 475.

(e) Decisions by associations of undertakings

2.082 **Examples of associations.**
Fn 393 For a further example of professional regulatory body, see C-1/12 *Ordem dos Técnicos Oficiais de Contas v Autoridade da Concorrência*, judgment of 28 February 2013, [2013] 4 CMLR 651 regarding a body which regulates chartered accountants.

2.083 **Decisions.**
Fn 406 The Commission's decision in COMP/38698 *CISAC Agreements*, decision of 16 July 2008, has been partially annulled by the General Court: Cases T-392, 398, 401, 410, 411, 413–422, 425, 428, 432–434, 442/08, judgments of 12 April 2013. See the update to paragraph 2.065, above.

4. The Prevention, Restriction or Distortion of Competition

(a) Generally

2.086 **Competition.**
Fn 418 See also the General Court's observations in Case T-587/08 *Del Monte Fresh Produce v Commission*, judgment of 14 March 2013, [2013] 4 CMLR 1091, paras 459–460; and Case T-588/08 *Dole Food Company v Commission*, judgment of 14 March 2013, para 65. On further appeal, Cases 293&294/13P *Fresh Del Monte Produce v Commission*, not yet decided; and Case 286/13P *Dole Food Company v Commission*, not yet decided.

2.091 **Restrictions of competition and restrictions of commercial freedom.**
Fn 436 The Commission's decision in COMP/38606 *Groupement des Cartes Bancaires*, decision of 17 October 2007 has been upheld by the General Court in Case T-491/07 *CB v Commission*, judgment of 29 November 2012, para 83. On further appeal, Case C-67/13P, not yet decided.

Restrictions of competition and detriment to consumers.　　　　　**2.093**
Fn 441　See also the General Court's observations in Case T-587/08 *Del Monte Fresh Produce v Commission*, judgment of 14 March 2013, [2013] 4 CMLR 1091, paras 459–460; and Case T-588/08 *Dole Food Company v Commission*, judgment of 14 March 2013, para 65. On further appeal, Cases 293&294/13P *Fresh Del Monte Produce v Commission*, not yet decided; and Case 286/13P *Dole Food Company v Commission*, not yet decided.

Fn 442　See also the General Court's observations in Case T-587/08 *Del Monte Fresh Produce v Commission*, judgment of 14 March 2013, [2013] 4 CMLR 1091, paras 459–460; and Case T-588/08 *Dole Food Company v Commission*, judgment of 14 March 2013, para 65. On further appeal, Cases 293&294/13P *Fresh Del Monte Produce v Commission*, not yet decided; and Case 286/13P *Dole Food Company v Commission*, not yet decided.

(b)　**Some basic concepts**

Inter-brand and intra-brand competition.　　　　　**2.098**
Fn 462　The Commission's decision in COMP/38606 *Groupement des Cartes Bancaires*, decision of 17 October 2007, has been upheld on other grounds by the General Court in Case T-491/07 *CB v Commission*, judgment of 29 November 2012. On further appeal, Case C-67/13P, not yet decided.

Per se and rule of reason.　　　　　**2.104**
Fn 490　See also *Federal Trade Commission v Actavis and others*, of 17 June 2013, 570 U.S. (2013), in which the Supreme Court clarified that in the United States the rule of reason approach is to be applied to antitrust scrutiny of patent settlement agreements.

No per se rules under Article 101(1).　　The Court of Justice held in Case C-226/11　**2.105**
Expedia Inc, judgment of 13 December 2012, [2013] 4 CMLR 439, paras 36–37, that an agreement that may affect trade between Member States and that has an anti-competitive object constitutes, by its nature and independently of any concrete effect that it may have, an appreciable restriction on competition. At the time of writing the Commission is consulting on a revised *De Minimis* Notice (see update to paragraphs 2.164 et seq, below) to take account of this judgment.

'Unfair competition' not deserving protection.　　An agreement intended to　**2.109**
exclude a competitor that had been operating illegally on the relevant market has also been held to infringe Article 101: Case C-68/12 *Protimonopolný úrad v Slovenská sporitel'ňa*, judgment of 7 February 2013, [2013] 4 CMLR 491, paras 19–21. The Supreme Court of the Slovak Republic subsequently upheld the infringement decision of the Antimonopoly Office on 22 May 2013: ECN Brief 03/2013, p35.

Restrictions must be appreciable.　　The Court of Justice held in Case C-226/11　**2.110**
Expedia Inc, judgment of 13 December 2012, [2013] 4 CMLR 439, paras 36–37,

that an agreement that may affect trade between Member States and that has an anti-competitive object constitutes, by its nature and independently of any concrete effect that it may have, an appreciable restriction on competition. At the time of writing the Commission is consulting on a revised *De Minimis* Notice (see paragraphs 2.164 et seq, and updates thereto) to take account of this judgment. The proposed revised Notice would make clear that the market share thresholds apply only to agreements which have the effect of preventing, restricting, or distorting competition.

(d) Restriction of competition by object

2.113 **Ascertaining object: analysis of the agreement in its context.** In Case C-32/11 *Allianz Hungária Bistozitó*, judgment of 14 March 2013, [2013] 4 CMLR 863, the Court of Justice considered whether vertical agreements between car insurance companies and car repair shops had the object of restricting competition. It held that as the agreements were likely to affect two markets, their object must be determined by reference to both markets (para 42), and it was relevant to consider that the insurance companies aimed to maintain or increase their market share by entering the agreements (para 44). The Court also provided detailed guidance on the legal and economic factors that were relevant, in that case, to determining the object of the agreements.

Where the agreement or concerted practice consists of exchanging commercially sensitive information, one aspect of the context of the agreement that requires consideration is whether the recipient of the information is active in the cartelised market: see Case T-380/10 *Wabco Europe v Commission (Bathroom Fittings)*, judgment of 16 September 2013, in particular at para 79, discussed in the update to paragraph 2.075, above.

2.115 **Object even if not implemented.** The General Court upheld the Commission's decision in COMP/38698 *CISAC Agreements*, decision of 16 July 2008, insofar as it found the membership clause infringed Article 101: Cases T-392, 401, 422, 432/08 judgments of 12 April 2013. It partially annulled the decision on other grounds in Cases T-392, 398, 401, 410, 411, 413–422, 425, 428, 432–434, 442/08, judgments of 12 April 2013.

2.116 **Object means no need to prove actual effects.** The General Court upheld the Commission's decision in COMP/39188 *Bananas*, decision of 15 October 2008, discussed in the main text in Case T-587/08 *Fresh Del Monte Produce v Commission*, judgment of 14 March 2013, [2013] 4 CMLR 1091 (reducing the fine but dismissing the appeal on liability); and Case T-588/08 *Dole Food Company v Commission*, judgment of 14 March 2013. On further appeal, Cases 293&294/13P *Fresh Del Monte Produce v Commission*, not yet decided; and Case 286/13P *Dole Food Company v Commission*, not yet decided.

Fn 554 On this aspect of the Commission's decision in particular, see Case T-587/08 *Fresh Del Monte Produce v Commission*, judgment of 14 March 2013,

[2013] 4 CMLR 1091, paras 427–440; and Case T-588/08 *Dole Food Company v Commission*, judgment of 14 March 2013, paras 332–354.

Fn 556 On this aspect of the Commission's decision in particular, see Case T-587/08 *Fresh Del Monte Produce v Commission*, judgment of 14 March 2013, [2013] 4 CMLR 1091, paras 304–308; and Case T-588/08 *Dole Food Company v Commission*, judgment of 14 March 2013, paras 69–71.

Fn 557 On this aspect of the Commission's decision in particular, see Case T-587/08 *Fresh Del Monte Produce v Commission*, judgment of 14 March 2013, [2013] 4 CMLR 1091, para 427–440; and Case T-588/08 *Dole Food Company v Commission*, judgment of 14 March 2013, paras 332–354.

Object does not remove the need for some effects analysis. The Court of Justice **2.117** held in Case C-226/11 *Expedia Inc*, judgment of 13 December 2012, [2013] 4 CMLR 439, paras 36–37, that an agreement that may affect trade between Member States and that has an anti-competitive object constitutes, by its nature and independently of any concrete effect that it may have, an appreciable restriction on competition. At the time of writing the Commission is consulting on a revised *De Minimis* Notice (see paragraphs 2.164 et seq, and the updates thereto) to take account of the judgment.

Market definition in object cases. The Court of Justice held in Case C-226/11 **2.118** *Expedia Inc*, judgment of 13 December 2012, [2013] 4 CMLR 439, paras 36–37, that an agreement that may affect trade between Member States and that has an anti-competitive object constitutes, by its nature and independently of any concrete effect that it may have, an appreciable restriction on competition. At the time of writing the Commission is consulting on a revised *De Minimis* Notice (see paragraphs 2.164 et seq, and the updates thereto) to take account of the judgment.

Fn 565 The Court of Justice dismissed the appeal in Case C-439/11P *Ziegler v Commission*, judgment of 11 July 2013. It confirmed that it is necessary to define the relevant market in order to determine whether there was an appreciable effect on trade between Member States in that market (para 63).

Fn 566 The Court of Justice dismissed the further appeal in Case C-444/11P *Team Relocations v Commission*, judgment of 11 July 2013.

Examples of horizontal object restrictions. The Court of Justice held in Case **2.121** C-68/12 *Protimonopolný úrad v Slovenská sporiteľňa*, judgment of 7 February 2013, [2013] 4 CMLR 491, paras 19–21, that an agreement that is intended to exclude a competitor from the relevant market is a restriction by object, and it is not relevant that that competitor had been operating on the market illegally. The Supreme Court of the Slovak Republic subsequently upheld the infringement decision of the Antimonopoly Office on 22 May 2013: ECN Brief 03/2013, p35.

2.122 Examples of vertical object restrictions.
Fn 581 For a further example see Case C-32/11 *Allianz Hungária Bistozitó*, judgment of 14 March 2013, [2013] 4 CMLR 863, paras 49–50, where the Court of Justice considered whether vertical agreements between car insurance companies and car repair shops had the object of restricting competition. It held that it was relevant to consider, *inter alia*, the fact that the terms of the agreements were based on a framework agreement, negotiated by the repair shops' trade association with the insurers, which contained recommended prices that insurers should pay to repairers for their work. There would be a restriction by object if the trade association had decided on recommended prices with the intention of harmonising prices, and the insurance companies confirmed those decisions in the framework agreement.

(e) Restriction of competition by effect

2.131 Effect on parties.
Fn 621 The Commission's decision in COMP/38606 *Groupement des Cartes Bancaires*, decision of 17 October 2007, has been upheld on other grounds by the General Court in Case T-491/07 *CB v Commission*, judgment of 29 November 2012. The General Court upheld the Commission's finding of an object infringement, and therefore did not go on to consider its findings on effect: see paras 269–272. On further appeal, Case C-67/13P, not yet decided.

(g) Ancillary restraints

2.147 Ancillary restraints.
Fn 663 For a further example, see COMP/39839 *Telefónica and Portugal Telecom*, decision of 23 January 2013, discussed in the update to paragraph 2.148, below (on appeal Cases T-208/13 *Portugal Telecom v Commission*; and T-216/13 *Telefónica v Commission*, not yet decided).

2.148 Directly related.   In COMP/39839 *Telefónica and Portugal Telecom*, decision of 23 January 2013, paras 367 et seq, the Commission held that a clause by which the parties agreed not to compete in the Iberian pensinsula was not directly related to (or necessary for) the acquisition by Telefónica of the Brazilian mobile operator, Vivo, which until then had been jointly owned by Telefónica and Portugal Telecom (on appeal Cases T-208/13 *Portugal Telecom v Commission*; and T-216/13 *Telefónica v Commission*, not yet decided).

2.149 Objectively necessary.   See also COMP/39839 *Telefónica and Portugal Telecom*, decision of 23 January 2013, discussed in the update to paragraph 2.148, above.

Fn 675 The Commission's decision in COMP/38606 *Groupement des Cartes Bancaires*, decision of 17 October 2007, has been upheld on other grounds by the General Court in Case T-491/07 *CB v Commission*, judgment of 29 November 2012. On further appeal, Case C-67/13P, not yet decided.

(h) Regulatory rules

Professional rules.   In *Ordem dos Técnicos Oficiais de Contas v Autoridade da*   **2.153**
Concorrência, judgment of 28 February 2013, [2013] 4 CMLR 651, paras 96–100,
the Court of Justice held that a requirement for chartered accountants to obtain
compulsory training through their professional association, or through training
providers approved by it, was neither necessary nor proportionate to ensuring the
quality of accountancy services.

Sporting rules.   **2.154**
Fn 692   The Court of Justice dismissed the further appeal in Case C-269/12P *Cañas v
Commission*, judgment of 20 June 2013, regarding the alleged anti-competitiveness
of certain anti-doping rules.

Other regulatory rules.   In Case T-451/08 *Föreningen Svenska Tonsättares*   **2.155**
Internationella Musikbyrå, judgment of 12 April 2013, [2013] 5 CMLR 577, paras
86 et seq, the General Court rejected the argument that the restriction of competition brought about by the concerted practice found by the Commission in
COMP/38698 *CISAC Agreements*, decision of 16 July 2008, [2009] 4 CMLR 577,
was inherent in, and proportional to, cultural objectives.

5. Appreciable Effect on Competition

Generally.   The Court of Justice held in Case C-226/11 *Expedia Inc*, judgment   **2.156**
of 13 December 2012, [2013] 4 CMLR 439, paras 36–37, that an agreement
that may affect trade between Member States and that has an anti-competitive
object constitutes, by its nature and independently of any concrete effect that it
may have, an appreciable restriction on competition. At the time of writing the
Commission is consulting on a revised *De Minimis* Notice (see paragraphs 2.164
et seq, and the update thereto) to take account of this judgment.

(b) Commission *De Minimis* Notice

In general.   At the time of writing the Commission is consulting on a revised   **2.164**
De Minimis Notice to take account of the Court of Justice's judgment in Case
C-226/11 *Expedia Inc*, judgment of 13 December 2012, [2013] 4 CMLR 439.
The Court held in paras 36–37 that an agreement that may affect trade between
Member States and that has an anti-competitive object constitutes, by its nature
and independently of any concrete effect that it may have, an appreciable restriction on competition. The proposed revised Notice would make clear that the market share thresholds apply only to agreements which have the effect of preventing,
restricting, or distorting competition.

De Minimis **Notice.**   At the time of writing the Commission is consulting on a   **2.165**
revised *De Minimis* Notice to take account of the Court of Justice's judgment in

Case C-226/11 *Expedia Inc*, judgment of 13 December 2012, [2013] 4 CMLR 439. The Court held in paras 36–37 that an agreement that may affect trade between Member States and that has an anti-competitive object constitutes, by its nature and independently of any concrete effect that it may have, an appreciable restriction on competition. The proposed revised Notice would make clear that the market share thresholds apply only to agreements which have the effect of preventing, restricting, or distorting competition.

2.166 **Status of the *De Minimis* Notice in Member States.** The Court of Justice has confirmed, in the preliminary reference from the French Cour de Cassation, that although NCAs may take account of the market share thresholds set by the Commission's *De Minimis* Notice when determining whether an agreement has an appreciable effect on competition, they are not required to do so: Case C-226/11 *Expedia Inc*, judgment of 13 December 2012, [2013] 4 CMLR 439, para 31.

Fn 743 The Court of Justice held in Case C-681/11 *Schenker*, judgment of 18 June 2013, [2013] 5 CMLR 831 (disagreeing with Advocate General Kokott's Opinion of 28 February 2013) that reliance by an undertaking on legal advice or a previous NCA decision that its conduct was not contrary to EU competition law as it was *de minimis*, is not sufficient to show that an infringement was not committed intentionally or negligently, and thereby to escape a fine.

3

ARTICLE 101(3)

1. Introduction

Guidelines on the application of Article 101(3) to particular agreements.   **3.005**
Fn 19 The Maritime Transport Guidelines, OJ 2008 C245/2: Vol II, App E20, expired on 26 September 2013, and the Commission has announced that it will not renew them: Press Release IP/13/122 (19 February 2013).

Application of Article 101(3) by NCAs. The Commission has proposed a   **3.008**
Directive on certain rules governing actions for damages under national law for infringements of the competition law provisions of the Member States and of the European Union (COM(2013) 404 final, COD 2013/0185) ('Draft Damages Directive'), issued on 16 June 2013, which includes a proposal that where a NCA has taken a decision finding an infringement of either EU or national competition laws, the national courts are also bound not to take a decision running counter to it. The proposal is, however, confined to 'infringement decisions', and will not apply to a decision that there are no grounds for action on their part: Articles 4(10) and 9 of the Draft Damages Directive.

2. Application in Individual Cases

(a) Generally

Agreements must satisfy all of the conditions in Article 101(3).   **3.013**
Fn 45 The Commission's decision in COMP/38606 *Groupement des Cartes Bancaires*, decision of 17 October 2007, has been upheld by the General Court in Case T-491/07 *CB v Commission*, judgment of 29 November 2012; on this issue see in particular para 377. On further appeal, Case C-67/13P, not yet decided.

(b) The first condition: benefits of an agreement

(i) Generally

3.030 **Commission's current approach.**
Fn 95 The Commission's decision in COMP/38698 *CISAC Agreements*, decision of 16 July 2008, [2009] 4 CMLR 577, has been partially annulled by the General Court, as the Commission had not established the existence of a concerted practice: Cases T-392, 398, 401, 410, 411, 413–422, 425, 428, 432–434, 442/08, judgments of 12 April 2013. However, in Case T-451/08 *Föreningen Svenska Tonsättares Internationella Musikbyrå v Commission*, judgment of 12 April 2013, [2013] 5 CMLR 15, the appellant did not contest the existence of a concerted practice, and the General Court went on to consider the practice's effects, and the potential application of Article 101(3) to it. The General Court dismissed the appeal, as a concerted practice limiting the territorial scope of licences was not indispensible for the maintenance of the national 'one-stop shops': see para 107. As the third condition was not met, the General Court did not consider the potential application of the other conditions.

Fn 99 Two of the appeals against COMP/398181 *Candle Waxes*, decision of 1 October 2008, on other grounds were largely dismissed: Cases T-548/08 *Total v Commission*, judgment of 13 September 2013; and T-566/08 *Total Raffinage Marketing*, judgment of 13 September 2013 (fine reduced on grounds of duration). The other appeals (Cases T-540/08, etc, not yet decided) are still pending.

The General Court upheld the Commission's decision in COMP/39188 *Bananas*, decision of 15 October 2008, in Case T-587/08 *Fresh Del Monte Produce v Commission*, judgment of 14 March 2013, [2013] 4 CMLR 1091 (reducing the fine but dismissing the appeal on liability); and Case T-588/08 *Dole Food Company v Commission*, judgment of 14 March 2013. On further appeal, Cases 293&294/13P *Fresh Del Monte Produce v Commission*, not yet decided; and Case 286/13P *Dole Food Company v Commission*, not yet decided.

3.031 **Proving that efficiencies will result from an agreement.**
Fn 103 In Case T-491/07 *CB v Commission*, judgment of 29 November 2012, paras 396–397, the General Court agreed that the Commission had erred in its interpretation of certain aspects of the economic evidence adduced in its decision in COMP/38606 *Groupement des Cartes Bancaires*, decision of 17 October 2007, but it rejected the complaint that that error was sufficient to indicate bias. It also upheld the decision in respect of the alleged benefits of the agreement: see para 374. On further appeal, Case C-67/13P, not yet decided.

(ii) Cost efficiencies

3.034 **Stability and flexibility of supply.**
Fn 115 Two of the appeals against COMP/398181 *Candle Waxes*, decision of 1 October 2008, on other grounds were largely dismissed: Cases T-548/08 *Total*

v Commission, judgment of 13 September 2013; and T-566/08 *Total Raffinage Marketing*, judgment of 13 September 2013 (fine reduced on grounds of duration). The other appeals (Cases T-540/08, etc, not yet decided) are still pending.

(iii) Qualitative efficiencies

Improved distribution. 3.039

Fn 144 The General Court upheld the Commission's decision in COMP/39188 *Bananas*, decision of 15 October 2008, in Case T-587/08 *Fresh Del Monte Produce v Commission*, judgment of 14 March 2013, [2013] 4 CMLR 1091 (reducing the fine but dismissing the appeal on liability); and Case T-588/08 *Dole Food Company v Commission*, judgment of 14 March 2013. On further appeal, Cases 293&294/13P *Fresh Del Monte Produce v Commission*, not yet decided; and Case 286/13P *Dole Food Company v Commission*, not yet decided.

Fn 154 The Commission's decision in COMP/38698 *CISAC Agreements*, decision of 16 July 2008, [2009] 4 CMLR 577, has been partially annulled by the General Court, as the Commission had not established the existence of a concerted practice: Cases T-392, 398, 401, 410, 411, 413–422, 425, 428, 432–434, 442/08, judgments of 12 April 2013. However, in Case T-451/08 *Föreningen Svenska Tonsättares Internationella Musikbyrå v Commission*, judgment of 12 April 2013, [2013] 5 CMLR 15, the appellant did not contest the existence of a concerted practice, and the General Court went on to consider the practice's effects, and the application of Article 101(3) to it. The General Court dismissed the appeal, concluding that a concerted practice limiting the territorial scope of licenses was not indispensible for the maintenance of the national 'one-stop shops': see para 107. As the third condition was not met, the General Court did not consider the potential application of the other conditions.

(iv) Improvements to market dynamics

Payment systems. The Commission's decision in COMP/38606 *Groupement* 3.046
des Cartes Bancaires, decision of 17 October 2007, has been upheld by the General Court in Case T-491/07 *CB v Commission*, judgment of 29 November 2012. On further appeal, Case C-67/13P, not yet decided.

(vi) Absence of benefit

No benefit from duplication of action by public authorities. 3.053

Fn 210 In Case C-68/12 *Protimonopolný úrad v Slovenská sporitel'ňa*, judgment of 7 February 2013, [2013] 4 CMLR 491, the Court of Justice held that an agreement between undertakings to eliminate a competitor from a market on which it had been operating illegally could not fall within Article 101(3) as it could not meet in particular the indispensibility criteria. The Court held that the undertakings could have reported the illegal activity to the competent authorities. The Supreme Court of the Slovak Republic subsequently upheld the infringement decision of the Antimonopoly Office, on 22 May 2013: ECN Brief 03/2013, p35.

(c) The second condition: fair share of benefits for consumers

3.056 'Consumers' includes all users.

Fn 214 The Commission's decision in COMP/38698 *CISAC Agreements*, decision of 16 July 2008, [2009] 4 CMLR 577, has been partially annulled by the General Court, as the Commission had not established the existence of a concerted practice: Cases T-392, 398, 401, 410, 411, 413–422, 425, 428, 432–434, 442/08, judgments of 12 April 2013. However, in Case T-451/08 *Föreningen Svenska Tonsättares Internationella Musikbyrå v Commission*, judgment of 12 April 2013, [2013] 5 CMLR 15, the appellant did not contest the existence of a concerted practice, and the General Court went on to consider the practice's effects, and the application of Article 101(3) to it. The General Court dismissed the appeal, concluding that a concerted practice limiting the territorial scope of licenses was not indispensible for the maintenance of the national 'one-stop shops': see para 107. As the third condition was not met, the General Court did not consider the potential application of the other conditions.

See also the Commission's decision in COMP/39839 *Telefónica / Portugal Telecom*, decision of 23 January 2013, in which the Commission rejected the argument that the agreement in question would not harm consumers as it was directed at the corporate sector: see para 445 (on appeal, Cases T-208/13 *Portugal Telecom v Commission*; and T-216/13 *Telefónica v Commission*, not yet decided).

3.060 Disadvantages for consumers.

Fn 237 The Commission's decision in COMP/38698 *CISAC Agreements*, decision of 16 July 2008, [2009] 4 CMLR 577, has been partially annulled by the General Court on appeal, as the Commission had not established the existence of a concerted practice: Cases T-392, 398, 401, 410, 411, 413–422, 425, 428, 432–434, 442/08, judgments of 12 April 2013. However, in Case T-451/08 *Föreningen Svenska Tonsättares Internationella Musikbyrå v Commission*, judgment of 12 April 2013, [2013] 5 CMLR 15, the appellant did not contest the existence of a concerted practice, and the General Court went on to consider the practice's effects, and the application of Article 101(3) to it. The General Court dismissed the appeal, concluding that a concerted practice limiting the territorial scope of licenses was not indispensible for the maintenance of the national 'one-stop shops': see para 107. As the third condition was not met, the General Court did not consider the potential application of the other conditions.

Fn 240 The Commission's decision in COMP/38606 *Groupement des Cartes Bancaires*, decision of 17 October 2007, has been upheld by the General Court in Case T-491/07 *CB v Commission*, judgment of 29 November 2012. On further appeal, Case C-67/13P, not yet decided.

(d) The third condition: indispensability of restrictions

Indispensability of individual restrictions.   **3.064**
Fn 257 The Commission's decision in COMP/38606 *Groupement des Cartes Bancaires*, decision of 17 October 2007, has been upheld by the General Court in Case T-491/07 *CB v Commission*, judgment of 29 November 2012. The General Court upheld the Commission's conclusion that the first condition for the application of Article 101(3) was not met, and so did not go on to consider the other conditions: see para 377. On further appeal, Case C-67/13P, not yet decided.

Hardcore restrictions.   A further example of a Commission decision concluding   **3.065**
that the requirement of indispensability could not be met in respect of a hardcore restriction is COMP/39839 *Telefónica / Portugal Telecom*, decision of 23 January 2013, in which the Commission found that an agreement not to compete on the Iberian telecommunications market breached Article 101. It rejected Telefónica's argument that unless it accepted a non-compete clause, the agreement (by which Telefónica acquired the Brazilian mobile operator, Vivo, which until then had been jointly owned by Telefónica and Portugal Telecom) would not have been concluded. The Commission recalled that the requirement of indispensability relates to efficiencies, not to the agreement itself: see para 444 (on appeal, Cases T-208/13 *Portugal Telecom v Commission*; and T-216/13 *Telefónica v Commission*, not yet decided).

Fn 262 The Commission's decision in COMP/38698 *CISAC Agreements*, decision of 16 July 2008, [2009] 4 CMLR 577, has been partially annulled by the General Court, as the Commission had not established the existence of a concerted practice: Cases T-392, 398, 401, 410, 411, 413–422, 425, 428, 432–434, 442/08, judgments of 12 April 2013. However, in Case T-451/08 *Föreningen Svenska Tonsättares Internationella Musikbyrå v Commission*, judgment of 12 April 2013, [2013] 5 CMLR 15, the appellant did not contest the existence of a concerted practice, and the General Court went on to consider the practice's effects, and the application of Article 101(3) to it. The General Court dismissed the appeal, concluding that a concerted practice limiting the territorial scope of licenses was not indispensible for the maintenance of the national 'one-stop shops': para 107.

(e) The fourth condition: no elimination of competition

Generally.   **3.067**
Fn 269 The Commission's decision in COMP/38698 *CISAC Agreements*, decision of 16 July 2008, [2009] 4 CMLR 577, has been partially annulled by the General Court, as the Commission had not established the existence of a concerted practice: Cases T-392, 398, 401, 410, 411, 413–422, 425, 428, 432–434, 442/08, judgments of 12 April 2013. However, in Case T-451/08 *Föreningen Svenska Tonsättares Internationella Musikbyrå v Commission*, judgment of

12 April 2013, [2013] 5 CMLR 15, the appellant did not contest the existence of a concerted practice, and the General Court went on to consider the practice's effects, and the application of Article 101(3) to it. The General Court dismissed the appeal, concluding that a concerted practice limiting the territorial scope of licenses was not indispensible for the maintenance of the national 'one-stop shops': para 107. As the third condition was not met, the General Court did not consider the potential application of the other conditions.

3.068 **Framework for analysis.**

Fn 271 The Commission's decision in COMP/38698 *CISAC Agreements*, decision of 16 July 2008, [2009] 4 CMLR 577, has been partially annulled by the General Court, as the Commission had not established the existence of a concerted practice: Cases T-392, 398, 401, 410, 411, 413–422, 425, 428, 432–434, 442/08, judgments of 12 April 2013. However, in Case T-451/08 *Föreningen Svenska Tonsättares Internationella Musikbyrå v Commission*, judgment of 12 April 2013, [2013] 5 CMLR 15, the appellant did not contest the existence of a concerted practice, and the General Court went on to consider the practice's effects, and the application of Article 101(3) to it. The General Court dismissed the appeal, concluding that a concerted practice limiting the territorial scope of licenses was not indispensible for the maintenance of the national 'one-stop shops': para 107. As the third condition was not met, the General Court did not consider the potential application of the other conditions.

3.071 **Channels of distribution.**

Fn 292 The Commission's decision in COMP/38698 *CISAC Agreements*, decision of 16 July 2008, [2009] 4 CMLR 577, has been partially annulled by the General Court on appeal, as the Commission had not established the existence of a concerted practice: Cases T-392, 398, 401, 410, 411, 413–422, 425, 428, 432–434, 442/08, judgments of 12 April 2013. However, in Case T-451/08 *Föreningen Svenska Tonsättares Internationella Musikbyrå v Commission*, judgment of 12 April 2013, [2013] 5 CMLR 15, the appellant did not contest the existence of a concerted practice, and the General Court went on to consider the practice's effects, and the application of Article 101(3). The General Court dismissed the appeal, concluding that a concerted practice limiting the territorial scope of licenses was not indispensible for the maintenance of the national 'one-stop shops': para 107. It upheld the Commission's decision in this regard, and against this appellant.

3. Block Exemption

(a) Generally

3.084 **Technology transfer agreements.** On 20 February 2013 the Commission launched a consultation on its proposals for a revised competition regime for technology transfer agreements. The consultation documents are available on the consultations section of the DG Comp website; see also Commission Press Release IP/13/120 (20 February 2013).

Maritime transport services.   **3.087**
Fn 353 The Commission has announced that it will not renew the Maritime Transport Guidelines, OJ 2008 C245/2: Vol II, App E20: Press Release IP/13/122 (19 February 2013).

4

MARKET DEFINITION

1. Introduction and Overview

(b) The concept of the relevant market

Meaning of a 'relevant market'.   **4.003**
Fn 9 The Court of Justice dismissed the further appeals in Case C-457/10P
AstraZeneca v Commission, judgment of 6 December 2012, [2013] 4 CMLR 233.

Fn 12 For extensive consideration of whether products were complements or substi-
tutes, see M.6166 *Deutsche Börse/NYSE Euronext* (1 February 2012), paras 305–367.
The decision is under appeal in Case T-175/12 *Deutsche Börse v Commission*, not yet
decided.

(c) Relevance of market definition in EU competition law

Anti-competitive object under Article 101(1). The Court of Justice held in Case   **4.006**
C-226/11 *Expedia Inc*, judgment of 13 December 2012, [2013] 4 CMLR 439,
paras 36–37, that an agreement that may affect trade between Member States and
that has an anti-competitive object constitutes, by its nature and independently
of any concrete effect that it may have, an appreciable restriction on competition.
At the time of writing the Commission is consulting on a revised *De Minimis*
Notice (see paragraphs 2.164 et seq, and the updates thereto) to take account of
this judgment.

The General Court's judgments in the appeals against the Commission's decision in COMP/39092 *Bathroom Fittings and Fixtures*, decision of 23 June 2010,
highlight that market definition may be important in determining both the
object and effect of an alleged infringement, where the behaviour in question
consists of information exchange: the Court observed in Case T-380/10 *Wabco
Europe v Commission (Bathroom Fittings)*, judgment of 16 September 2013,
para 79:

> 'it cannot be presumed that an agreement or a concerted practice whereby under-
> takings exchange information which is commercially sensitive but which relates to a

product sold on a market on which they are not competitors has an anti-competitive object or effect on that market. A practice whereby an undertaking which is active on two distinct product markets provides to its competitors – which are present on one market – commercially sensitive information which relates to a second market – on which those competitors are not present – is not capable, in principle, of having an impact on competition on the second market.'

See also Joined Cases T-379&381/10 *Keramag Keramische Werke and Others v Commission ('Bathroom Fittings')*, judgment of 16 September 2013, paras 92 and 221.

Fn 20 The Court of Justice dismissed the further appeal in Case C-439/11P *Ziegler v Commission*, judgment of 11 July 2013. It confirmed that it is necessary to define the relevant market in order to apply a market share criterion (in that case, to determine whether there was an appreciable effect on trade between Member States in that market) (para 63) but held that the Commission had in fact provided a sufficiently detailed description of the services with which its decision was concerned to constitute a definition of the market for these purposes (paras 67–73). See also Case T-82/08 *Guardian Industries Corp v Commission*, para 90.

Fn 23 The Court of Justice dismissed the further appeal, on other grounds, in Case C-510/11P *Kone v Commission ('Elevators and Escalators')*, judgment of 24 October 2013.

Fn 28 Two of the appeals against COMP/398181 *Candle Waxes*, decision of 1 October 2008, on other grounds, were largely dismissed: Cases T-548/08 *Total v Commission*, judgment of 13 September 2013; and T-566/08 *Total Raffinage Marketing*, judgment of 13 September 2013 (fine reduced). The other appeals (Cases T-540/08, etc, not yet decided) are still pending.

See also Case T-135/09 *Nexans France v Commission*, judgment of 14 November 2012, [2013] 4 CMLR 195, paras 89–91 (Commission did not have reasonable grounds for ordering an inspection covering markets for which it had no evidence justifying an inspection). On further appeal, Case C-37/13P, not yet decided.

4.007 Anti-competitive effect under Article 101(1).
Fn 33 The Court of Justice dismissed the appeal in Case C-439/11P *Ziegler v Commission*, judgment of 11 July 2013. It confirmed that it is necessary to define the relevant market in order to apply a market share criterion (in that case, to determine whether there was an appreciable effect on trade between Member States in that market) (para 63) but held that the Commission had in fact provided a sufficiently detailed description of the services with which its decision was concerned to constitute a definition of the market for these purposes (paras 67–73).

(c) Methodology for defining the relevant market

(i) *Jurisprudence and guidelines*

Quantitative and qualitative approaches to market definition.   **4.011**
Fn 50 The Court of Justice dismissed the further appeals in Case C-457/10P
AstraZeneca v Commission, judgment of 6 December 2012, [2013] 4 CMLR 233.

(ii) *Factors relevant to defining relevant markets*

Market definitions are contextual.   **4.014**
Fn 62 The Commission's decision in COMP/38606 *Groupement des Cartes
Bancaires*, decision of 17 October 2007, has been upheld by the General Court in
Case T-491/07 *CB v Commission*, judgment of 29 November 2012: see, in particu-
lar, paras 83 and 104. On further appeal, Case C-67/13P, not yet decided.

Fn 64 Two of the appeals against COMP/398181 *Candle Waxes*, decision of
1 October 2008, on other grounds, were largely dismissed: Cases T-548/08 *Total
v Commission*, judgment of 13 September 2013; and T-566/08 *Total Raffinage
Marketing*, judgment of 13 September 2013 (fine reduced). The other appeals
(Cases T-540/08, etc, not yet decided) are still pending.

Fn 66 See M.6266 *Johnson & Johnson/Synthes* (18 April 2012), para 23, for a discussion of possible bundled markets (rejected for lack of evidence).

Fn 68 See also M.6663 *Ryanair / Aer Lingus III* (27 February 2013), paras 69–73,
in which the Commission treated as 'important factual elements which it takes
into account in its assessment' its analyses of markets affected by an earlier proposal by Ryanair to acquire control over Aer Lingus, which had been upheld by
the General Court (M.4439 *Ryanair/Aer Lingus* (27 June 2007); upheld in Case
T-342/07 *Ryanair Holdings plc v European Commission* [2010] ECR II-03457). The
Commission sought to ascertain whether there had been 'any significant changes
in the market circumstances such as to warrant a different conclusion than the one
reached in the 2007 Decision', but concluded that there had not. On appeal, Case
T-260/13 *Ryanair v Commission*, not yet decided.

'One-way' markets.   **4.015**
Fn 71 The Court of Justice dismissed the appeals in Case C-457/10P *AstraZeneca
v Commission*, judgment of 6 December 2012, [2013] 4 CMLR 233. In particular,
see paras 46–51, and the Court's finding at para 47 that 'the gradual nature of the
increase in sales of a new product being substituted for an existing product does
not necessarily mean that that latter product exercised on the former a significant
competitive constraint'.

(iv) *Limitations on the SSNIP test*

The 'cellophane fallacy'.   **4.025**
Fn 107 The *Mastercard* decision is on further appeal in Case C-382/12P, not yet
decided.

2. Relevant Product Market

(a) Demand-side substitution

4.029 **Product characteristics and functional interchangeability**
Fn 115 See also M.6458 *Universal Music Group / EMI Music* (21 September 2012), eg para 127, in which the Commission considers the different characteristics of recorded music in physical and digital formats.

4.030 **Switching data.**
Fn 127 The Court of Justice dismissed the further appeals in Case C-457/10P *AstraZeneca v Commission*, judgment of 6 December 2012, [2013] 4 CMLR 233: see, in particular, paras 46–51.

Fn 128 The Court of Justice dismissed the further appeals in Case C-457/10P *AstraZeneca v Commission*, judgment of 6 December 2012, [2013] 4 CMLR 233: see, in particular, paras 46–51.

4.033 **Switching costs and other barriers.**
Fn 135 For an example of a decision considering high switching costs and other barriers, see COMP/39230 *Rio Tinto Alcan*, decision of 20 December 2012, para 23.

4.037 **Different absolute price levels.**
Fn 144 In M.5830 *Olympic/Aegean Airlines* (26 January 2011), the Commission stated at para 259 that 'Difference in price, in a differentiated products environment, provides a proxy of the distance in the product space between the two products. The larger this difference, the lower the likelihood that these two products are considered substitutable by a significant proportion of customers'. The appeal against the decision in Case T-202/11 *Aeroporia Aigaiou Aeroporiki and Marfin Investment Group Symmetochon v Commission*, was withdrawn on 10 September 2013.

See also, for example, M.6203 *Western Digital Ireland/Viviti Technologies* (23 November 2011), paras 150–151, 199–200, and 341, in which the Commission concluded that two products formed separate markets because, although there was scope to switch between them, the price differences meant that it would not be economic to do so; and M.6266 *Johnson & Johnson/Synthes* (18 April 2012), paras 76–77.

Fn 147 The Court of Justice dismissed the further appeals in Case C-457/10P *AstraZeneca v Commission*, judgment of 6 December 2012, [2013] 4 CMLR 233.

4.038 **Price elasticity of demand.**
Fn 158 In M.5830 *Olympic/Aegean Airlines* (26 January 2011), para 249 the Commission found that 'Critical Loss Analysis is not an appropriate tool for the evaluation of the SSNIP test for the airline industry in view of the extent of price

discrimination and the difficulties in evaluating appropriately gross margins'. The appeal against the decision in Case T-202/11 *Aeroporia Aigaiou Aeroporiki and Marfin Investment Group Symmetochon v Commission*, was withdrawn on 10 September 2013.

In M.6166 *Deutsche Börse/NYSE Euronext* (1 February 2012) the limitations of critical loss analysis are described at paras 344–349 (on appeal, Case T-175/12 *Deutsche Börse v Commission*, not yet decided).

Price correlations.   4.040
Fn 163 See also M.6663 *Ryanair / Aer Lingus III* (27 February 2013), section 7.3.3 and Annex 1 (on appeal, Case T-260/13 *Ryanair v Commission*, not yet decided).

Trade relationships.   4.042
Fn 174 The Commission's decision in Case M.6281 *Microsoft/Skype* (7 October 2011) is under appeal in Case T-79/12 *Cisco Systems and Messagenet v Commission*, not yet decided.

Evidence from internal company documents.   4.045
Fn 184 The Commission's decision in COMP/34579 *Mastercard*, decision of 19 December 2007, is on further appeal in Case C-382/12P, not yet decided.

(b) Supply-side substitution

Conditions for consideration of supply-side substitution.   4.048
Fn 192 In respect of suppliers being able to switch 'without incurring significant additional costs or risks', see M.6101 *UPM/Myllykoski and Rhein Paper* (13 July 2011), para 61.

(c) Particular issues in determining the relevant product market

(i) *Connected markets*

Connected markets   4.054
Fn 208 See also Case COMP/39839 *Telefónica/Portugal Telecom*, decision of 23 January 2013, para 191, in which the Commission described the retail mobile market as including a 'cluster' of services.

Interaction between connected markets. The Court of Justice dismissed the   4.055
further appeal in Case C-56/12P *European Federation of Ink and Ink Cartridge Manufacturers (EFIM) v Commission*, judgment of 19 September 2013. The Court confirmed the General Court's, and Commission's, approach of considering whether the markets for printers and cartridges were closely related, such that competition in the primary market for printers could exercise an effective discipline on the market for printer cartridges, by reference to the criteria set out in the main text: see paras 36 et seq.

Market definition in two-sided markets.   4.060
Fn 233 The Commission's decision in COMP/34579 *Mastercard*, decision of 19 December 2007, is on further appeal in Case C-382/12P, not yet decided. The

Commission's decision in COMP/38606 *Groupement des Cartes Bancaires*, decision of 17 October 2007, has been upheld by the General Court in Case T-491/07 *CB v Commission*, judgment of 29 November 2012, in particular para 104. On further appeal, Case C-67/13P, not yet decided.

3. Relevant Geographic Market

(b) Demand-side substitution

4.079 Demand-side substitution evidence: internal company documents.
Fn 311 For a further instance of the use by the Commission of internal company documents, in the context of defining the geographic market, see M.6203 *Western Digital Ireland/Viviti Technologies* (23 November 2011), paras 394 et seq.

(c) Supply-side substitution

4.084 Legislative requirements or other barriers to switching by suppliers.
Fn 325 The Commission's decision in COMP/38698 *CISAC Agreements*, decision of 16 July 2008, [2009] 4 CMLR 577, has been partially annulled by the General Court: Cases T-392, 398, 401, 410, 411, 413–422, 425, 428, 432–434, 442/08, judgments of 12 April 2013.

(d) Particular issues in determining the geographic market

4.086 Markets for transport services.
Fn 333 See also M.5830 *Olympic/Aegean Airlines* (26 January 2011) in which, on one route, air services and ferry services were found to be part of the same product market as regards time sensitive passengers: para 269. The appeal in Case T-202/11 *Aeroporia Aigaiou Aeroporiki and Marfin Investment Group Symmetochon v Commission* was withdrawn on 10 September 2013.

See also COMP/39595 *Continental/United/Lufthansa/Air Canada*, decision of 23 May 2013, paras 17–19; and M.6663 *Ryanair / Aer Lingus III* (27 February 2013), section 7.2 (on appeal, Case T-260/13 *Ryanair v Commission*, not yet decided).

4. Temporal Market

4.087 Existence of a temporal dimension.
Fn 339 See also Case COMP/39654 *Reuters Instrument Codes*, decision of 20 December 2012, paras 28–30, identifying a market for certain types of 'real-time datafeeds'.

5

CARTELS

1. An Overview

Cartels are an enforcement priority.   5.001
Fn 1 In 2012 the Commission took five decisions, involving 37 undertakings or
associations of undertakings, and imposed fines totalling €1.875 billion. The highest fine to date is that which was imposed on the participants in COMP/39437 *TV
and computer monitor tubes*, decision of 5 December 2012, of €1.47billion: decision not yet published, but see Press Release IP/12/1317 (5 December 2012).

(a) The typical subject-matter of cartel activity

The definition of cartels.   5.003
Fn 4 The Commission now publishes a 'Questions and Answers' page in the
Cartels section of the DG Comp website (at the time of writing, it was last updated
in April 2012).

Restrictions ancillary to the cartel agreements.   5.006
Fn 8 The General Court dismissed the appeals against the Commission's decision in COMP/39180 *Aluminium Fluoride*, decision of 25 June 2008, in Cases
T-404/08 *Fluorsid and Minmet v Commission*, judgment of 18 June 2013, [2013]
5 CMLR 902; and Case T-406/08 *Industries chimiques du fluor v Commission*,
judgment of 18 June 2013 (on further appeal, Case C-467/13P, not yet decided).

Fn 14 The Court of Justice dismissed the further appeals against the decision in
COMP/37766 *Netherlands Beer Market*, decision of 18 April 2007, in Case C-452/11P
Heineken Nederland and Heineken v Commission, judgment of 19 December
2012; and C-445/11P *Bavaria v Commission*, judgment of 19 December 2012.

(b) How cartels operate

Single continuous infringement.   The approach laid down by the General Court 5.008
in Case T-204&208/12 *Team Relocations v Commission (International Removal
Services)* [2011] ECR II-3569, [2011] 5 CMLR 889 was upheld by the Court of

Justice in Case C-444/11P *Team Relocations v Commission*, judgment of 11 July 2013, paras 51 et seq.

5.009 **Participation in a cartel.** On participation, and the circumstances in which an undertaking will be treated as having distanced itself from a cartel, see also the updates to paragraphs 2.079 et seq, above.

5.010 **Liability of undertaking for the overall cartel.** On liability for cartel activities in which the undertaking did not directly participate, see also the updates to paragraphs 2.076 et seq, above.

Fn 27 The Court of Justice dismissed the further appeal on liability in Case C-70/12P *Quinn Barlo v Commission* ('*Methacrylates*'), judgment of 30 May 2013, [2013] 5 CMLR 637.

Fn 28 The General Court has ruled on the appeals against the Commission decisions noted in the footnote. The Commission's findings of infringement in decision COMP/39406 *Marine Hoses*, decision of 28 January 2009, were upheld, but the decision was partially annulled on other grounds, in Case T-146/09, etc, *Parker ITR and Parker-Hannifin v Commission (Marine Hoses)*, judgments of 17 May 2013, [2013] 5 CMLR 712 (on further appeal, Case C-434/13P *Commission v Parker Hannifin Manufacturing and Parker-Hannifin*, not yet decided). The appeals against the Commission's decision in COMP/39180 *Aluminium Fluoride*, decision of 25 June 2008, were dismissed in Cases T-404/08 *Fluorsid and Minmet v Commission*, judgment of 18 June 2013, [2013] 5 CMLR 902; and Case T-406/08 *Industries chimiques du fluor v Commission*, judgment of 18 June 2013 (on further appeal, Case C-467/13P, not yet decided).

5.011 **Cartel 'consultancy'.**
Fn 31 The Commission's finding of infringement in decision COMP/39406 *Marine Hoses*, decision of 28 January 2009, were upheld, but the decision was partially annulled on other grounds, in Case T-146/09, etc, *Parker ITR and Parker-Hannifin v Commission (Marine Hoses)*, judgments of 17 May 2013, [2013] 5 CMLR 712 (on further appeal, Case C-434/13P *Commission v Parker Hannifin Manufacturing and Parker-Hannifin*, not yet decided). Two of the appeals against COMP/398181 *Candle Waxes*, decision of 1 October 2008, were largely dismissed: Cases T-548/08 *Total v Commission*, judgment of 13 September 2013; and T-566/08 *Total Raffinage Marketing*, judgment of 13 September 2013 (fine reduced on grounds of duration). The other appeals (Cases T-540/08, etc, not yet decided) are still pending.

(c) **Arguments typically used to justify cartels**

5.013 **No effects.**
Fn 36 In the appeals against the Commission's decision in COMP/38456 *Dutch Bitumen*, decision of 13 September 2006, the General Court reduced the fine

imposed on Shell in Case T-343/06 *Shell Petroleum v Commission*, judgment of 27 September 2012, [2012] 5 CMLR 1064 (on further appeal in Case C-585/12P, not yet decided), and dismissed the other appeals, on other grounds, in Cases T-344/06 etc, judgments of 27 September 2012 (further appeal by Kuwait Petroleum in C-581/12P *Kuwait Petroleum v Commission*, not yet decided).

Fn 37 The General Court upheld the Commission's decision in COMP/39188 *Bananas*, decision of 15 October 2008, in Case T-587/08 *Fresh Del Monte Produce v Commission*, judgment of 14 March 2013 (reducing the fine but dismissing the appeal on liability) paras 305–308; and Case T-588/08 *Dole Food Company v Commission*, judgment of 14 March 2013, paras 67–71. On further appeal, Cases 293&294/13P *Fresh Del Monte Produce v Commission*, not yet decided; and Case 286/13P *Dole Food Company v Commission*, not yet decided.

In Case T-404/08 *Fluorsid and Minmet v Commission*, judgment of 18 June 2013, [2013] 5 CMLR 902, para 96, the General Court rejected an argument that implementation of an agreement, found by the Commission to have an anticompetitive object in COMP/39810 *Aluminium Fluoride*, decision of 25 June 2008, was 'impossible'.

No interest in or benefit from the cartel.　　　　　　　　　　　　　　**5.014**

Fn 40 The General Court has upheld the Commission's decision in COMP/39188 *Bananas*, decision of 15 October 2008, in Case T-587/08 *Fresh Del Monte Produce v Commission*, judgment of 14 March 2013 (reducing the fine but dismissing the appeal on liability); and Case T-588/08 *Dole Food Company v Commission*, judgment of 14 March 2013. On further appeal, Cases 293&294/13P *Fresh Del Monte Produce v Commission*, not yet decided; and Case 286/13P *Dole Food Company v Commission*, not yet decided.

Fn 42 The General Court dismissed the appeals against the Commission's decision in COMP/39810 *Aluminium Fluoride*, decision of 25 June 2008, in Case T-404/08 *Fluorsid and Minmet v Commission*, judgment of 18 June 2013, [2013] 5 CMLR 902; and Case T-406/08 *Industries chimiques du fluor v Commission*, judgment of 18 June 2013 (on further appeal, Case C-467/13P, not yet decided). In *Fluorsid and Minment*, para 96, the General Court rejected an argument that implementation of an agreement found by the Commission to have an anti-competitive object in was 'impossible', as it was not necessary to examine the effects of the agreement once its anti-competitive object had been established.

Fn 43 The General Court upheld the Commission's decision in *Bananas* on other grounds: see the update to footnote 40 above.

Participation under compulsion.　　　　　　　　　　　　　　　　**5.015**

Fn 44 See also Case T-154/09 *Manuli Rubber Industries v Commission (Marine Hoses)*, judgment of May 2013, paras 182 et seq, in which the General Court rejected a contention that the undertaking maintained contact with the other cartelists in order to give the impression it had an interest in relaunching the cartel, and to protect itself against reprisals. See also paras 233 et seq, in which it rejected a contention that this could bear upon the gravity of the infringement for the purpose of determining the percentage of relevant sales on which to set the fine, and paras 285 et seq in which it rejected the contention that the Commission should have considered this a factor mitigating the fine.

5.016   **Not active on the cartelised market.**   The General Court has distinguished its judgment in *Industrial Thread*, noted in the main text (Joined Cases T-456&457/05 *Gütermann and Zwicky v Commission* [2010] ECR II-1443) in Case T-380/10 *Wabco Europe v Commission (Bathroom Fittings)*, judgment of 16 September 2013. Where the alleged cartel includes an exchange of commercially sensitive information, it is necessary that the recipient of the information be active on the cartelised market, such that there is potential for that recipient to modify its behaviour as a result of receiving the information, in order for the exchange to infringe Article 101. The Court emphasised at para 79 that:

> 'it cannot be presumed that an agreement or a concerted practice whereby undertakings exchange information which is commercially sensitive but which relates to a product sold on a market on which they are not competitors has an anti-competitive object or effect on that market. A practice whereby an undertaking which is active on two distinct product markets provides to its competitors – which are present on one market – commercially sensitive information which relates to a second market – on which those competitors are not present – is not capable, in principle, of having an impact on competition on the second market.'

The Court held that its judgment in Joined Cases T-456&457/05 *Gütermann and Zwicky v Commission* [2010] ECR II-1443, relied upon by the Commission, would apply to a disclosure of commercially sensitive information with a view to restricting competition in the market on which the recipient of the information is active, by a disclosing party that is not itself active on that market; whereas in the decision under appeal, COMP/39092 *Bathroom Fittings*, decision of 23 June 2010, the Commission had (as the Court held, wrongly) found that the purpose of the disclosure was to restrict competition in a market on which the disclosing party was active but the recipient was not: see paras 98–99. See also Joined Cases T-379&381/10 *Keramag Keramische Werke and Others (Bathroom Fittings) v Commission*, judgment of 16 September 2013, paras 92 and 221.

5.017   **Industry crisis.**

Fn 49   In Case T-404/08 *Fluorsid and Minmet v Commission*, judgment of 18 June 2013, [2013] 5 CMLR 902, para 96; and Case T-406/08 *Industries chimiques du fluor v Commission*, judgment of 18 June 2013 (on further appeal, Case C-467/13P, not yet decided) para 90, the General Court confirmed that the Commission did not need to prove the effects of the cartel found in COMP/39810 *Aluminium Fluoride*, decision of 25 June 2008. In *Fluorsid and Minmet* it rejected an argument that implementation of the agreement, found by the Commission to have an anti-competitive object, was 'impossible', as it was not necessary to examine the effects of the agreement, once its anti-competitive object had been established.

Response to anti-competitive behaviour by other firms.   The Court of Justice **5.018** confirmed in Case C-68/12 *Protimonopolný úrad v Slovenská sporitel'ňa*, judgment of 7 February 2013, [2013] 4 CMLR 491, paras 19–21, that if an agreement is intended to exclude a competitor from the relevant market, it is not relevant that that competitor had been operating on the market illegally. The Supreme Court of the Slovak Republic subsequently upheld the infringement decision of the Antimonopoly Office on 22 May 2013: ECN Brief 03/2013, p35.

Government connivance.   See also Case C-444/11P *Team Relocations v* **5.019** *Commission*, judgment of 11 July 2013, paras 148–150, in which the Court of Justice dismissed a complaint that the Commission had itself sought out cover prices from the cartelists.

Fn 53 Two of the appeals against COMP/398181 *Candle Waxes*, decision of 1 October 2008, on other grounds were largely dismissed: Cases T-548/08 *Total v Commission*, judgment of 13 September 2013; and T-566/08 *Total Raffinage Marketing*, judgment of 13 September 2013 (fine reduced on grounds of duration). The other appeals (Cases T-540/08, etc, not yet decided) are still pending.

(d) Investigation and enforcement

Information requests and inspections.   On the Commission's powers to gather **5.021** information and to conduct inspections, see also the updates to paragraphs 13.011 et seq, below.

The Leniency Notice.   A revised Model Leniency Programme was issued in **5.022** November 2012, and is available on DG Comp's website.

Fn 56 The Commission now publishes a 'Questions and Answers' page in the Cartels section of the DG Comp website (at the time of writing, it was last updated in April 2012).

Proving the infringement.   **5.024**
Fn 68 The Court of Justice dismissed the further appeal against the decision in COMP/37766 *Netherlands Beer Market*, decision of 18 April 2007, in Cases C-452/11P *Heineken Nederland and Heineken v Commission*, judgment of 19 December 2012; and C-445/11P *Bavaria v Commission*, judgment of 19 December 2012.

Fn 71 Two of the appeals against COMP/398181 *Candle Waxes*, decision of 1 October 2008, were largely dismissed: Cases T-548/08 *Total v Commission*, judgment of 13 September 2013 (appeal on other grounds dismissed); and T-566/08 *Total Raffinage Marketing*, judgment of 13 September 2013 (appeal on liability dismissed, fine reduced on grounds of duration). The other appeals (Cases T-540/08, etc, not yet decided) are still pending.

5.026   **Contemporaneous documents.**
Fn 80 The Court of Justice dismissed the further appeals against the decision in COMP/37766 *Netherlands Beer Market*, decision of 18 April 2007, in Cases C-452/11P *Heineken Nederland and Heineken v Commission*, judgment of 19 December 2012; and C-445/11P *Bavaria v Commission*, judgment of 19 December 2012.

5.028   **Credibility of statements made by a leniency applicant.**
Fn 89 The Court of Justice dismissed the further appeal in Case C-70/12P *Quinn Barlo v Commission* ('*Methacrylates*'), judgment of 30 May 2013, [2013] 5 CMLR 637. The General Court dismissed an appeal against COMP/398181 *Candle Waxes*, decision of 1 October 2008 in Case T-566/08 *Total Raffinage Marketing*, judgment of 13 September 2013, paras 63 et seq (fine reduced on grounds of duration). The appeal, on other grounds, in Case T-548/08 *Total v Commission*, judgment of 13 September 2013, was also dismissed. The other appeals (Cases T-540/08, etc, not yet decided) are still pending.

On the economic benefits of submitting a leniency application, and the consequent impact upon the credibility of the applicant, see the discussion in the General Court's judgment in Case T-588/08 *Dole Food Company v Commission*, judgment of 14 March 2013, paras 86 et seq. Dole argued that the leniency application had been made in order to secure the completion of an acquisition by the leniency applicant of another company: the banks that had been asked to finance the acquisition had expressed concerns about the leniency applicant's operations, and had only agreed to provide the financing once immunity had been granted. The General Court rejected the argument that this undermined the leniency applicant's credibility. It held that 'the existence of a personal interest in reporting the existence of a concerted practice does not necessarily mean that the person doing so is unreliable' (para 92). The existence of the banks' concerns reinforced the credibility of the evidence that the cartel existed (para 93), and any economic benefits that the leniency applicant obtained as a result of being granted immunity had to be balanced against the exposure to third party damages actions that would arise as a result of its admissions (para 94).

Fn 90 In Case T-462/07 *Galp Energía España v Commission*, judgment of 16 September 2013, paras 129 et seq the General Court dismissed a complaint that two leniency applicants appeared to have coordinated their applications.

Fn 91 The Court of Justice dismissed the further appeal in Case C-70/12P *Quinn Barlo v Commission* ('*Methacrylates*'), judgment of 30 May 2013, [2013] 5 CMLR 637. On this point in particular, see also the General Court's judgment in Case T-588/08 *Dole Food Company v Commission*, judgment of 14 March 2013, para 91.

Fn 92 The Court of Justice dismissed the further appeal in Case C-70/12P *Quinn Barlo v Commission* ('*Methacrylates*'), judgment of 30 May 2013, [2013] 5 CMLR 637.

(e) Sanctions and redress

The harm caused by cartels.   **5.031**
Fn 100 The General Court upheld the Commission's decision in COMP/39188 *Bananas*, decision of 15 October 2008, and specifically rejected the contention that it was necessary to show the infringement had led to higher prices for consumers: Case T-587/08 *Fresh Del Monte Produce v Commission*, judgment of 14 March 2013, paras 459–460; and Case T-588/08 *Dole Food Company v Commission*, judgment of 14 March 2013, paras 64–65. On further appeal, Cases 293&294/13P *Fresh Del Monte Produce v Commission*, not yet decided; and Case 286/13P *Dole Food Company v Commission*, not yet decided.

Fines—overview.   The approach of the General Court in the appeals against the   **5.032**
Commission's decision in COMP/38543 *International Removals Services*, decision of 11 March 2008, has been upheld by the Court of Justice in Case C-444/11P *Team Relocations v Commission*, judgment of 11 July 2013, paras 139–141.

See also the updates to Chapter 14, below.

Deterrence.   On the uplift of fines for deterrence, see also the update to para-   **5.033**
graph 14.071, below.

Repeat infringements and other aggravating factors.   On recidivism and other   **5.034**
aggravating factors, see also the updates to paragraphs 14.040 et seq, below.

Fn 110 In Case C-508/11P *Commission v Eni*, judgment of 8 May 2013, the Court of Justice dismissed the Commission's appeal against the General Court's judgment in Case T-39/07 *ENI v Commission*, judgment of 13 July 2011. The Commission issued a second statement of objections to Eni and Versalis on 1 March 2013, providing the explanation held by the General Court to have been absent from the decision in COMP/38638 *Butadeine Rubber and Emulsion Styrene Butadeine Rubber*, decision of 29 November 2006, [2009] 4 CMLR 421 (namely of the capacity in which, or extent to which, the undertaking was considered to have participated in a previous infringement) and reaching the provisional conclusion that an uplift should be imposed for recidivism: COMP/40032 *BR/ESBR Recidivism*, Press Release IP/13/179 (1 March 2013).

Joint and several liability for payment of the fine.   On joint and several liability,   **5.035**
see also the updates to paragraphs 14.087, below.

Criminal sanctions.   The Enterprise and Regulatory Reform Act 2013 received   **5.036**
Royal Assent in April 2013. Section 47 amends s 188 of the Enterprise Act 2002 to remove the dishonesty requirement from the cartel offence, and adds ss 188A

and 188B to clarify the circumstances in which the offence is committed. These provide:

(a) Under s 188A, parties to an arrangement that would otherwise be within the scope of the offence may bring the arrangement outside the scope, if they satisfy certain notification requirements. These are: (a) the notification exclusion (under the terms of the arrangement customers would be given relevant information about the arrangements before they enter into agreements for the supply to them of the product or service affected); (b) the bid-rigging notification exclusion (the person requesting bids would be given relevant information about the arrangements at or before the time when a bid is made); or (c) the publication exclusion (relevant information about the arrangement would be published, before the arrangements are implemented, in the manner specified at the time of the making of the agreement in an order made by the Secretary of State). 'Relevant information' for the purpose of these exclusions is defined as the names of the undertakings to which the arrangements relate; a description of the nature of the arrangements which is sufficient to show why they are or might be arrangements which fall within the scope of the offence; the products or services to which they relate; and any other information as may be specified in an order made by the Secretary of State.

(b) Under s 188B, three statutory defences are created. These are: (a) where the arrangements would affect supply in the UK, the individual did not intend that the nature of the arrangements would be concealed from customers before they enter into agreements for the supply to them of the product or service; (b) the individual did not intend that the nature of the arrangements would be concealed from the Competition and Markets Authority; (c) before making the agreement, the individual took reasonable steps to ensure that the nature of the arrangements would be disclosed to professional legal advisers, for the purpose of obtaining advice about them before they were made or implemented.

The provisions will enter force in April 2014.

5.037 **Private actions for damages arising from cartel activity.**   The Commission has proposed a Directive on certain rules governing actions for damages under national law for infringements of the competition law provisions of the Member States and of the European Union (COM(2013) 404 final, COD 2013/0185) ('Draft Damages Directive'), issued on 16 June 2013. The detailed proposals are discussed in the updates to Chapter 16, below.

2. Prices and Pricing Restrictions

5.040 **Effect of price-fixing on prices.**
Fn 126 The General Court upheld the Commission's decision in COMP/39188 *Bananas*, decision of 15 October 2008, and applied the approach laid down in

Case C-8/08 *T-Mobile v Netherlands* [2009] ECR I-4529, in Case T-587/08 *Fresh Del Monte Produce v Commission*, judgment of 14 March 2013 (reducing the fine but dismissing the appeal on liability), paras 459–460; and Case T-588/08 *Dole Food Company v Commission*, judgment of 14 March 2013, paras 64–65. On further appeal, Cases 293&294/13P *Fresh Del Monte Produce v Commission*, not yet decided; and Case 286/13P *Dole Food Company v Commission*, not yet decided.

Fn 131 On this aspect of the Commission's decision in particular, see Case T-587/08 *Fresh Del Monte Produce v Commission*, judgment of 14 March 2013, paras 305–308; and Case T-588/08 *Dole Food Company v Commission*, judgment of 14 March 2013, paras 67–71.

Price-fixing. The Commission's findings of infringement in decision **5.041** COMP/39406 *Marine Hoses*, decision of 28 January 2009, discussed in the main text, were upheld but the decision was partially annulled on other grounds, in Case T-146/09, etc, *Parker ITR and Parker-Hannifin v Commission (Marine Hoses)*, judgments of 17 May 2013, [2013] 5 CMLR 712 (on further appeal, Case C-434/13P *Commission v Parker Hannifin Manufacturing and Parker-Hannifin*, not yet decided).

Fn 135 The OFT's *Dairy Retail Prices Initiative* decision, of 26 July 2011, was partially annulled on appeal by the CAT, in *Tesco v OFT* [2012] CAT 31.

Fn 141 See also Joined Cases T-379&381/10 *Keramag Keramische Werke and Others v Commission ('Bathroom Fittings')*, judgment of 16 September 2013, paras 59 et seq. The General Court confirmed that the coordination of indicative list prices is an object infringement.

Fn 144 See also *BA / Virgin*, OFT decision of 19 April 2012, where the parties notified each other of their intentions to increase fuel surcharges, prior to those increases being announced publicly.

Agreement to fix recommended or maximum prices. As well as the forms of **5.042** 'recommended' prices noted in the main text, coordination of indicative list prices is an infringement by object, as list prices serve as a starting point for subsequent price negotiations: Joined Cases T-379&381/10 *Keramag Keramische Werke and Others v Commission ('Bathroom Fittings')*, judgment of 16 September 2013, paras 59 et seq.

Elements added to price. **5.043**
Fn 158 The Commission's findings of infringement in decision COMP/39406 *Marine Hoses*, decision of 28 January 2009, were upheld, but the decision was partially annulled on other grounds in Case T-146/09, etc, *Parker ITR and Parker-Hannifin v Commission (Marine Hoses)*, judgments of 17 May 2013, [2013] 5 CMLR 712 (on further appeal, Case C-434/13P *Commission v Parker Hannifin Manufacturing and Parker-Hannifin*, not yet decided).

5.045 **Other contractual provisions related to pricing.**
Fn 162 The Commission's decisions in COMP/39847 *E-books*, decision of 12 December 2012 (OJ 2012 C283/7), and of 25 July 2013 (Press Release IP/13/746 (25 July 2013)) accepted commitments from five publishing companies, and Apple, *inter alia* not to enter into most favoured nation clauses for five years. See also M.6458 *Universal Music Group / EMI Music* (21 September 2012), in which the Commission cleared a merger upon Universal committing *inter alia* not to include most favoured national clauses in its licensing agreements with digital music services in the EEA for five years.

5.046 **Price transparency.**   The General Court has upheld the Commission's decision in COMP/39188 *Bananas*, decision of 15 October 2008, in Case T-587/08 *Fresh Del Monte Produce v Commission*, judgment of 14 March 2013 (reducing the fine but dismissing the appeal on liability); and Case T-588/08 *Dole Food Company v Commission*, judgment of 14 March 2013. On further appeal, Cases 293&294/13P *Fresh Del Monte Produce v Commission*, not yet decided; and Case 286/13P *Dole Food Company v Commission*, not yet decided.

Fn 168 See also *BA / Virgin*, OFT decision of 19 April 2012.

5.047 **Price agreements among distributors.**
Fn 174 The test laid down by the Court of Appeal in *Argos & Littlewoods and JJB Sports v Office of Fair Trading* [2006] EWCA Civ 1318 was applied by the Competition Appeal Tribunal in *Tesco v OFT* [2012] CAT 31, which discusses in detail the state of mind required to satisfy the test.

5.052 **Fixing of purchase prices.**
Fn 191 The further appeal against Case T-38/05 *Agroexpansion* [2011] ECR II-7005 was dismissed by the Court of Justice in Case C-668/11P *Alliance One International v Commission*, judgment of 26 September 2013. The further appeal against T-41/05 *Dimons* [2011] ECR II-7101 was dismissed in Case C-679/11P *Alliance One International v Commission*, judgment of 26 September 2013.

Fn 192 The further appeal in Case C-593/11P *Alliance One International* was dismissed as manifestly unfounded in part, and inadmissible in part, by Order of 13 December 2012. The Court of Justice upheld the appeal in Case C-652/11P *Mindo*, judgment of 13 April 2013, [2013] 4 CMLR 1, and has referred the case back to the General Court (remitted case not yet decided). The further appeal in Case C-654/11P *Transcatab* was dismissed by Order of 13 December 2012.

5.054 **Resale price maintenance for books.**
Fn 200 The Commission's decisions in COMP/39847 *E-books*, decision of 12 December 2012 (OJ 2012 C283/7), and of 25 July 2013 (Press Release IP/13/746 (25 July 2013)), accepted commitments from five publishing companies, and Apple, under which the undertakings agreed to terminate their agency agreements,

to allow retailers full discretion to set their e-book prices for at least two years, and not to enter into most favoured nation clauses for five years.

Price-fixing and Article 101(3). The General Court has ruled on appeals 5.057 against the two Commission decisions referred to in the main text. In respect of COMP/398181 *Candle Waxes*, decision of 1 October 2008, two of the appeals on other grounds were largely dismissed: Cases T-548/08 *Total v Commission*, judgment of 13 September 2013, and T-566/08 *Total Raffinage Marketing*, judgment of 13 September 2013 (reducing the fine but dismissing the appeal on liability). The other appeals (Cases T-540/08, etc, not yet decided) are still pending. In respect of COMP/39188 *Bananas*, decision of 15 October 2008, the General Court upheld the decision on other grounds in Case T-587/08 *Fresh Del Monte Produce v Commission*, judgment of 14 March 2013 (reducing the fine but dismissing the appeal on liability); and Case T-588/08 *Dole Food Company v Commission*, judgment of 14 March 2013. On further appeal, Cases 293&294/13P *Fresh Del Monte Produce v Commission*, not yet decided; and Case 286/13P *Dole Food Company v Commission*, not yet decided.

Relevance of legislative price controls.   5.059
Fn 219 Two of the appeals against COMP/398181 *Candle Waxes*, decision of 1 October 2008, on other grounds were largely dismissed: Cases T-548/08 *Total v Commission*, judgment of 13 September 2013; and T-566/08 *Total Raffinage Marketing*, judgment of 13 September 2013 (reducing the fine but dismissing the appeal on liability). The other appeals (Cases T-540/08, etc, not yet decided) are still pending.

4. Market-sharing and Customer Allocation

(a) Generally

Market-sharing.   5.065
Fn 241 The Commission's findings of infringement in decision COMP/39406 *Marine Hoses*, decision of 28 January 2009, discussed in the main text were upheld, but the decision was partially annulled on other grounds, in Case T-146/09, etc, *Parker ITR and Parker-Hannifin v Commission (Marine Hoses)*, judgments of 17 May 2013, [2013] 5 CMLR 712 (on further appeal, Case C-434/13P *Commission v Parker Hannifin Manufacturing and Parker-Hannifin*, not yet decided).

Market-sharing between producers.   5.066
Fn 242 See also COMP/39839 *Telefónica and Portugal Telecom*, decision of 23 January 2013, concerning an agreement under which the parties agreed not to compete in the Iberian pensinsula, following the acquisition by Telefónica of the Brazilian mobile operator, Vivo, which until then had been jointly owned by

Telefónica and Portugal Telecom (on appeal Cases T-208/13 *Portugal Telecom v Commission*; and T-216/13 *Telefónica v Commission*, not yet decided).

Fn 244 See also COMP/39839 *Telefónica and Portugal Telecom*, decision of 23 January 2013, referred to in the update to footnote 242, above. The Commission's finding of infringement in this regard in COMP/398181 *Candle Waxes*, decision of 1 October 2008, was upheld in Case T-566/08 *Total Raffinage Marketing*, judgment of 13 September 2013, paras 192 et seq (fine reduced on other grounds). The appeal on other grounds in Case T-548/08 *Total v Commission*, judgment of 13 September 2013, was dismissed, and the other appeals (Cases T-540/08, etc, not yet decided) are still pending. The findings of infringement in COMP/39406 *Marine Hoses*, decision of 28 January 2009, were also upheld, but the decision was partially annulled on other grounds, in Cases T-146/09, etc, *Parker ITR and Parker-Hannifin v Commission (Marine Hoses)*, judgments of 17 May 2013, [2013] 5 CMLR 712 (on further appeal, Case C-434/13P *Commission v Parker Hannifin Manufacturing and Parker-Hannifin*, not yet decided).

5.068 Market-sharing between purchasers.
Fn 249 The further appeal against Case T-38/05 *Agroexpansion* [2011] ECR II-7005 was dismissed by the Court of Justice in Case C-668/11P *Alliance One International v Commission*, judgment of 26 September 2013. The further appeal against Case T-41/05 *Dimons* [2011] ECR II-7101 was dismissed in Case C-679/11P *Alliance One International v Commission*, judgment of 26 September 2013.

5.073 Market-sharing under Article 101(3).
Fn 266 Two of the appeals against COMP/398181 *Candle Waxes*, decision of 1 October 2008, on other grounds were largely dismissed: Cases T-548/08 *Total v Commission*, judgment of 13 September 2013; and T-566/08 *Total Raffinage Marketing*, judgment of 13 September 2013 (reducing the fine but dismissing the appeal on liability). The other appeals (Cases T-540/08, etc, not yet decided) are still pending.

(d) Customer allocation

5.083 Customer allocation.
Fn 292 The General Court has ruled on appeals against a number of the decisions referred to in the footnote:

The Commission's finding of infringement in COMP/398181 *Candle Waxes*, decision of 1 October 2008, was upheld in Case T-566/08 *Total Raffinage Marketing*, judgment of 13 September 2013, paras 209 et seq (fine reduced on other grounds). The appeal on other grounds in Case T-548/08 *Total v Commission*, judgment of 13 September 2013, was dismissed, and the other appeals (Cases T-540/08, etc, not yet decided) are still pending.

Four of the appeals against COMP/39396 *Calcium Carbide and magnesium based reagents*, decision of 22 July 2009 (appeals only in respect of fines) were dismissed: Cases T-352/09 *Nováckechemické závody v Commission*, judgment of 12 December 2012, [2013] 4 CMLR 734; T-392/09 *1. garantovana v Commission*, judgment of 12 December 2012 (on further appeal C-90/13P, not yet decided); T-400/09 *Ecka Granulate v Commission*, judgment of 12 December 2012; and T-410/09 *Almamet v Commission*, judgment of 12 December 2012, [2013] 4 CMLR 788. The appeals in Cases T-384/09, etc, are still pending.

5. Information Exchange

Information exchange ancillary to a cartel. The General Court has ruled on **5.085** a number of appeals against the decisions referred to in the main text. In respect of COMP/39406 *Marine Hoses*, decision of 28 January 2009, the General Court upheld the Commission's finding of infringement but the decision was partially annulled on other grounds, in Cases T-146/09, etc, *Parker ITR and Parker-Hannifin v Commission (Marine Hoses)*, judgments of 17 May 2013, [2013] 5 CMLR 712 (on further appeal, Case C-434/13P *Commission v Parker Hannifin Manufacturing and Parker-Hannifin*, not yet decided). In respect of COMP/39188 *Bananas*, decision of 15 October 2008, the General Court upheld the decision in Case T-587/08 *Fresh Del Monte Produce v Commission*, judgment of 14 March 2013 (reducing the fine but dismissing the appeal on liability); and Case T-588/08 *Dole Food Company v Commission*, judgment of 14 March 2013. On further appeal, Cases 293 & 294/13P *Fresh Del Monte Produce v Commission*, not yet decided; and Case 286/13P *Dole Food Company v Commission*, not yet decided. In *Dole* in particular the General Court upheld the distinction the Commission had drawn between infringements by object and effect, based on whether the information was exchanged before or after transaction prices were set.

The General Court has emphasised that in order for the exchange of sensitive information to constitute a breach of Article 101, the undertakings concerned must be competitors in the relevant product market, such that there is potential for the recipient of the information to modify its conduct as a result of having received that information. In appeals against the Commission's decision in COMP/39092 *Bathroom Fittings*, decision of 23 June 2010, which concerned a single and continuous infringement across three separate product markets, the General Court held that:

> 'it cannot be presumed that an agreement or a concerted practice whereby undertakings exchange information which is commercially sensitive but which relates to a product sold on a market on which they are not competitors has an anti-competitive object or effect on that market. A practice whereby an undertaking which is active on two distinct product markets provides to its competitors – which are present on

one market – commercially sensitive information which relates to a second market – on which those competitors are not present – is not capable, in principle, of having an impact on competition on the second market.'

See Case T-380/10 *Wabco Europe v Commission (Bathroom Fittings)*, judgment of 16 September 2013, paras 78 et seq; and Joined Cases T-379&381/10 *Keramag Keramische Werke and Others (Bathroom Fittings) v Commission*, judgment of 16 September 2013, paras 92 and 221.

Fn 295 In Case T-404/08 *Fluorsid and Minmet v Commission*, judgment of 18 June 2013, [2013] 5 CMLR 902, para 94; and Case T-406/08 *Industries chimiques du fluor v Commission*, judgment of 18 June 2013 (on further appeal, Case C-467/13P, not yet decided), paras 88 and 106, the General Court upheld the Commission's decision in COMP/39810 *Aluminium Fluoride*, decision of 25 June 2008, in respect of the exchange of information.

6. Collective Exclusive Dealing

(b) Joint tendering and bid-rigging

5.090 Generally.
Fn 312 See also COMP/39748 *Automotive Wire Harnesses*, decision of 10 July 2013, Press Release IP/13/673 (10 July 2013).

The Commission's finding of infringement in COMP/39406 *Marine Hoses*, decision of 28 January 2009, were upheld, but the decision was partially annulled on other grounds, in Case T-146/09 *Parker ITR and Parker-Hannifin v Commission (Marine Hoses)*, judgments of 17 May 2013, [2013] 5 CMLR 712 (on further appeal, Case C-434/13P *Commission v Parker Hannifin Manufacturing and Parker-Hannifin*, not yet decided).

The further appeal against COMP/38823 *Elevators and Escalators*, decision of 21 February 2007, in Case C-493/11P, etc, *United Technologies*, has been dismissed as partly inadmissible, and partly clearly unfounded, by Order of 15 June 2012.

In the further appeals against the Commission's decision in COMP/38543 *International Removals Services*, decision of 11 March 2008, the Court of Justice in Case C-441/11P *Commission v Verhuizingen Coppens*, judgment of 6 December 2012, [2013] 4 CMLR 312 reversed the General Court's judgment, holding that it had erred in annulling the decision entirely. The Court instead upheld the Commission's decision in respect of Coppens' participation in cover pricing, and annulled it partially. The Court dismissed the further appeals in Case C-439/11P *Ziegler v Commission*, judgment of 11 July 2013; and Case C-444/11P *Team Relocations v Commission*, judgment of 11 July 2013.

Bid-rigging. The Commission's finding of infringement in decision **5.091** COMP/39406 *Marine Hoses*, decision of 28 January 2009, were upheld, but the decision was partially annulled on other grounds, in Cases T-146/09, etc, *Parker ITR and Parker-Hannifin v Commission (Marine Hoses)*, judgments of 17 May 2013, [2013] 5 CMLR 712 (on further appeal, Case C-434/13P *Commission v Parker Hannifin Manufacturing and Parker-Hannifin*, not yet decided).

Fn 319 The Danish Competition and Consumer Authority published guidelines on fighting bid rigging in public procurement 29 November 2012: ECN Brief 01/2013, p3.

Cover pricing. **5.093**
Fn 323 The Court of Justice in Case C-441/11P *Commission v Verhuizingen Coppens*, judgment of 6 December 2012, [2013] CMLR 312, set aside the General Court's judgment, and instead annulled the Commission decision only in respect of Verhuizingen Coppens' participation in the cartel activities beyond cover pricing, and the attribution to it of a single and continuous infringement.

6

NON-COVERT HORIZONTAL
COOPERATION

1. Introduction

(c) Sources of law and general principles for assessment

De minimis and safe harbours.   6.10

Fn 34 At the time of writing, the Commission is consulting on a revised *De Minimis* Notice (see paragraphs 2.164 et seq, and the updates thereto) to take account of the Court of Justice's judgment in Case C-226/11 *Expedia Inc*, judgment of 13 December 2012, [2013] 4 CMLR 439, paras 36–37, in which the Court held that an agreement that may affect trade between Member States and that has an anti-competitive object constitutes, by its nature and independently of any concrete effect that it may have, an appreciable restriction on competition.

Centre of gravity of cooperation.   6.013

Fn 39 The General Court upheld the Commission's decision in COMP/38698 *CISAC Agreements*, decision of 16 July 2008, insofar as it found that the exclusivity clause (Cases T-401/08 *Säveltäjäin Tekijänoikeustoimisto Teosto v Commission*, judgment of 12 April 2013, [2013] 5 CMLR 15) and membership clause (Cases T-392, 401, 422, 432/08, judgments of 12 April 2013, [2013] 5 CMLR 15) in the agreements infringed Article 101. It partially annulled the decision, in respect of the Commission's conclusions as to the existence of a concerted practice, in Cases T-392, 398, 401, 410, 411, 413–422, 425, 428, 432–434, 442/08, judgments of 12 April 2013.

Ancillary restraints.   6.016

Fn 62 See also the Commission's decision in COMP/39839 *Telefónica/Portugal Telecom*, decision of 23 January 2013, paras 367 et seq, concerning a clause in which the parties agreed not to compete in the Iberian pensinsula following the acquisition by Telefónica of the Brazilian mobile operator, Vivo, which until then had been jointly owned by Telefónica and Portugal Telecom (on appeal, Cases T-208/13 *Portugal Telecom v Commission*; and T-216/13 *Telefónica v Commission*, not yet decided).

2. Information Exchange

(b) Information exchange amounting to an agreement, concerted practice or decision by an association of undertakings

6.020 **Direct or indirect sharing of data.** In order for the exchange of information to constitute a breach of Article 101 the undertakings concerned must be competitors in the relevant product market, such that there is potential for the recipient of the information to modify its conduct as a result of having received that information. The General Court emphasised in Case T-380/10 *Wabco Europe v Commission (Bathroom Fittings)*, judgment of 16 September 2013, paras 78 et seq that:

> 'it cannot be presumed that an agreement or a concerted practice whereby undertakings exchange information which is commercially sensitive but which relates to a product sold on a market on which they are not competitors has an anti-competitive object or effect on that market. A practice whereby an undertaking which is active on two distinct product markets provides to its competitors – which are present on one market – commercially sensitive information which relates to a second market – on which those competitors are not present – is not capable, in principle, of having an impact on competition on the second market.': see in particular para 79.

The Court distinguished its earlier case law in Joined Cases T-456&457/05 *Gütermann and Zwicky v Commission* [2010] ECR II-1443, relied upon by the Commission, on the basis that that judgment would apply to a disclosure of commercially sensitive information with a view to restricting competition in the market on which the recipient of the information is active, by a disclosing party that is not itself active on that market, whereas in the decision under appeal, COMP/39092 *Bathroom Fittings*, decision of 23 June 2010, the Commission had (as the Court held, wrongly) found that the purpose of the disclosure was to restrict competition in a market on which the disclosing party was active but the recipient was not: see paras 98–99. See also Joined Cases T-379&381/10 *Keramag Keramische Werke and Others (Bathroom Fittings) v Commission*, judgment of 16 September 2013, paras 92 and 221.

6.022 **Dissemination of information by an association of undertakings.** There is also a risk, where an undertaking is a member of an umbrella association, or cross-product association, that it will be considered to be aware of the anti-competitive behaviour of the other members: see Case T-378/10 *Masco and others v Commission*, judgment of 16 September 2013, paras 61–62 and 82, in which the General Court upheld the Commission's conclusion in COMP/39092 *Bathroom Fittings*, decision of 23 June 2010, finding that the undertaking concerned must have been aware of the anti-competitive behaviour of the other members, for the purposes of finding a single and continuous infringement (see paragraphs 2.076 et seq, and the updates thereto).

'Hub and spoke' or 'ABC' collusion.　　　　　　　　　　　　　　　　　　**6.023**
Fn 86 The Commission's preliminary assessment in its commitments decision in
COMP/39847 *E-Books*, decision of 12 December 2012 (OJ 2012 C283/7), was
that the publishing companies had each entered into agreements with Apple, having also discussed the arrangements between themselves: paras 29 and 34.

Hub and spoke agreements in national enforcement.　　　　　　　　　　**6.024**
Fn 87 The OFT's *Dairy Retail Prices Initiative* decision was partially annulled on
appeal by the Competition Appeal Tribunal, in *Tesco v OFT* [2012] CAT 31.

Fn 88 The state of mind required to satisfy the test laid down by the Court of
Appeal in *Argos & Littlewoods and JJB Sports v OFT* [2006] EWCA Civ 1318,
para 141 was discussed at length by the Competition Appeal Tribunal in *Tesco v
OFT* [2012] CAT 31. At stage (i) it is not sufficient to show retailer A knew supplier
B 'might' pass on the information (para 78), and the Tribunal expressed doubts as
to whether anything short of intention or actual foresight that supplier B will pass
on the information will suffice (paras 350–354).

(c) **Analysis of the competitive effects of information exchanges**

Object restrictions: practices facilitating the fixing of purchase or selling　**6.027**
prices.　 See also the General Court judgments in Case T-380/10 *Wabco
Europe v Commission (Bathroom Fittings)*, judgment of 16 September 2013,
paras 78–79; and Joined Cases T-379&381/10 *Keramag Keramische Werke and
Others (Bathroom Fittings) v Commission*, judgment of 16 September 2013,
paras 92 and 221, discussed in the update to paragraph 6.020, above.

Pre-pricing communications and exchange of quotation prices.　 The General　**6.028**
Court upheld the Commission's decision in COMP/39188 *Bananas*, decision
of 15 October 2008, in Case T-587/08 *Fresh Del Monte Produce v Commission*,
judgment of 14 March 2013 (reducing the fine but dismissing the appeal on
liability); and Case T-588/08 *Dole Food Company v Commission*, judgment of
14 March 2013. On further appeal, Cases C-293 & 294/13P *Fresh Del Monte
Produce v Commission*, not yet decided; and Case 286/13P *Dole Food Company v
Commission*, not yet decided.

Fn 101 Although the appeal by Weichert was dismissed as inadmissible, it inter-
vened in the appeal by its parent company, Del Monte. The General Court reduced
the fine imposed on the undertaking by a further 10 per cent to reflect the relative
gravity of its participation in the cartel: Case T-587/08 *Fresh Del Monte Produce v
Commission*, judgment of 14 March 2013, paras 816–817 (on further appeal Cases
C-293 & 294/13P *Fresh Del Monte Produce v Commission*, not yet decided).

Fn 102 On this aspect of the appeal, see Case T-588/08 *Dole v Commission*, judgment of 14 March 2013, paras 53 et seq, where the General Court dismisses the
argument. On further appeal, Case 286/13P, not yet decided.

6.030 Disclosure of pricing information: cases at the national level. The OFT decision in *BA / Virgin*, decision of 19 April 2012, is a further example of an NCA decision finding that exchanges of information are an object infringement. The OFT condemned the sharing of confidential future pricing information by one airline with another regarding increases in fuel surcharges.

Fn 111 The OFT's *Dairy Retail Prices Initiative* decision was partially annulled on appeal by the Competition Appeal Tribunal, in *Tesco v OFT* [2012] CAT 31.

5. Joint Purchasing Agreements

6.067 Competition concerns.
Fn 301 The further appeal in Case C-593/11P *Alliance One International* was dismissed as manifestly unfounded in part, and inadmissible in part, by Order of 13 December 2012. The Court of Justice upheld the appeal in Case C-652/11P *Mindo*, judgment of 13 April 2013, [2013] 4 CMLR 1381, and has referred the case back to the General Court (remitted case not yet decided). The further appeal in Case C-654/11P *Transcatab* was dismissed by Order of 13 December 2012.

(a) Assessment under Article 101(1)

6.071 Effect restrictions.
Fn 319 The Maritime Transport Guidelines, OJ 2008 C245/2: Vol II, App E20, expired on 26 September 2013, and the Commission has announced that it will not renew them: Press Release IP/13/122 (19 February 2013).

7. Standardisation Agreements and Agreements on Standard Terms

(a) Assessment under Article 101(1)

6.085 Restrictions by object.
Fn 390 For a further example, see the decision of the Belgian Competition Council finding that three Belgian cement producers, their trade association, and the National Centre for Technical and Scientific Research for the cement industry had all colluded, in breach of Article 101, with the aim of delaying the adoption of a licence, and of the standards, that would make it possible to use a particular alternative component in ready-mix concrete in Belgium. Sales of cement as a component in ready-mix concrete were secured by the delay: ECN Brief 04/2013, p33.

FRAND commitments.   **6.087**

Fn 402 The appeals by Hynix Semiconductor (now trading as SK Hynix Inc) in Joined Cases T-148&149/10 against COMP/38636 *Rambus*, decision of 9 December 2009, were withdrawn on 5 July 2013.

On the Commission's ongoing investigation into alleged abusive conduct in relation to IPR used in international telecoms standards, see Press Release IP/12/1448 (21 December 2012) regarding the statement of objections sent in COMP/39939 *Samsung – enforcement of ETSI standards essential patents* and IP/13/406 (6 May 2013) regarding the statement of objections sent in COMP/39985 *Motorola – enforcement of ETSI standards essential patents*. The Commission's preliminary view is that it is an abuse of dominance, contrary to Article 102, for the holder of a standard essential patent to seek injunctions for patent infringement in circumstances where it has given a commitment that it will grant licences on FRAND terms and where the potential licensee has agreed to accept a binding determination of the terms of a FRAND licence by a third party. At the time of writing, the Commission is consulting on commitments proposed by Samsung under which it would agree, in essence, for a period of five years not to seek an injunction before any court or tribunal in the EEA for infringement of its standard essential patents (including all existing and future patents) implemented in smartphones and tablets against a potential licensee that agrees to, and complies with, a particular framework for determining the terms of a licence: see OJ 2013 C302/11.

The Landgericht of Düsseldorf has referred to the Court of Justice for a preliminary ruling various questions concerning the circumstances in which it is an abuse for an undertaking to seek an injunction for breach of its standard essential patent: Case C-170/13 *Huawei Technologies v ZTE*, not yet decided.

8. Trade Associations

(a) Membership rules

Restrictions on ceasing membership or membership of competing organ-   **6.096**
isations.   See also the Commission's findings in respect of the membership clause in the model contract drawn up by CISAC for use by its members, in COMP/38698 *CISAC Agreements*, decision of 16 July 2008, [2009] 4 CMLR 577. The General Court dismissed the appeals against this aspect of the Commission's decision: Cases T-392, 401, 422, 432/08, judgments of 12 April 2013, [2013] 5 CMLR 15. The decision was partially annulled on other grounds: Cases T-392, 398, 401, 410, 411, 413–422, 425, 428, 432–434, 442/08, judgments of 12 April 2013.

9. Horizontal Cooperation Agreements—Illustrations from Specific Sectors

(a) Airlines

6.100 **Collaborative arrangements.**
Fn 449 See also COMP/39595 *Continental/United/Lufthansa/Air Canada*, decision of 23 May 2013 accepting commitments under Article 9 of Regulation 1/2003.

(b) Banking and payment services

6.102 **Generally.**   See also the Report on Competition Policy (2012). The Commission observes that 'a viable, transparent and competitive banking system providing finance to the real economy is a necessary precondition to restore sustainable growth' (p2).

6.103 **Competition, the single market and regulation of financial services.**   Regulation 924/2009 was amended by Regulation 260/2012 establishing technical and business requirements for credit transfers and direct debits in euro and amending Regulation 924/2009, OJ 2012 L94/22, which was adopted on 12 March 2012. This obliges all users to move to the new Single Euro Payment Area systems established by the European Payments Council. Following the Green Paper 'Towards an integrated European market for card, internet and mobile payments' COM/2011/0941 final (11 January 2012), the Commission adopted on 24 July 2013 a legislative package which includes a proposed revised Directive on payment services in the internal market (COM(2013) 547 final, 2013/0264 (COD)) and a proposed Regulation on interchange fees for card-based payment transactions (COM(2013) 550 final, 2013/0265 (COD)).

6.105 **Price-fixing in the banking sector.**   The Commission has taken steps to address the manipulation by various banks of the benchmark used in derivatives trading, in particular of the London Interbank Offered Rate (LIBOR) and the Euro Interbank Offered Rate (EURIBOR). An amendment to the proposed Market Abuse Regulation (proposal for a Regulation on indices used as benchmarks in financial instruments and financial contracts, COM(2013)0641 final, 2013/0314(COD)) was agreed by the Parliament and Council in June 2013 to make the manipulation of benchmarks a criminal offence. The Commission is also pursuing a number of antitrust investigations into these benchmarks: Report on Competition Policy (2012) p27.

Fn 475 The Commission's decision in COMP/38606 *Groupement des Cartes Bancaires*, decision of 17 October 2007, has been upheld by the General Court in Case T-491/07 *CB v Commission*, judgment of 29 November 2012, para 83. On further appeal, Case C-67/13P, not yet decided.

Exclusion of competitors from horizontal arrangements. The Commission **6.106** has issued a statement of objections in COMP/39745 *CDS – Information Market*, regarding agreements between thirteen investment banks, the International Swaps and Derivatives Association and a data service provider, by which they prevented two exchanges from entering the credit derivatives market. The ISDA and data service provider were instructed by the investment banks which controlled them not to grant licences for data and index benchmarks to two exchanges that sought to enter the market: see Press Release IP/613/630 (1 July 2013). The investigation in COMP/39730 *CDS – Clearing* is ongoing.

Fn 481 Regulation 924/2009 was amended by Regulation 260/2012 establishing technical and business requirements for credit transfers and direct debits in euro and amending Regulation (EC) No 924/2009, which was adopted on 12 March 2012. This obliges all users to move to the new Single Euro Payment Area systems established by the European Payments Council.

Multilateral Interchange Fees. On 24 July 2013 the Commission adopted a leg- **6.107** islative package which includes a proposed revised Directive on payment services in the internal market (COM(2013) 547 final, 2013/0264 (COD)) and a proposed Regulation on interchange fees for card-based payment transactions (COM(2013) 550 final, 2013/0265 (COD)).

Fn 482 Following the Commission's investigation of Visa's MIFs for transactions with consumer credit cards, Visa has offered commitments under Article 9 of Regulation 1/2003 to reduce its fees: see MEMO 13/431 (14 May 2013).

MIFs: Scrutiny by Member States and the Commission. **6.108**
Fn 491 On 6 May 2013 the Autorité de la Concurrence began market testing commitments by both Visa and Mastercard to reduce the level of their fees in France on payments/withdrawals on their Visa and Mastercard 'only' cards (ie those outside the *Cartes Bancaires* system): ECN Brief 03/2013, p35.

(c) Professional services

(i) *Measures adopted by a professional association*

Decisions by associations of undertakings. **6.110**
Fn 499 See also Case C-1/12 *Ordem dos Técnicos Oficiais de Contas v Autoridade da Concorrência*, judgment of 28 February 2013, [2013] 4 CMLR 651, para 48.

(ii) *Analysing the competitive effects of professional rules*

Other professional rules. The Court of Justice confirmed in Case C-1/12 **6.113** *Ordem dos Técnicos Oficiais de Contas v Autoridade da Concorrência*, judgment of 28 February 2013, [2013] 4 CMLR 651, that Article 101 applies to the rules of a professional association for chartered accountants requiring them to obtain compulsory ongoing professional training through the association itself, or under-takings approved by it.

Fn 516 See also Case C-1/12 *Ordem dos Técnicos Oficiais de Contas v Autoridade da Concorrência*, judgment of 28 February 2013, [2013] 4 CMLR 651, which was a preliminary reference arising from appeal proceedings following an infringement decision by the Autoridade da Concorrência (the Portuguese NCA), against the Order of Chartered Accountants in respect of their rules on compulsory ongoing professional training.

The Italian Competition Authority has also issued an infringement decision on 23 April 2013 against five Bar Associations for imposing additional registration requirements on non-Italian lawyers: ECN Brief 03/2013, p35.

(d) Sporting bodies and competitions

6.117 *Meca-Medina* and 'sporting rules'.
Fn 531 The Court of Justice dismissed the further appeal in Case C-269/12P *Cañas v Commission*, judgment of 20 June 2013, regarding the alleged anti-competitiveness of certain anti-doping rules.

(f) E-commerce platforms

6.124 E-commerce platforms: generally.
Fn 533 See also M.6314 *Telefónica UK/Vodafone UK/EE/JV* (4 September 2012), in which the Commission considered a full-function JV established by three of the leading UK MNOs to operate in the nascent 'mCommerce' sector (or mobile commerce sector) which encompasses mobile payments, mobile advertising, and data analytics, and which has developed with the rapid emergence and market penetration of smartphone technology; and equivalent decisions clearing JVs intended to operate in Spain, M.6956 *Telefónica/Caixabank/Banco Santander/JV* (14 August 2013); and Belgium, M.6967 *BNP Paribas Fortis/Belgacom/Belgian MobileWallet JV* (11 October 2013).

7

VERTICAL AGREEMENTS AFFECTING DISTRIBUTION OR SUPPLY

2. Vertical Agreements: General Principles

(c) Approach to the application of Article 101

Vertical restraints of minor importance. The Court of Justice held in Case **7.020** C-226/11 *Expedia Inc*, judgment of 13 December 2012, [2013] 4 CMLR 439, paras 36–37, that an agreement that may affect trade between Member States and that has an anti-competitive object constitutes, by its nature and independently of any concrete effect that it may have, an appreciable restriction on competition. At the time of writing the Commission is consulting on a revised *De Minimis* Notice (see paragraphs 2.164 et seq, and the updates thereto) to take account of this judgment.

3. Regulation 330/2010

(a) Scope

Retailers' associations. **7.029**
Fn 80 For an illustration, see Case C-32/11 *Allianz Hungária Bistozitó*, judgment of 14 March 2013, [2013] 4 CMLR 863, in which the Court of Justice was asked to consider whether vertical agreements between car insurance companies and car repair shops had the object of restricting competition. It held that it was relevant to consider, *inter alia*, the fact that the terms of the agreements were based on a framework agreement, negotiated by the repair shops' trade association with the insurers, which contained recommended prices that insurers should pay to repairers for their work. There would be a restriction by object if the trade association had decided on recommended prices with the intention of harmonising prices, and the insurance companies confirmed those decisions in the framework agreement.

(c) **Hardcore restrictions**

(i) Resale price maintenance

7.040   **RPM is a restriction by object under Article 101(1).**
Fn 114 See also the Commission's decisions in COMP/39847 *E-books*, decisions of 12 December 2012 (OJ 2012 C283/7) and of 25 July 2013 (Press Release IP/13/746 (25 July 2013)) accepting commitments from five publishing companies, and Apple.

4. Exclusive Distribution and Supply Agreements

(b) **Restrictions on sales outside the exclusive grant**

7.069   **'Active' and 'passive' sales.**   The Irish High Court held in *SRI Apparel v Revolution Workwear and others* [2013] IEHC 289, para 61, that the use by a distributor (in that case, a distributor in a selective distribution agreement) of the website Amazon was active selling rather than passive, and that an agreement to restrict such activity was therefore within the scope of Article 4(b)(i) of Regulation 330/2010 (the Vertical Block Exemption).

(d) **Other common clauses in exclusive agreements**

7.087   **Exchange of information between supplier and distributor.**
Fn 280 The test laid down by the Court of Appeal in *Argos & Littlewoods and JJB Sports v Office of Fair Trading* [2006] EWCA Civ 1318 was applied by the Competition Appeal Tribunal in *Tesco v OFT* [2012] CAT 31, which discusses in detail the state of mind required to satisfy the test.

5. Selective Distribution Systems

(b) **The principles established by the EU Courts**

7.101   **Limits on internet sales by authorised resellers.**   The Irish High Court held in *SRI Apparel v Revolution Workwear and others* [2013] IEHC 289, para 61, that the use by a distributor of the website Amazon was active selling rather than passive, and that an agreement to restrict such activity was within the scope of Article 4(b)(i) of Regulation 330/2010 (the Vertical Block Exemption).

See also the OFT's decision CE/9578-12 *'Roma-branded mobility scooters: prohibitions on online sales and online price advertising'*, decision of 5 August 2013, in which the OFT found that an agreement or concerted practice in which a manufacturer prevented the distributors in its selective distribution system from selling its products online, or advertising their prices online, was a restriction of competition by object.

Hardcore restrictions: resale to end-users or other authorised distributors.   **7.108**
Fn 392 On sales via the internet, see also the update to paragraph 7.101, above.

9. Agency Agreements

Agent acting for more than one principal.   See also the Commission's decisions   **7.184**
in COMP/39847 *E-Books*, decisions of 12 December 2012 (OJ 2012 C283/7) and
of 25 July 2013 (Press Release IP/13/746 (25 July 2013)). The Commission's preliminary assessment was that five publishing companies had engaged in a concerted practice by all moving the sales of their electronically formatted books to
Apple from a wholesale model to an agency model, employing the same terms
in the agency agreements, and discussing among themselves their intention to
move to that model. It accepted commitments from the five publishing companies
and Apple.

11. Waste Packaging Recycling Arrangements

Licence fees for the use of the Green Dot logo.   The Supreme Court of the   **7.204**
Slovak Republic held in *Železničná spoločnosť Cargo Slovakia*, on 23 May 2013,
that ENVI-PAK, which held the licence to the Green Dot mark in Slovakia,
had abused its dominant position by setting the fees for sub-licensing the use
of the dot in such a way that it was payable only where the companies used the
waste collection, recovery and recycling services of its competitors, and not where
they used ENVI-PAK's own services: ECN Brief 03/2013, p35. The Commission
submitted written observations to the Supreme Court pursuant to Article 15(3)
of Regulation 1/2003 (see paragraph 15.051 of the main text on Article 15(3)
of Regulation 1/2003), which are available on the 'Cooperation with national
courts' section of the DG Comp website (at the time of writing, not yet available
in English).

8

MERGER CONTROL

1. Introduction

(b) Commission guidance

Implementing Regulation and Notices.   On 27 March 2013 the Commission   **8.007**
launched a consultation on its proposals for simplifying procedures under
the Merger Regulation. These include a draft Regulation amending the
Implementing Regulation; draft revised annexes including a revised Form CO,
Form RS, and Short Form; and a draft revised Simplified Procedure Notice. The
consultation documents are available on the consultations section of the DG
Comp website; see also Commission Press Release IP/13/288 (27 March 2013).

(c) Case law and statistics

Statistics.   The statistics in the main text can be updated, as follows, for the   **8.010**
period 1 August 2012 – 31 October 2013:

(a) Total number of notifications and referrals by year

Year	Notifications to Commission	Referrals from Member States to Commission		Referrals from Commission to Member States	
		Pre notification (Art 4(5))	post-notification (Art 22)	Pre notification (Art 4(4))	post-notification (Art 9)
2012	283	22	2	12	2
2013 (to 31 October)	219	10	1	7	0
Total	3009	249	20	82	29

(b) Different Phase I outcomes by year

Year	Clearance decisions				Referred to Phase II		Notifications withdrawn during Phase I	
	Unconditional		Conditional					
2012	254	(92%)	9	(3%)	10	(4%)	4	(1%)
2013 (to 31 October)	196	(94%)	9	(4%)	3	(1%)	1	(1%)
Total	2721	(91%)	127	(4%)	86	(3%)	55	(2%)

(c) Different Phase II outcomes by year

Year	Clearance decisions				Prohibition decisions		Notifications withdrawn during Phase II	
2012	1	(11%)	6	(67%)	1	(11%)	1	(11%)
2013 (to 31 October)	2	(33%)	2	(33%)	2	(33%)	0	(0%)
Total	30	(34%)	36	(41%)	6	(7%)	16	(18%)

2. Jurisdictional Scope of the Merger Regulation

(b) Concentrations

(i) In general

8.017 **State-controlled undertakings.**
Fn 43 See also M.6801 *Rosneft/TNK-BP* (8 March 2013), taking into account the other entities owned by the Russian state in the oil and gas sector.

(iv) Sole control

8.028 **Acquisition of sole control.**
Fn 71 On the reference by the OFT to the Competition Commission of Ryanair's acquisition of a minority shareholding in Aer Lingus, the Competition Commission concluded in *Ryanair Holdings and Aer Lingus Group*, decision of 28 August 2013, that the acquisition of a minority shareholding in Aer Lingus has led, or may be expected to lead, to a substantial lessening of competition in the markets for air passenger services between Great Britain and the Republic of Ireland, and ordered partial divestiture. An application for review is pending in the Competition Appeal Tribunal (Case no.1219/4/8/13).

8.029 **Sole control through minority shareholding.** The General Court dismissed the appeal in Case T-332/09 *Electrabel v Commission*, judgment of 12 December

2012. It upheld the Commission's approach of basing its analysis of whether or not sole control exists on the evidence of the presence of shareholders at shareholder meetings in previous years, and rejected the argument that it is necessary to look at the situation at general meetings for several years *after* the increase in capital likely to give rise to sole control, in order to confirm whether such control does in fact exist (paras 45 et seq, in particular para 48). On the appeal against the fine imposed, see the update to paragraph 8.188, below.

Other factors leading to *de facto* control.
Fn 85 The Commission's decision in M.6447 *IAG/bmi* (30 March 2012) is under **8.032**
appeal, Case T-344/12 *Virgin Atlantic Airways v Commission*, not yet decided.

(v) Joint control

Concept of joint control. **8.033**
Fn 86 See, for example, M.6439 *AGRANA/RWA/JV* (4 April 2012), para 14: the
Commission considered joint control arose because the business plan for the first
five years of the JV had to be adopted by mutual consent of the parent companies.

(vii) Interrelated transactions

'Warehousing' arrangements. **8.049**
Fn 129 The Court of Justice dismissed the further appeal in Case C-551/10P
Éditions Odile Jacob v Commission, judgment of 6 November 2012, [2013] 4
CMLR 11. It held that even if the General Court had erred in its conclusion
that the transactions did not enable Lagardère to acquire control, or joint control, of the target assets, that had no consequences other than that the notification of the concentration might be found to have been made late, or, that the
concentration might be found to have been implemented prematurely. That
may expose the parties to penalties, but it does not lead to the Commission
decision being annulled as it does not bear upon whether the concentration is
compatible with the common market: see paras 37–38.

(viii) Specific operations that are not concentrations

Article 3(5)(a) in practice. The Court of Justice dismissed the further **8.051**
appeal in Case C-551/10P *Éditions Odile Jacob v Commission*, judgment of
6 November 2012, [2013] 4 CMLR 11. It held that even if the General Court
had erred in its conclusion that the transactions did not enable Lagardère
to acquire control, or joint control, of the target assets, that had no consequences other than that the notification of the concentration might be found
to have been made late, or, that the concentration might be found to have been
implemented prematurely. That may expose the parties to penalties, but it
does not lead to the Commission decision being annulled as it does not bear
upon whether the concentration is compatible with the common market: see
paras 37–38.

(d) EU dimension

(iii) Undertakings concerned

8.075 **Acquisitions by State-controlled companies.**
Fn 208 See also M.6801 *Rosneft/TNK-BP* (8 March 2013), in which the Commission considered, though ultimately did not need to decide, whether Rosneft has power of decision independently from the Russian state.

(iv) Identification of a 'group' for the purpose of calculating turnover

8.076 **Group turnover for the purposes of Article 5(4).**
Fn 212 The Commission's decision in M.6447 *IAG/bmi* (30 March 2012) is under appeal, Case T-344/12 *Virgin Atlantic Airways v Commission*, not yet decided.

(e) Pre-notification reallocation of jurisdiction

(i) Article 4(4) referrals from Commission to NCAs

8.082 **Voluntary procedure.** On 27 March 2013 the Commission launched a consultation on its proposals for simplifying procedures under the Merger Regulation, which include a draft Regulation amending the Implementing Regulation, and draft revised annexes including a revised Form RS. The consultation documents are available on the consultations section of the DG Comp website; see also Press Release IP/13/288 (27 March 2013).

8.084 **Consequences of Article 4(4) referral.**
Fn 230 At the time of writing, the Commission has made two further partial referrals, in addition to those noted in the footnote: M.6753 *Orkla/Rieber & Son* (25 January 2013), in which the Commission agreed to a request to refer the Norwegian aspects of the case to the Norwegian NCA and retained jurisdiction over the rest of the transaction; and M.6982 *Altor Fund III/Tryghedsgruppen/Elixia/ HFN Group* (23 October 2013) (decision not yet published).

(ii) Article 4(5) referrals to Commission

8.086 **Voluntary procedure.** On 27 March 2013 the Commission launched a consultation on its proposals for simplifying procedures under the Merger Regulation, which include a draft Regulation amending the Implementing Regulation, and draft revised annexes including a revised Form RS. The consultation documents are available on the consultations section of the DG Comp website; see also Press Release IP/13/288 (27 March 2013).

(iii) Formalities and review

8.089 **Form RS.**
Fn 239 On 27 March 2013 the Commission launched a consultation on its proposals for simplifying procedures under the Merger Regulation, which include a

draft Regulation amending the Implementing Regulation. Article 1(2) of the proposed Regulation would amend Article 3(2) of the Implementing Regulation to clarify that the number of copies to be provided, and their format, is that specified by the Commission from time to time in the Official Journal.

Croatia's joining the EU, on 1 July 2013, has not affected the number of copies of Form RS that must be submitted.

Review of pre-notification referral procedures. On 27 March 2013 the **8.090** Commission launched a consultation on its proposals for simplifying procedures under the Merger Regulation, which include a draft Regulation amending the Implementing Regulation, and draft revised annexes including a revised Form RS. The consultation documents are available on the consultations section of the DG Comp website; see also Press Release IP/13/288 (27 March 2013).

(f) Post-notification reallocation of jurisdiction

(i) Article 9 referrals from Commission to NCAs

Legal requirements under Article 9. **8.091**
Fn 244 A further example is M.6321 *Buitenfood/AD Van Geloven Holding/JV (Article 9(3) decision)* (13 January 2012): partial referral at the request of the Dutch competition authority, as the concentration would significantly affect competition in the market for frozen snacks in the Netherlands.

Commission's discretion under Article 9(2)(a). **8.092**
Fn 248 The Commission's decision in M.5960 *Credit Agricole/Cassa di Risparmio della Spezia/Agences Intesa San Paolo* (10 November 2010) is under appeal in Case T-45/11 *Italy v Commission*, not yet decided.

Fn 251 See, for example, M.6321 *Buitenfood/AD Van Geloven Holding/JV* (13 January 2012): partial referral at the request of the Dutch competition authority, as the concentration would significantly affect competition in the market for frozen snacks in the Netherlands, and a decision taken the same day clearing the aspects of the concentration not related to the Netherlands.

3. Procedure

(a) In general

(ii) Pre-notification contacts

Initial contact. On 27 March 2013 the Commission launched a consulta- **8.109** tion on its proposals for simplifying procedures under the Merger Regulation, which include a draft Regulation amending the Implementing Regulation and draft revised annexes including a revised Form CO. The consultation documents underline the Commission's view that pre-notification contacts are useful, and encourage parties to engage in them. The consultation documents are available on the consultations section of the DG Comp website; see also Press Release IP/13/288 (27 March 2013).

(iii) Obligation to notify

8.114 **Waivers regarding provision of information.** On 27 March 2013 the Commission launched a consultation on its proposals for simplifying procedures under the Merger Regulation, which include encouraging parties *inter alia* to approach the Commission about obtaining a waiver from the obligation to provide information that would otherwise be required, and specifying the particular information that, in the Commission's experience, is not required in a significant number of cases and might be appropriate for a waiver application. The consultation documents are available on the consultations section of the DG Comp website; see also Press Release IP/13/288 (27 March 2013).

(iv) Formalities

8.117 **Form CO.** On 27 March 2013 the Commission launched a consultation on its proposals for simplifying procedures under the Merger Regulation, which include a draft Regulation amending the Implementing Regulation and revised annexes including a revised Form CO. The draft revised Form CO will, if approved:

(a) redefine what is to be considered an 'affected market' (see the update to paragraph 8.194, below);
(b) encourage parties voluntarily to submit a description of the data that each of the undertakings collects and holds (including the type of data, the level of disaggregation, the time period covered, and the format in which it is held) in cases where a quantitative economic analysis of the affected markets is likely to be useful;
(c) encourage parties voluntarily to facilitate international cooperation between the Commission and the competition authorities of non-EEA countries that are also reviewing the concentration, by submitting a list of which non-EEA competition authorities are reviewing the concentration and by waiving confidentiality to allow the Commission to engage in discussions with those authorities.

The consultation documents are available on the consultations section of the DG Comp website; see also Press Release IP/13/288 (27 March 2013).

8.118 **Submission of notification and supporting documentation.**
Fn 338 On 27 March 2013 the Commission launched a consultation on its proposals for simplifying procedures under the Merger Regulation, which include a draft Regulation amending the Implementing Regulation. Article 1(2) of the proposed Regulation would amend Article 3(2) of the Implementing Regulation

to clarify that the number of copies to be provided, and their format, is that specified by the Commission from time to time in the Official Journal.

Fn 340 See the update to footnote 338, above. Croatia's joining the EU, on 1 July 2013, has not affected the number of copies of Form CO that must be submitted.

Fn 342 See the update to paragraph 8.117, above, on the Commission's proposed amendment to Form CO to encourage parties to take steps to facilitate cooperation between the Commission and the competition authorities of non-EEA countries.

(v) Simplified procedure

Generally. On 27 March 2013 the Commission launched a consultation on its **8.122** proposals for simplifying procedures under the Merger Regulation. The proposals recognise that a larger number of concentrations should be notified using the simplified procedure, in order to simplify and expedite the process. The Commission has proposed a draft Regulation amending the Implementing Regulation, draft revised annexes including a revised Short Form, and a draft revised Simplified Procedure Notice. See, in particular, Recital (3) to the Commission's proposed Regulation amending the Implementing Regulation, and the update to paragraph 8.123, below, regarding the Commission's detailed proposals. The consultation documents are available on the consultations section of the DG Comp website; see also Commission Press Release IP/13/288 (27 March 2013).

Eligible cases. On 27 March 2013 the Commission launched a consultation **8.123** on its proposals for simplifying procedures under the Merger Regulation. The Commission has proposed *inter alia* a draft revised Simplified Procedure Notice. The Commission's proposals would, if approved, revise the categories of cases in which the simplified procedure is available:

(a) it will no longer be available in cases where the parties are in neither a horizontal nor a vertical relationship;

(b) the combined market share threshold for parties in a horizontal relationship would be increased from 15 per cent to 20 per cent;

(c) the market share threshold for parties in a vertical relationship would be increased from 25 per cent to 30 per cent; and

(d) it will become available in cases where on all plausible market definitions the combined market share of parties in a horizontal relationship is below 50 per cent, and the increment ('delta') of the Herfindahl-Hirschman Index ('HHI') resulting from the concentration is below 150 (for the HHI, and calculation of the delta, see paragraph 8.213 and footnote 663 in the main text).

The consultation documents, including the draft revised Simplified Procedure Notice, are available on the consultations section of the DG Comp website; see also Commission Press Release IP/13/288 (27 March 2013).

8.124 **Short Form.** On 27 March 2013 the Commission launched a consultation on its proposals for simplifying procedures under the Merger Regulation, which include a draft Regulation amending the Implementing Regulation, and a draft revised Short Form. The consultation documents are available on the consultations section of the DG Comp website; see also Press Release IP/13/288 (27 March 2013). Article 1(2) of the proposed Regulation would amend Article 3(2) of the Implementing Regulation to clarify that the number of copies to be provided, and their format, is that specified by the Commission from time to time in the Official Journal.

Croatia's joining the EU, on 1 July 2013, has not affected the number of copies of the Short Form that must be submitted.

8.125 **Exceptions.**
Fn 361 On 27 March 2013 the Commission launched a consultation on its proposals for simplifying procedures under the Merger Regulation, which include a draft revised Simplified Procedures Notice that proposes to expand paras 6–11 of the current Simplified Procedure Notice. The consultation documents are available on the consultations section of the DG Comp website; see also Commission Press Release IP/13/288 (27 March 2013).

(vi) Suspension of concentrations

8.130 **Completion in breach.**
Fn 372 The Court of Justice dismissed the appeal in Case T-332/09 *Electrabel v Commission*, judgment of 12 December 2012. On the appeal against the fine imposed, see the update to paragraph 8.188, below.

(c) In-depth Phase II investigation

(i) Phase II process

8.149 **Notifying parties' access to file and key documents.**
Fn 438 On 27 March 2013 the Commission launched a consultation on its proposals for simplifying procedures under the Merger Regulation, which include a draft Regulation amending the Implementing Regulation. Article 1(7) of the proposed Regulation would amend Article 17(3) of the Implementing Regulation to include correspondence between the Commission and the competition authorities of non-EEA countries.

(iv) Possible outcomes at Phase II

8.159 **Decisions following a Phase II investigation.**
Fn 478 At the time of writing, there have been 24 prohibition decisions: see the update to table (c) at paragraph 8.010, above. Recent prohibition decisions are M.6570 *UPS/TNT Express* (30 January 2013) (on appeal, Case T-194/13 *United Parcel Service v Commission*, not yet decided); and M.6663 *Ryanair/Aer Lingus III* (27 February 2013) (on appeal, Case T-260/13 *Ryanair v Commission*, not yet decided).

The appeal in Case T-202/11 *Aeroporia Aigaiou Aeroporiki and Marfin Investment Group Symmetochon v Commission*, was withdrawn on 10 September 2013.

(d) Commitments to enable clearance

(i) Commitments at Phase I or Phase II

Phase I commitments.   8.168
Fn 501 See also M.6503 *LaPoste/Swiss Post/JV* (4 July 2012).

Phase II commitments.   8.169
Fn 507 On 27 March 2013 the Commission launched a consultation on its proposals for simplifying procedures under the Merger Regulation, which include a draft Regulation amending the Implementing Regulation. Article 1(8) of the proposed Regulation would amend Article 19(2) of the Implementing Regulation to clarify that where offered commitments are modified on day 55 or thereafter, the time limit is extended to 105 working days. The consultation documents, including the draft Regulation, are available on the consultations section of the DG Comp website; see also Commission Press Release IP/13/288 (27 March 2013).

(ii) Scope of commitments

Structural and behavioural commitments.   8.171
Fn 516 See also M.6459 *Sony/Mubadala Development/EMI Music Publishing* (19 April 2012) (divestment of certain rights in works and future works, and non-solicitation agreement).

Fn 571 For an example in the telecommunications sector, see M.6497 *Hutchinson 3G Austria/Orange Austria* (12 December 2012) in which the Commission granted clearance at phase II, subject to two conditions: that Hutchinson divest itself of spectrum frequency bands, and that it enter into network access agreements to grant mobile virtual network operators (MVNOs) wholesale access to up to 30 per cent of its network capacity in the coming 10-year period.

Fn 518 See also M.6455 *SCA/Georgia–Pacific Europe* (5 July 2012), paras 288–297.

Fn 527 See also M.6564 *ARM/Giesecke & Devrient/Gemalto/JV* (7 November 2012): upstream undertaking to provide interoperability information on the same terms to the JV and to its competitors.

Divestiture.   8.172
Fn 531 In M.6690 *Syniverse/Mach* (29 May 2013) Mach gave commitments to divest itself of a significant part of its assets in the EEA, including its entire EEA data clearing services and EEA near trade roaming data exchange services, to obtain clearance at Phase II: see Press Release IP/13/481 (29 May 2013).

Fn 537 In M.6570 *UPS/TNT Express* (30 January 2013) the Commission prohibited the concentration as an upfront buyer commitment had not been offered, and the attempt to sign an agreement before the end of the Commission's investigation did not materialise: see Press Release IP/13/68 (30 January 2013). On appeal, Case T-194/13 *United Parcel Service v Commission*, not yet decided.

(iii) Implementation of commitments

8.175 **Role of trustees.**
Fn 547 The Court of Justice in Cases C-553 & 554/10P *Commission v Éditions Odile Jacob*, judgment of 6 November 2012, [2013] 4 CMLR 55, disagreed with Advocate General Mazák's Opinion of 27 March 2012 and upheld the General Court's judgment in Case T-452/04 *Éditions Odile Jacob v Commission* [2010] ECR II-4713. The Court of Justice held that the trustee in that case was not independent of the parties, as required by their commitments, and the General Court was correct in concluding that that alone was sufficient basis for annulling the decision approving the purchaser. The Court of Justice rejected the argument that it was necessary to establish that the lack of independence had actually affected the trustee's choice of purchaser: see para 52. The parallel appeal in Case C-551/10P *Éditions Odile Jacob*, judgment of 6 November 2012, [2013] 4 CMLR 11 (against the General Court judgment in Case T-279/04 *Éditions Odile Jacob v Commission* [2010] ECR II-0185, upholding the Commission's decision to clear the concentration) was dismissed.

(e) Commission's powers of investigation

(iii) Confidentiality and business secrets

8.184 **Public access to documents.**   The General Court has confirmed that, in addition to the exceptions from disclosure provided for in Article 4(2) of Regulation 1049/2001, discussed in the main text, the Commission's internal documents prepared in the course of merger control proceedings may also fall within the exception in Article 4(3) of Regulation 1049/2001. That exception will apply where the Commission's decision-making process may be prejudiced by disclosure of the document, and in particular in circumstances where its investigation has closed but its decision is under appeal and the possibility remains that it will be required to re-open its proceedings: Case T-561/12 *Beninca v Commission*, judgment of 25 October 2013, paras 28 et seq, in particular para 36 (request for disclosure of an internal Commission memorandum which related to M.6166 *NYSE Euronext/ Deutsche Börse* (1 February 2012)).

(f) Commission's powers of sanction

(i) In general

8.185 **Measures following a prohibition decision.**
Fn 581 No further decisions imposing remedies under Article 8(4) were issued between 1 August 2012 and 31 October 2013. The total number of decisions remains four.

(ii) Fines and penalty payments

Fines for substantive infringements.   In Case T-332/09 *Electrabel v Commission*,   **8.188**
judgment of 12 December 2012, the General Court upheld the Commission's conclusion that Electrabel had acquired control in December 2003 (on the acquisition
of control, see the update to paragraph 8.029, above), and rejected a complaint
that the fine was disproportionate. It observed that €20 million represented only
0.42 per cent of the legal maximum that the Commission could have imposed (paras
225–226, 283, and 303), and held *inter alia* that the Commission was correct to
conclude that a failure to notify is a serious infringement (para 235); that it was not
relevant that the question of whether control was acquired was complex, because
Electrabel should have erred on the side of caution and contacted the Commission
in those circumstances (paras 248–255); and that the overall proportionality of
the fine could not usefully be assessed by reference to earlier Commission decisions
which are distinguishable on their facts, or to the fines imposed in cartel cases
which pursue particular objectives linked to the secret nature of cartels, or to decisions taken by NCAs (see paras 284–286 on earlier Commission decisions, para
292 on cartel decisions, and para 301 on decisions of NCAs).

4. Substantive Appraisal of Concentrations

(b) Market definition

(i) Affected markets for Form CO purposes

Market definition and relevant markets.   On 27 March 2013 the Commission   **8.194**
launched a consultation on its proposals for simplifying procedures under the
Merger Regulation, which include a draft Regulation amending the Implementing
Regulation, and a draft revised Form CO. The Commission's proposals would, if
approved, increase these market share thresholds:

(a) *horizontally affected markets:* the combined market share threshold would be
increased from 15 per cent to 20 per cent; and
(b) *vertically affected markets:* the market share threshold for parties in a vertical
relationship would be increased from 25 per cent to 30 per cent.

It would also clarify that the market share thresholds are to be applied to all plausible market definitions. The consultation documents are available on the consultations section of the DG Comp website; see also Press Release IP/13/288 (27
March 2013).

Relevant geographic market.   **8.198**
Fn 615 See also Case T-405/08 *SPAR Österreichische Warenhandel v Commission*,
judgment of 7 June 2013, paras 115 et seq, in which the General Court upheld
the Commission's decision in M.5047 *REWE/ADEG* (29 April 2011), finding

the relevant geographic market to be national but analysing competitive effects also at the subnational level of political districts.

(c) SIEC test

(ii) Relationship with concept of dominance

8.203 **Dominance remains a relevant consideration.**
Fn 628 In M.6503 *LaPoste/Swiss Post/JV* (4 July 2012) the Commission noted the 'very strong position' of La Poste, as the incumbent operator on a market which had been liberalised fairly recently and in which 'no entrants are to be expected in the medium term': para 85. It considered the JV would strengthen that position, and cleared the merger after accepting divestiture commitments at Phase I. In M.6690 *Syniverse/Mach* (29 May 2013) the Commission considered a proposed merger between the largest and second largest operators in a number of markets for roaming technology services provided to telecommunications companies, such as data clearing and financial settlement, that would have created a dominant player with virtual monopoly market shares. It cleared the concentration after accepting commitments at Phase II to divest a significant part of Mach's assets in the EEA: see Press Release IP/13/481 (29 May 2013).

(iv) General content of assessment

8.208 **Counterfactual.**
Fn 630 The Commission's decision in M.6447 *IAG/bmi* (30 March 2012) is under appeal, Case T-344/12 *Virgin Atlantic Airways v Commission*, not yet decided.

8.211 **Priority principle for contemporaneous transactions.**
Fn 656 Western Digital's challenges to the lawfulness of the Commission's priority rule in Cases T-452/11 and 60/12 were withdrawn on 20 September 2012.

(d) Unilateral effects

(i) In general

8.213 **Relevance of market shares and concentration levels.**
Fn 663 Although the Commission may consider the HHI, it is not obliged to do so: Case T-405/08 *SPAR Österreichische Warenhandel v Commission*, judgment of 7 June 2013, paras 66–69.

(f) Vertical and conglomerate effects

(i) Vertical effects

8.230 **Degree of market power.**   On 27 March 2013 the Commission launched a consultation on its proposals for simplifying procedures under the Merger Regulation, which include a draft Regulation amending the Implementing Regulation, and a draft revised Form CO. The Commission's proposals would, if approved, increase the combined market share threshold for parties in a vertical relationship from 25 per cent to 30 per cent, and require it to be applied to all plausible market definitions. The consultation documents are available on the consultations section of the DG Comp website; see also Press Release IP/13/288 (27 March 2013).

Input foreclosure.   In M.6314 *Telefónica UK/Vodafone UK/EE/JV* (4 September **8.231** 2012) the Commission sought the assistance of an industry regulator, OFCOM, to understand whether the parties had the ability to engage in input foreclosure, including whether the regulatory system was such that their incentives to do so were affected (paras 294 et seq).

Fn 726 See also M.6568 *Cisco Systems/NDS Group* (23 July 2012), paras 113–115; M.6560 *EQT VI/BSN Medical* (7 August 2012).

Customer foreclosure.   **8.232**
Fn 730 See, for example, M.6314 *Telefónica UK/Vodafone UK/EE/JV* (4 September 2012) para 249.

(ii) Conglomerate effects

Anti-competitive foreclosure.   On whether the merged entity would have the **8.235** economic incentive to foreclose, see for example M.6671 *LBO France/Aviapartner* (30 November 2012), paras 152 et seq; and M.6584 *Vodafone/Cable & Wireless Worldwide* (3 July 2012), para 109.

Fn 736 On 27 March 2013 the Commission launched a consultation on its proposals for simplifying procedures under the Merger Regulation, which include a draft Regulation amending the Implementing Regulation, and a draft revised Form CO. The Commission's proposals would, if approved, increase the market share threshold on closely related markets from 25 per cent to 30 per cent and require it to be applied to all plausible market definitions. The consultation documents are available on the consultations section of the DG Comp website; see also Press Release IP/13/288 (27 March 2013).

Fn 738 See also M.6671 *LBO France/Aviapartner* (30 November 2012), paras 152 et seq.

Tying or bundling of related products.   **8.237**
Fn 746 See also M.6568 *Cisco Systems/NDS Group* (23 July 2012), paras 97–103 and 110–112.

Concerns regarding interoperability.   In M.6564 *ARM/Giesecke & Devrient/* **8.238** *Gemalto/JV* (7 November 2012) the Commission considered that ARM had the necessary market power in the market upstream from the JV, and an incentive, to degrade the interoperability of its product with the downstream products of the JV's competitors. The Commission accepted commitments to make interoperability information available on the same terms to the JV and its competitors, and granted Phase I clearance. In M.6490 *EADS/Israel Aerospace Industries/JV* (16 July 2012), para 28, the Commission considered that where a joint venture was established to develop a new product for towing aircraft, a key part of its commercial strategy was to ensure the product's interoperability with different types of aircraft. There was no incentive to restrict interoperability, as that would reduce demand for the new product.

The Commission's decision in M.6281 *Microsoft/Skype* (7 October 2011), discussed in the main text, is under appeal in Case T-79/12 *Cisco Systems & Messagenet v Commission*, not yet decided.

(g) Other considerations relevant to substantive appraisal

(i) Buyer power

8.241 Customers' countervailing buyer power.
Fn 755 See also M.6843 *Siemens/Invensys Rail* (18 April 2013), paras 52–53, finding that customers' sophisticated tendering procedures gave them significant countervailing buyer power.

Fn 758 See also M.6535 *Glory/Talaris Topco* (3 July 2012), paras 47–49.

Fn 759 See also M.6611 *Arla Foods/Milk Link* (27 September 2012), paras 114–118.

(ii) Efficiencies

8.242 **Efficiencies.** In M.6490 *EADS/Israel Aerospace Industries/JV* (16 July 2012), paras 20 et seq, the Commission considered that a JV set up to develop and produce an entirely new product 'is *a priori* unlikely to have negative effects on final consumers'.

8.243 **Proving efficiencies.**
Fn 764 In M.6497 *Hutchinson 3G Austria/Orange Austria* (12 December 2012), paras 403 et seq the Commission found the efficiencies claimed were not sufficiently verifiable, but went on to grant Phase II clearance subject to two conditions.

(iii) Failing firm defence

8.244 **Criteria of failing firm defence.** In two recent decisions, the Commission has concluded that the criteria of the failing firm defence are met. In M.6360 *Nynas/Shell/Harburg* (2 September 2013) it accepted that the operator of the Harburg refinery for napthenic base and process oils was economically unsustainable and would exit the market if the concentration did not proceed. As there were no alternative buyers for the assets, the most likely alternative scenario to the proposed transaction would be the closure of the refinery, such that the reduction of the number of competitors in the market would occur anyway and would not be caused by the acquisition itself. Moreover, the closure of the refinery would lead to EEA demand being met by imports and consequently higher prices for consumers due to import costs: see Press Release IP/13/804 (2 September 2013). In M.6796 *Aegean /Olympic II* (9 October 2013) the Commission approved the merger it had previously prohibited in M.5830 *Olympic/Aegean Airlines* (26 January 2011). It was satisfied that Olympic was likely to go out of business if the concentration did not proceed, as its sole shareholder had indicated an intention to withdraw its financial support and there were no alternative buyers for the assets: see Press Release IP/13/927 (10 October 2013). The decision contrasts with that in M.6447 *IAG/bmi* (30 March 2012) (on appeal in Case T-344/12 *Virgin Atlantic Airways v Commission*, not yet decided), section VII, where the Commission considered that the failing firm defence was not met as the assets of bmi consisted primarily in slot pairs at Heathrow airport, and these assets were not likely to exit the market.

Fn 766 The Commission's decision in M.6447 *IAG/bmi* (30 March 2012) is under appeal, Case T-344/12 *Virgin Atlantic Airways v Commission*, not yet decided. See also the update to the main text, above, on M.6796 *Aegean /Olympic II* (9 October 2013).

(h) Coordinative aspects of certain full-function joint ventures

(i) In general

Spill-over effects. In M.6477 *BP/Chevron/ENI/Sonangol/Total/JV* (16 May **8.245** 2012), paras 30–31, the Commission noted that the JV agreements included a mechanism to prevent the parents acquiring commercially sensitive information, and that the market was not sufficiently transparent to facilitate coordination.

Fn 770 See also M.6485 *Euler Hermes/Mapfre/Mapfre CC* (20 September 2012), para 23; M.6314 *Telefónica UK/Vodafone UK/EE/JV* (4 September 2012), para 585.

7. National Merger Control and International Cooperation

(a) National merger control regimes within EEA

National control where application of the Merger Regulation is contested. The **8.289** European Commission has prohibited the concentration notified in M.6663 *Ryanair/Aer Lingus III* (27 February 2013) (on appeal, Case T-260/13 *Ryanair v Commission*, not yet decided). The Competition Commission subsequently concluded in *Ryanair Holdings and Aer Lingus Group*, decision of 28 August 2013, that Ryanair's acquisition of a minority shareholding in Aer Lingus has led, or may be expected to lead, to a substantial lessening of competition in the markets for air passenger services between Great Britain and the Republic of Ireland, and ordered partial divestiture. An application for review is pending in the

Competition Appeal Tribunal (Case no.1219/4/8/13) contending, *inter alia*, that the Competition Commission breached the duty of sincere cooperation under Article 4(3) TEU by issuing its decision while Ryanair's appeal to the General Court was pending.

8.291 **Outline of national merger control rules in the EEA.** As at 31 October 2013, the following entries should be substituted at the appropriate place in the table:

(c) Cooperation with countries outside EEA

Belgium	(a) combined turnover in Belgium in excess of €100m; and (b) at least two parties each have turnover in Belgium in excess of €40m	Mandatory prior notification to Belgian Competition Authority
Italy	(a) combined turnover in Italy of €474m; or (b) target has turnover in Italy of €47m *(These thresholds are revised annually to take account of inflation; above figures were revised in September 2012.)*	Mandatory prior notification to the Autorità Garante della Concorrenza e del Mercato (Competition Authority)
Germany	(a) combined worldwide turnover of €500m; and (b) at least one party has turnover in Germany of €25m, and (c) at least one other party has turnover in Germany of €5m Exceptionally notification may not be necessary if: (a) there is an independent (non-affiliated) undertaking, merging with another undertaking, which has worldwide turnover of not more than €10m; *(NB: If the only relevant market is a minor market where goods/services have been offered for at least five years and total annual turnover was less than €15m in the last calendar year, the transaction must be notified. However, such transaction will not be prohibited.)*	Mandatory prior notification to Bundeskartellamt (Federal Cartel Office or BKartA)

8.297 **Canada, Japan and Korea and Switzerland.** The EU has signed a cooperation agreement on competition matters with the Swiss Confederation, subject to ratification: see Press Release IP/13/444 (17 May 2013).

9

INTELLECTUAL PROPERTY RIGHTS

1. Introduction

Generally. The Court of Justice upheld the legality of the Council's decision **9.008**
authorising the use of the enhanced cooperation procedure under Article 20 TEU
in the area of the creation of a unitary patent (Council Decision 2011/167/EU of 10
March 2011): see Joined Cases C-274 & 295/11 *Spain & Italy v Council*, judgment
of 16 April 2013.

2. Free Movement and Intellectual Property Rights

(b) The right of production or reproduction

Trade marks. In Case C-561/11 *Fédération Cynologique Internationale v* **9.014**
Federación Canina Internacional de Perros de Pura Raza, judgment of 21 February
2013, the Court of Justice held that a 'third party', whom a trade mark proprietor
would be justified under Article 36 in suing for infringement of his mark, includes
a third-party proprietor of a later registered Community trade mark. The later
registered trade mark does not have to be declared invalid before the proprietor
of the earlier trade mark can enforce his rights. In Case C-661/11 *Martin Y Paz
v David Depuydt*, judgment of 19 September 2013, paras 57 et seq, the Court
confirmed that a trade mark proprietor who has previously consented to shared
use of his trade mark is entitled to withdraw that consent and regain exclusive use.

(c) The right of distribution

(ii) Conditions for the exhaustion of the distribution right

Goods in transit through Union territory. **9.026**
Fn 67 See also Regulation 608/2013 concerning customs enforcement of intellectual property rights and repealing Regulation 1383/2003, adopted on 12 June
2013: OJ 2013 L181/15.

(e) The exclusive right to provide services

9.040 **Public performance.**   In Case C-283/10 *Circul Globus Bucureşti*, [2011] ECR I-12031, para 41, the Court of Justice clarified that the concept of 'communication to the public' in Article 3(1) Directive 2001/29 (the Copyright Directive) is limited to situations where the public is not present at the place where the performance or direct presentation takes place. It does not include, therefore, a communication which is carried out directly in a place open to the public, such as a circus.

9.042 **Exhaustion of rights:** *Coditel (No.1).*   In Case C-607/11 *ITV Broadcasting and others*, judgment of 7 March 2013, [2013] 3 CMLR 1 the Court of Justice considered the position under Directive 2001/29 (the Copyright Directive) in connection with a company that captures television broadcasts and retransmits them via the internet in realtime. It held that the original broadcast does not exhaust the right to communicate to the public, and the retransmission via the internet constitutes a 'communication to the public' within Article 3(1) that the copyright holder is entitled to prohibit. The Court of Justice held that it was immaterial whether the retransmitting company could be considered a competitor of the broadcasters: see para 47.

The Bundesgerichtshof has referred to the Court of Justice for a preliminary ruling a question concerning whether rebroadcasting by wire, to persons who receive the broadcast in private or family circles, for profit constitutes a 'communication to the public' for these purposes: Case C-416/12 *Wikom Electrik v VG Media*, not yet decided.

9.043 **Exhaustion of rights:** *Football Association Premier League.*   The Outer House of the Scottish Court of Sessions has followed the Court of Justice's judgment in Cases C-403 & 429/08 *Football Association Premier League v QC Leisure / Murphy v Media Protection Services*, judgment of 4 October 2011, [2012] 1 CMLR 769, in *Scottish Premier League Limited v Lisini Pub Management Company Limited* [2013] CSOH 48, judgment of 25 March 2013.

3. Articles 101 and 102 and the Enforcement of Intellectual Property Rights

(b) Other abusive conduct

9.059 **Abuse of regulatory process.**   The Court of Justice dismissed the appeals in Case C-457/10P *AstraZeneca v Commission*, judgment of 6 December 2012, [2013] 4 CMLR 233. It was argued that deliberate fraud or deceit should be required in order to find an abuse in the context of alleged misrepresentations to public authorities for the purposes of acquiring exclusive rights: para 71. The Court of Justice did not directly rule on the point, but held that AstraZeneca had, on the facts of that case, deliberately misled the relevant patent offices, and that a consideration of whether a dominant undertaking has misled the authorities 'may' vary according to the circumstances of each case: paras 74 et seq. It suggested, however, that not every objectively wrong representation will be an abuse, where it was made unintentionally and immediately rectified: para 99.

Patent ambushes.   **9.060**
Fn 183 The appeals by Hynix Semiconductor (now trading as SK Hynix Inc) in Joined Cases T-148&149/10 against COMP/38636 *Rambus*, decision of 9 December 2009, were withdrawn on 5 July 2013.

As part of its ongoing investigation into alleged abusive conduct in relation to IPR used in international telecoms standards, the Commission has issued statements of objection to Samsung and Motorola: see Press Release IP/12/1448 (21 December 2012) regarding COMP/39939 *Samsung – enforcement of ETSI standards essential patents*; and Press Release IP/13/406 (6 May 2013) regarding COMP/39985 *Motorola – enforcement of ETSI standards essential patents*. The Commission's preliminary view is that it is an abuse of dominance, contrary to Article 102, for the holder of a standard essential patent to seek injunctions for patent infringement in circumstances where it has given a commitment that it will grant licences on fair, reasonable, and non-discriminatory ('FRAND') terms and where the potential licensee has agreed to accept a binding determination of the terms of a FRAND licence by a third party. At the time of writing, the Commission is consulting on commitments proposed by Samsung under which it would agree, in essence, for a period of five years not to seek an injunction before any court or tribunal in the EEA for infringement of its standard essential patents (including all existing and future patents) implemented in smartphones and tablets against a potential licensee that agrees to, and complies with, a particular framework for determining the terms of a licence: see OJ 2013 C302/11.

The Landgericht of Düsseldorf has referred to the Court of Justice for a preliminary ruling various questions concerning the circumstances in which it is an abuse for an undertaking to seek an injunction for breach of its standard essential patent: Case C-170/13 *Huawei Technologies v ZTE*, not yet decided.

The pharmaceutical sector inquiry report.   The Commission has continued to   **9.061**
monitor patent settlements between originator and generics companies, and its Reports are also available on the DG Comp website: First Report of 5 July 2010, in respect of the period mid-2008 to end 2009; Second Report of 6 July 2011, in respect of the period January to December 2010; and Third Report of 25 July 2012, in respect of the period January to December 2011.

Following the sector inquiry report, the Commission has initiated enforcement proceedings against several originator companies and the generic companies with which they entered patent settlement agreements: it has issued a decision against

Lundbeck and four groups of generics companies for 'reverse' settlement agreements reached in respect of the drug citalopram in COMP/39226 *Lundbeck*: see Press Release IP/13/563 (19 June 2013). The decision is under appeal: Cases T-460/13, etc, not yet decided. Investigations are ongoing in COMP/39612 *Perindopril (Servier)* and COMP/39685 *Johnson & Johnson and Novartis*. The enforcement action taken by the Commission since the sector inquiry report is summarised in MEMO/12/593 (25 July 2012). Similar concerns regarding patent settlements have arisen in the United States, and the US Supreme Court judgment in *Federal Trade Commission v Actavis and others*, of 17 June 2013, 570 U.S. (2013), has clarified that in the United States a 'rule of reason' approach is to be applied to antitrust scrutiny of such agreements, that is, the courts will consider in the light of all the relevant facts and circumstances whether a particular agreement has overall pro-competitive or anti-competitive effects on the relevant market (see further paragraphs 2.104 et seq of the main text).

See also the decision of the French Autorité de la concurrence, of 14 May 2013, fining Sanofi-Aventis €40.6 million for abusing its dominant position by adopting a strategy of denigrating its generic competitors. Sanofi-Aventis manufactures clopidogrel, an anti-platelet medication used to prevent relapses of serious cardiovascular diseases. It adopted a strategy of questioning, with doctors and pharmacists, the efficacy and safety of the generics' products, and intimating that the doctors/pharmacists could be held liable for any problems they caused, in order to limit generic entry and protect the market position of its branded clopidogrel 'Plavix', and its own generic 'Clopidogrel Winthrop': see ECN Brief 03/2013, p2. On appeal to the Cour d'Appel de Paris, not yet decided.

4. Collective Licensing of Intellectual Property Rights

(b) Copyright collecting societies

9.070 Pooling protected works. The General Court has upheld the Commission's decision in COMP/38698 *CISAC Agreements*, decision of 16 July 2008, [2009] 4 CMLR 577, regarding the clause in the collecting societies' agreement that prevented them from adding to their rights pools the rights of persons having nationality of one of the countries in which a competing society operates (referred to in the General Court's judgments as the 'membership clause'): Cases T-392, 401, 422, 432/08, judgments of 12 April 2013, [2013] 5 CMLR 15. It partially annulled the decision on other grounds in Cases T-392, 398, 401, 410, 411, 413–422, 425, 428, 432–434, 442/08, judgments of 12 April 2013.

The Commission adopted, on 11 July 2012, a proposal for a Directive on collective management of copyright and related rights and multi-territorial licensing of rights in musical works for online uses in the internal market (COM(2012) 372 final, 2012/0180 (COD)).

5. Licensing Intellectual Property Rights

(b) Typical clauses in licensing agreements

(i) Clauses concerning royalties

Abusive royalties. In respect of the Green Dot scheme, the Supreme Court of **9.092**
the Slovak Republic held in *Železničná spoločnosť Cargo Slovakia*, on 23 May 2013,
that ENVI-PAK, which held the licence to the Green Dot mark in Slovakia, had
abused its dominant position by setting the fees for sub-licensing the use of the dot
in such a way that it was payable only where the companies used the waste collection, recovery and recycling services of its competitors, and not where they used
ENVI-PAK's own services: ECN Brief 03/2013, p35. The Commission submitted
written observations to the Supreme Court pursuant to Article 15(3) of Regulation
1/2003 (see paragraph 15.051 of the main text on Article 15(3) of Regulation
1/2003), which are available on the 'Cooperation with national courts' section of
the DG Comp website (not yet available in English).

(iv) Restrictions concerning the licensee's provision of services

Territorial allocation: mere grant of an exclusive licence. **9.113**
Fn 373 The Commission's decision in COMP/38698 *CISAC Agreements*, decision
of 16 July 2008, [2009] 4 CMLR 577, has been partially annulled by the General
Court, on other grounds: Cases T-392, 398, 401, 410, 411, 413–422, 425, 428,
432–434, 442/08, judgments of 12 April 2013.

Market-sharing as opposed to territorial allocation. The Commission's deci- **9.115**
sion in COMP/38698 *CISAC Agreements*, decision of 16 July 2008, has been partially annulled by the General Court: Cases T-392, 398, 401, 410, 411, 413–422,
425, 428, 432–434, 442/08, judgments of 12 April 2013. The Court held that
the Commission did not have sufficient evidence to establish the existence of a
concerted practice, and that the need for the societies to monitor rights uses did
provide a plausible explanation for their parallel behaviour.

Market-sharing: justification. The Commission's decision in COMP/38698 **9.116**
CISAC Agreements, decision of 16 July 2008, [2009] 4 CMLR 577, has been partially annulled by the General Court: Cases T-392, 398, 401, 410, 411, 413–422,
425, 428, 432–434, 442/08, judgments of 12 April 2013. The Court held that
the Commission did not have sufficient evidence to establish the existence of a
concerted practice, and that the need for the societies to monitor rights uses did
provide a plausible explanation for their parallel behaviour.

(v) Other restrictions on the licensee

Tying and bundling obligations. In COMP/39230 *Rio Tinto Alcan*, decision **9.120**
of 20 December 2012, the Commission accepted commitments from Rio Tinto

to amend its technology transfer agreements for its aluminium smelting technology, which had required licensees to purchase speciality cranes used in aluminium smelters from its subsidiary.

(vi) Obligations extending after expiry of the licence or of the rights

9.129 **Settlement of litigation or disputes.**   The Commission has issued a decision in COMP/39226 *Lundbeck*: see Press Release IP/13/563 (19 June 2013). It has found that agreements between Lundbeck and several groups of generics companies to settle patent litigation in respect of the drug citalopram, on terms that included the generics refraining from entering the market independently, Lundbeck paying significant sums to the generics, and Lundbeck guaranteeing the generics a profit margin on a distribution agreement, breached Article 101. The decision is under appeal: Cases T-460/13, etc, not yet decided.

Fn 417 See also COMP/39685 *Johnson & Johnson and Novartis*, investigation ongoing.

6. The Block Exemption for Technology Transfer Agreements

(h) Review of Regulation 772/2004

9.175 **Review of block exemption.**   On 20 February 2013 the Commission launched a consultation on its proposals for a revised competition regime for technology transfer agreements. The consultation documents are available on the consultations section of the DG Comp website; see also Press Release IP/13/120 (20 February 2013).

10

ARTICLE 102

1. Introduction

(b) Relationship between Article 102 and other competition rules

Link between dominant position and abuse. 10.009

Fn 38 The Court of Justice dismissed the appeals in Case C-457/10P *AstraZeneca v Commission*, judgment of 6 December 2012, [2013] 4 CMLR 233.

Fn 44 The Court of Justice dismissed the appeals in Case C-457/10P *AstraZeneca v Commission*, judgment of 6 December 2012, [2013] 4 CMLR 233.

2. Dominant Position

(a) Generally

Indicators of dominance. 10.020

Fn 81 The Court of Justice dismissed the appeals in Case C-457/10P *AstraZeneca v Commission*, judgment of 6 December 2012, [2013] 4 CMLR 233. In dismissing the cross-appeal by the European Federation of Pharmaceutical Industries and Associations ('EFPIA'), the Court upheld the General Court's conclusions on market power. It rejected the argument that insufficient weight had been attached to the powers of the State as a monopsonist purchaser and as price regulator, both as inadmissible and as unfounded: see paras 175–181. The complaint that the General Court erred in taking into account AstraZeneca's first-mover status and financial resources was held to be inadmissible, and the complaint that it erred in taking into account AstraZeneca's intellectual property rights was dismissed: paras 185–188.

Caution about market shares. 10.022

Fn 89 The Court of Justice dismissed the appeals in Case C-457/10P *AstraZeneca v Commission*, judgment of 6 December 2012, [2013] 4 CMLR 233. On this point, see in particular para 177.

(b) The market position of the undertaking itself and its competitors

10.024   **Market share levels.**
Fn 101   The Court of Justice dismissed the appeals in Case C-457/10P *AstraZeneca v Commission*, judgment of 6 December 2012, [2013] 4 CMLR 233.

Fn 102   The Court of Justice dismissed the appeals in Case C-457/10P *AstraZeneca v Commission*, judgment of 6 December 2012, [2013] 4 CMLR 233. On this point, see in particular para 188.

10.025   **Market shares of competitors.**
Fn 108   The Court of Justice dismissed the appeals in Case C-457/10P *AstraZeneca v Commission*, judgment of 6 December 2012, [2013] 4 CMLR 233.

10.026   **Stability of market shares.**
Fn 111   Advocate General Wathelet has suggested, in his Opinion of 26 September 2013 in Case C-295/12P *Telefónica de España v Commission*, not yet decided, that the appeal on liability should be dismissed as partly inadmissible, partly unfounded, but the appeal on fines should be upheld and the case remitted to the General Court for reconsideration.

10.029   **Overall size and strength.**
Fn 117   The Court of Justice dismissed the appeals in Case C-457/10P *AstraZeneca v Commission*, judgment of 6 December 2012, [2013] 4 CMLR 233. In dismissing the cross-appeal by the European Federation of Pharmaceutical Industries and Associations ('EFPIA'), the Court held to be inadmissible the complaint that the General Court erred in taking into account AstraZeneca's first-mover status and financial resources, and it dismissed the complaint that the General Court erred in taking into account AstraZeneca's intellectual property rights: see paras 185–188.

10.030   **Incumbency and 'first mover advantage'.**
Fn 121   The Court of Justice dismissed the appeals in Case C-457/10P *AstraZeneca v Commission*, judgment of 6 December 2012, [2013] 4 CMLR 233. The cross-appeal by the European Federation of Pharmaceutical Industries and Associations ('EFPIA') against the General Court taking into account AstraZeneca's first-mover status was dismissed as inadmissible: see para 185.

(c) Barriers to entry and expansion

10.034   **Technical barriers.**
Fn 133   The Court of Justice dismissed the appeals, on other grounds, in Case C-457/10P *AstraZeneca v Commission*, judgment of 6 December 2012, [2013] 4 CMLR 233.

Fn 134   The appeals by Hynix Semiconductor (now trading as SK Hynix Inc) in Joined Cases T-148&149/10 against the Commission's decision in

COMP/38636 *Rambus*, decision of 9 December 2009, were withdrawn on 5 July 2013.

Structural barriers: vertical integration.   **10.036**
Fn 143 The Court of Justice dismissed the appeals in Case C-457/10P *AstraZeneca v Commission*, judgment of 6 December 2012, [2013] 4 CMLR 233. On this point, see in particular para 188.

Fn 145 Advocate General Wathelet has suggested, in his Opinion of 26 September 2013 in Case C-295/12P *Telefónica de España v Commission*, not yet decided, that the appeal on liability should be dismissed as partly inadmissible, partly unfounded, but the appeal on fines should be upheld and the case remitted to the General Court for reconsideration.

Strategic barriers: conduct as evidence of dominance. The Court of Justice **10.038**
dismissed the appeals in Case C-457/10P *AstraZeneca v Commission*, judgment of 6 December 2012, [2013] 4 CMLR 233. On this point, see in particular para 185.

(d) Countervailing market power

Countervailing buyer power.   **10.041**
Fn 164 The Court of Justice dismissed the appeals in Case C-457/10P *AstraZeneca v Commission*, judgment of 6 December 2012, [2013] 4 CMLR 233. The cross-appeal by the European Federation of Pharmaceutical Industries and Associations ('EFPIA'), which contended that the General Court had attached insufficient weight to the powers of the State as a monopsonist purchaser and as price regulator, was dismissed both as inadmissible and as unfounded: see paras 175–181.

Separate market for spare parts and ancillary services. The Danish Competition **10.046**
Council on 12 June 2013 found that Deutz, a German engine manufacturer, had abused its dominant position by preventing the supply of spare parts for its engines (which were used in trains owned and operated by the Danish State Railway) outside of its exclusive dealership network. The Competition Council also found that the agreement between Deutz and its Danish distributor infringed Article 101 TFEU as it prevented parallel imports: see ECN Brief 03/2013, p2.

Fn 172 In Case C-56/12P *European Federation of Ink and Ink Cartridge Manufacturers (EFIM) v Commission*, judgment of 19 September 2013, the Court of Justice dismissed the appeal against the General Court's conclusion that there were separate markets for printers and ink-jet cartridges, and upheld its rejection of the complaint alleging abuse of dominance in the market for the supply of ink cartridges. The case is discussed in paragraph 4.055, and the update thereto.

3. Abuse of a Dominant Position

(b) Some basic concepts

10.058 **Anti-competitive intent.**

Fn 231 In C-457/10P *AstraZeneca v Commission*, judgment of 6 December 2012, [2013] 4 CMLR 233, it was argued that deliberate fraud or deceit should be required in order to find an abuse in the context of alleged misrepresentations to public authorities for the purposes of acquiring exclusive rights: para 71. The Court of Justice did not directly rule on the point, but held that AstraZeneca had, on the facts of that case, deliberately misled the relevant patent offices, and that a consideration of whether a dominant undertaking has misled the authorities 'may' vary according to the circumstances of each case: paras 74 et seq. It suggested, however, that not every objectively wrong representation will be an abuse, where it was made unintentionally and immediately rectified: para 99.

Fn 236 The Court of Justice dismissed the appeals in Case C-457/10P *AstraZeneca v Commission*, judgment of 6 December 2012, [2013] 4 CMLR 233. On this point, see in particular para 129.

10.059 **Anti-competitive effects.**

Fn 238 See also C-457/10P *AstraZeneca v Commission*, judgment of 6 December 2012, [2013] 4 CMLR 233, para 112.

Fn 241 The Court of Justice dismissed the appeals in Case C-457/10P *AstraZeneca v Commission*, judgment of 6 December 2012, [2013] 4 CMLR 233. On this point, see in particular para 112: 'it is sufficient to demonstrate that there is a potential anti-competitive effect'. In Case C-295/12P *Telefónica de España v Commission*, not yet decided, Advocate General Wathelet has suggested in his Opinion of 26 September 2013 that the appeal on liability should be dismissed as partly inadmissible, partly unfounded, but the appeal on fines should be upheld and the case remitted to the General Court for reconsideration.

10.062 **Proportionality.**

Fn 249 The Court of Justice dismissed the appeals, on other grounds, in Case C-457/10P *AstraZeneca v Commission*, judgment of 6 December 2012, [2013] 4 CMLR 233.

(e) Own market abuses

(iv) Exclusive dealing and long-term contracts

10.101 **Exclusive dealing.**

Fn 381 See also the decision of the Danish Competition Council of 12 June 2013 finding an abuse of dominance by Deutz, a German engine manufacturer, in preventing the supply of spare parts for its engines (which were used in trains owned and operated by the Danish State Railway) outside of its exclusive dealership network. The Competition Council also found that the agreement between Deutz and its Danish distributor infringed Article 101 TFEU as it prevented parallel imports: ECN Brief 03/2013, p2.

(v) Excessive pricing

Royalties for intellectual property rights. The Competition Council of Latvia has fined the Latvian collective copyright management association, which has exclusive rights to license public use of musical works in Latvia, for abusing its dominant position by imposing excessive royalty tariffs. The Competition Council compared the level of tariffs imposed across Europe, and in particular in neighbouring Lithuania and Estonia, with those in Latvia and found that the tariffs in Latvia were 50–100 per cent higher than in other Member States: ECN Brief 02/2013, p2.   **10.110**

(d) Related market abuses

(i) Generally

Margin squeezing is a distinct abuse.   **10.114**
Fn 434 The finding of abuse of dominance against TeliaSonera has since been upheld by the Swedish Market Court, although the fine imposed on it by the City Court was reduced: ECN Brief 02/2013, p33.

Fn 433 Advocate General Wathelet has suggested, in his Opinion of 26 September 2013 in Case C-295/12P *Telefónica de España v Commission*, not yet decided, that the appeal on liability should be dismissed as partly inadmissible, partly unfounded, but the appeal on fines should be upheld and the case remitted to the General Court for reconsideration.

Fn 436 Advocate General Wathelet has suggested, in his Opinion of 26 September 2013 in Case C-295/12P *Telefónica de España v Commission*, not yet decided, that the appeal on liability should be dismissed as partly inadmissible, partly unfounded, but the appeal on fines should be upheld and the case remitted to the General Court for reconsideration.

(ii) Margin squeeze

Margin squeezing: remedies.   **10.120**
Fn 466 In *Albion Water v Dŵr Cymru Cyfyngedig* [2013] CAT 6, the Competition Appeal Tribunal rejected Dŵr Cymru's argument that for the purposes of quantifying the damage that Albion had suffered as a result of the margin squeeze it had to determine what price could lawfully have been charged. It held that where a dominant undertaking could have charged a range of prices, absent its unlawful conduct, the counterfactual should be constructed using a figure in the middle of the range of lawful prices, not the highest that could lawfully have been charged: paras 69–71.

(iv) Tying and bundling

10.124 **Two distinct products must be tied**
Fn 479 The Commission exercised its power under Article 23(2)(c) of Regulation 1/2003 for the first time in COMP/39530 *Microsoft – Tying*, decision of 6 March 2013, when Microsoft failed to comply with the commitment decision of 16 December 2009. It imposed a fine of €561 million. The General Court dismissed the appeal in Case T-74/11 *Omnis Group v Commission*, judgment of 30 May 2013, as there was not sufficient evidence to establish that there was or might be an abuse.

10.127 **Tying of other ancillary services.**
Fn 491 The Commission has accepted commitments offered by Rio Tinto Alcan to address concerns relating to the tying of its aluminium smelting technology to the supply of its aluminium smelter equipment: COMP/39230 *Rio Tinto Alcan*, decision of 20 December 2012.

10.128 **Objective justification of tying practices.** In COMP/39230 *Rio Tinto Alcan*, decision of 20 December 2012, paras 86 et seq the putatively dominant undertaking wished to rely on alleged efficiencies, and the Commission's preliminary assessment was that it could not do so as it did not meet the four criteria outlined in its Article 102 Enforcement Priorities Guidance, para 30. Moreover, it considered that 'any efficiency enhancing tying must be driven by customer preferences for joint consumption' (para 89).

(v) Refusal to supply

10.131 **Constructive refusal to supply.**
Fn 505 See also the decision of the Italian Competition Authority of 9 May 2013 finding Telecom Italia, the incumbent in telecommunications markets in Italy, had constructively refused to supply access to its network by rejecting a large proportion of competitors' wholesale orders. The Competition Authority found that the orders were rejected as a result of the different delivery processes Telecom Italia used to provide wholesale services as compared with those it used internally, and that Telecom Italia could have adjusted the delivery processes to reduce the level of rejections of wholesale orders by competitors: ECN Brief 02/2013, p2.

10.133 **Exclusion of downstream competition.**
Fn 516 See also, for example, the decision of the Slovakian Antimonopoly Office finding an abusive refusal to supply electric locomotives to the dominant company's competitors in the freight rail transport market, who were only able to access less efficient and more costly diesel locomotives: ECN Brief 04/2013, p2. Decision on appeal, not yet decided.

10.141 **Refusal to satisfy demand generated by parallel trade.** In *Chemistree Homecare v Abbvie* [2013] EWHC 264 (Ch), paras 43–44, the High Court (Roth J.) held that where a dominant undertaking has chosen to distribute its product by supplying only to retailers, and has a policy of not supplying wholesalers, then orders placed by a customer for the undisclosed purpose of reselling the product on the wholesale market are not ordinary (upheld, on other grounds, in *Chemistree Homecare v Abbvie* [2013] EWCA Civ 1338, where the Court of Appeal agreed that dominance could not be established).

(e) Other forms of abuse

Generally.   10.142
Fn 555 See also the decision of the French Autorité de la concurrence, of 14 May 2013, fining Sanofi-Aventis €40.6 million for abusing its dominant position by denigrating its competitors. Sanofi-Aventis manufactures clopidogrel an anti-platelet medication used to prevent relapses of serious cardiovascular diseases. It adopted a strategy of denigrating its generic competitors, in particular by questioning, with doctors and pharmacists, the efficacy and safety of the generics' products and intimating that the doctors/pharmacists could be held liable for any problems they caused, in order to limit generic entry and protect the market position of its branded clopidogrel 'Plavix', and its own generic 'Clopidogrel Winthrop': see ECN Brief 03/2013, p2. On appeal to the Cour d'Appel de Paris, not yet decided.

Abuse by sporting bodies.   10.146
Fn 573 The Court of Justice dismissed the further appeal in Case C-269/12P *Cañas v Commission*, judgment of 20 June 2013, regarding the alleged anti-competitiveness of certain anti-doping rules.

Abusive use of litigation.   10.151
Fn 592 The Court of Justice dismissed the appeals, on other grounds, in Case C-457/10P *AstraZeneca v Commission*, judgment of 6 December 2012, [2013] 4 CMLR 233.

11

THE COMPETITION RULES AND
THE ACTS OF MEMBER STATES

2. State Compulsion

Scope for residual competition.   **11.006**
Fn 19 The Court of Justice dismissed the further appeal in Case C-181/11P
Compañía española de tabaco en rama v Commission, judgment of 12 July 2012.

3. The Application and Enforcement of the
Prohibition in Article 106(1)

Undertakings granted special or exclusive rights.   Similarly to the authors'   **11.012**
rights society case considered in the main text, in Case T-55/08 *UEFA v Commission*
[2011] ECR II-0271, paras 165–171, the General Court held that broadcasters that benefited from being able to broadcast events designated by a Member
State as events of major importance for society within that Member State (under
Directive Article 3a(1) of Council Directive 89/552/EEC of 3 October 1989 on
the coordination of certain provisions laid down by law, regulation or administrative action in Member States concerning the pursuit of television broadcasting activities (OJ 1989 L 298, p23)) are not within the scope of Article 106(1),
because it was open to all broadcasters to acquire the right to broadcast such
events. The fact that in practice certain broadcasters would not be interested in
acquiring the right, because they were only interested in exclusive broadcasting,
was not sufficient to render the rights granted 'exclusive' within Article 106(1).
The Court upheld the Commission's decision that the designation by the UK of
the European Football Championship as an event of major importance for UK
society was compatible with EU law. The Court of Justice dismissed the further
appeal in Cases C-201, 204, 205/11P *UEFA and FIFA v Comission*, judgment of
18 July 2013, paras 78–79.

6. Derogations under Articles 106(2) and 346

(a) Article 106(2) TFEU: services of general interest

11.048 Article 106(2) and State aids.
Fn 165 The Commission has issued a new Staff Working Document, in April 2013 (SWD(2013) 53/final 2, '*Guide to the application of the European Union rules on state aid, public procurement and the internal market to services of general economic interest, and in particular to social services of general interest*'.

11.049 **The act of entrustment.** The Commission has issued a new Staff Working Document, in April 2013 (SWD(2013) 53/final 2, '*Guide to the application of the European Union rules on state aid, public procurement and the internal market to services of general economic interest, and in particular to social services of general interest*'. It contains the same indication as to the requirements of an 'act of entrustment': see section 3.2.2, in particular para 55.

11.051 **Member States' discretion in defining SGEIs.** The Commission has issued a new Staff Working Document, in April 2013 (SWD(2013) 53/final 2, '*Guide to the application of the European Union rules on state aid, public procurement and the internal market to services of general economic interest, and in particular to social services of general interest*'. On the definition of SGEIs, see section 2, in particular para 5.

11.054 **Activities which are not SGEIs.** In Case C-1/12 *Ordem dos Técnicos Oficiais de Contas v Autoridade da Concorrência*, judgment of 28 February 2013, [2013] 4 CMLR 651, para 105, the Court of Justice expressed doubts as to whether the provision of compulsory training to chartered accountants is within the scope of Article 106(2).

Fn 194 The Commission's decision in COMP/38698 *CISAC Agreements*, decision of 16 July 2008, has been partially annulled by the General Court on other grounds: Cases T-392, 398, 401, 410, 411, 413–422, 425, 428, 432–434, 442/08, judgments of 12 April 2013, [2013] 5 CMLR 536.

Fn 197 The Commission has issued a new Staff Working Document, in April 2013 (SWD(2013) 53/final 2, '*Guide to the application of the European Union rules on state aid, public procurement and the internal market to services of general economic interest, and in particular to social services of general interest*'. On activities consisting in advertising, e-commerce, the use of premium-rate telephone numbers in prize games, sponsorship and merchandising, see para 7.

Fn 198 In the revised Staff Working Document, see para 10.

12

SECTORAL REGIMES

2. Electronic Communications

(a) Regulatory framework

Revised regulatory framework. 12.006

Fn 13 Two sets of proceedings are extant: Cases C-330/12 *Commission v Poland* and C-407/12 *Commission v Slovenia*, not yet decided. C-325/12 *Commission v Portugal* was withdrawn by Order of 5 November 2012.

(i) Framework Directive

Obligations on NRAs. 12.009

Fn 37 On the role of the NRA in resolving disputes where it has not imposed *ex ante* regulation, see *Telefónica O2 UK v OFCOM* [2012] EWCA Civ 1002. On further appeal to the Supreme Court, not yet decided.

Fn 38 The Verwaltungsgerichtshof (Administrative Court) of Austria has referred to the Court of Justice for a preliminary ruling a question concerning the rights of competitor undertakings to appeal against a regulatory decision concerning the right to use radio frequencies: see Case C-282/13 *T-Mobile Austria GmbH v Telefon-Kontrol-Kommission*, not yet decided.

(iii) Authorisation Directive

General authorisation regime. 12.027

Fn 137 In *Recall Support Services Ltd et al v Secretary of State for Culture, Media and Sport* [2013] EWHC 3091 (Ch), the High Court of England and Wales (Rose J.) held that the UK's decision to impose a specific licence requirement, going beyond a general authorisation, on the commercial provision of communications services to multiple users through GSM gateway devices was justified on grounds of public security under Article 5 of the Authorisation Directive. The High Court did not accept that a licensing requirement was justified in relation to the commercial provision of communications services to a single user through a GSM gateway device.

Fn 144 Questions have been referred to the Court of Justice for a preliminary ruling on whether Articles 12 and 13 of the Authorisation Directive precludes Member States from imposing a tax on telecommunications infrastructure: see Cases C-346/13 *Ville de Mons v KPM Group Belgium*, not yet decided; and C-454/13 *Belgacom v Commune d-Etterbeek*, not yet decided.

Fn 145 In Case C-375/11 *Belgacom v Belgium*, judgment of 21 March 2013, [2013] 3 CMLR 185, three Belgian mobile operators challenged spectrum renewal fees imposed under Belgian national law as incompatible with Article 12 of Directive 2002/20 (the Authorisation Directive). The Court of Justice held that a renewal fee for rights to use the spectrum falls under Article 13 of the Authorisation Directive: paras 37–39. Therefore, provided such a fee complies with the requirements of Article 13, it is not precluded by Articles 12 and 13: para 48. The infraction proceedings against Hungary for its 'telecoms tax', referred to in the main text, is Case C-462/12 *Commission v Hungary*, not yet decided.

(iv) Universal Service Directive

12.032 **Designation and financing of undertakings.**
Fn 170 The infraction proceedings against Portugal for its failure to designate a universal services provider, referred to in the main text, is Case C-325/12 *Commission v Portugal*, not yet decided.

(v) Directive on competition in the market for ECNs and ECSs

12.033 **Abolition of special and exclusive rights.**   The Commission has commenced infraction proceedings against Bulgaria in respect of its national scheme for the allocation of radio frequencies used for digital terrestrial broadcasting, alleging that it breaches the requirements of Directive 2002/77 (the Telecommunications Competition Directive): see Case C-376/13 *Commission v Bulgaria*, not yet decided.

(b) Application of competition law

(iii) Application of Article 101

12.047 **Prevalence of agreements.**   In COMP/39839 *Telefónica and Portugal Telecom*, decision of 23 January 2013, the Commission concluded that the agreement between Telefónica and Portugal Telecom not to compete on the Iberian telecommunications market for a period of time following the acquisition by Telefónica of sole control over the Brazilian mobile operator, Vivo, which had previously been owned by both parties (as noted in footnote 241) breached Article 101 and fined the parties €79 million. On appeal, Cases T-208/13 *Portugal Telecom v Commission*; and T-216/13 *Telefónica v Commission*, not yet decided.

Price agreements.   **12.049**
Fn 248 The Commission issued decisions in COMP/39847 *E-books*, decisions of 12 December 2012 (OJ 2012 C283/7) and of 25 July 2013 (Press Release IP/13/746 (25 July 2013)) accepting commitments from five publishing companies and Apple, to abandon the most favoured nation clauses.

Interplay between agreements on standards and intellectual property rights.   **12.054**
Fn 258 The appeals by Hynix Semiconductor (now trading as SK Hynix Inc) in Joined Cases T-148&149/10 against COMP/38636 *Rambus*, decision of 9 December 2009, were withdrawn on 5 July 2013.

On the Commission's ongoing investigation into alleged abusive conduct in relation to IPR used in international telecoms standards, see also Press Release IP/12/1448 (21 December 2012) regarding the statement of objections sent in COMP/39939 *Samsung – enforcement of ETSI standards essential patents*; and IP/13/406 (6 May 2013) regarding the statement of objections sent in COMP/39985 *Motorola – enforcement of ETSI standards essential patents*. The Commission's preliminary view is that it is an abuse of dominance, contrary to Article 102, for the holder of a standard essential patent to seek injunctions for patent infringement in circumstances where it has given a commitment that it will grant licences on fair, reasonable, and non-discriminatory ('FRAND') terms and where the potential licensee has agreed to accept a binding determination of the terms of a FRAND licence by a third party. At the time of writing, the Commission is consulting on commitments proposed by Samsung under which it would agree, in essence, for a period of five years not to seek an injunction before any court or tribunal in the EEA for infringement of its standard essential patents (including all existing and future patents) implemented in smartphones and tablets against a potential licensee that agrees to, and complies with, a particular framework for determining the terms of a licence: see OJ 2013 C302/11.

(iv) Joint ventures and mergers

Mergers and full-function joint ventures.   **12.066**
Fn 289 See also M.6314 *Telefónica UK/Vodafone UK/EE/JV* (4 September 2012) (a full-function JV created to operate in the nascent 'mCommerce' sector, which consists of mobile payment applications, mobile advertising, and data analytics services); and equivalent decisions clearing JVs intended to operate in Spain M.6956 *Telefónica/Caixabank/Banco Santander/JV* (14 August 2013); and Belgium, M.6967 *BNP Paribas Fortis/Belgacom/Belgian MobileWallet JV* (11 October 2013).

Mergers in the mobile communications sector.   In M.6497 *Hutchinson 3G*   **12.068**
Austria/Orange Austria (12 December 2012) the Commission granted clearance at phase II, subject to two conditions: that Hutchinson divest itself of spectrum frequency bands, and that it enter into network access agreements to grant mobile virtual network operators (MVNOs) wholesale access to up to

30 per cent of its network capacity in the coming 10 year period. In M.6990 *Vodafone/Kabel Deutschland* (20 September 2013) the Commission granted unconditional Phase I clearance to the acquisition by Vodafone (primarily active in the mobile telephony sector) of Kabel Deutschland (primarily active in cable TV, fixed line telephony and internet access services), as it considered that the parties' economic activities are largely complementary, and the incremental increase in their market shares in those markets where they do overlap will not appreciably alter competition.

(v) Application of Article 102

12.083 **Examples of margin squeeze.**
Fn 388 Advocate General Wathelet has suggested, in his Opinion of 26 September 2013 in Case C-295/12P *Telefónica de España v Commission*, not yet decided, that the appeal on liability should be dismissed as partly inadmissible, partly unfounded, but the appeal on fines should be upheld and the case remitted to the General Court for reconsideration.

3. Energy

(a) Introduction

12.091 **Energy 2020.**
Fn 358 Croatia also joined the EU, on 1 July 2013.

(c) Electricity

(ii) Long-term arrangements and exclusivity

12.104 **Capacity withholding.**
Fn 398 In COMP/39727 *CEZ* the Commission accepted commitments that include CEZ divesting itself of generation capacity: Press Release IP/13/320 (10 April 2013).

(iii) Imports and exports

12.106 **Discrimination and the internal market.** The Commission has opened investigations into whether Article 102 is breached by an agreement that prescribes where energy is to be delivered, and thereby prevents its export (COMP/39767 *BEH*, Press Release IP/12/1307 (3 December 2012)); and has issued a statement of objections in respect of a requirement imposed by a national power exchange that all participants on spot markets be established in that Member State (COMP/39984 *Romanian Power Exchange*, Press Release IP/13/486 (30 May 2013)).

Fn 405 In COMP/39727 *CEZ* the Commission accepted commitments that include CEZ divesting itself of generation capacity: Press Release IP/13/320 (10 April 2013).

(d) Gas

(ii) Application of the competition rules

Capacity management issues leading to divestment. The Commission has **12.113**
opened an investigation into whether Article 102 has been breached by the
Bulgarian gas supplier and transmission asset owner, by refusing or delaying third
party access to its infrastructure: Press Release IP/13/656 (5 July 2013).

Similarly to the decision discussed in the main text, COMP/39402 *RWE Gas
Foreclosure*, decision of 18 March 2009, see also the decision of the Greek NCA,
of 30 April 2013, fining the Hellenic Gas Transmission System Operator,
which is a wholly owned subsidiary of DEPA, the incumbent supplier of natural
gas in Greece, for having denied access to the gas transmission network to an
undertaking that is a customer and potential competitor of DEPA: ECN Brief
03/2013, p2.

Territorial restrictions.
Fn 435 The Commission has opened an investigation into whether Article 102 **12.116**
has been breached by the Russian gas producer and supplier Gazprom, by *inter alia*
restricting the flow of gas between Member States: COMP/39816 *Upstream gas supplies in Central and Eastern Europe*; see Press Release IP/12/937 (4 September 2012).

Mergers. **12.117**
Fn 437 A recent example of a decision clearing a merger in the gas and oil sector is
M.6081 *Rosneft/TNK-BP* (8 March 2013).

4. Insurance

Insurance intermediaries. In Case C-32/11 *Allianz HungáriaBistozító*, judg- **12.133**
ment of 14 March 2013, [2013] 4 CMLR 863, paras 46–48, the Court of Justice
held that vertical agreements between insurers and car dealers which made the
dealers' remuneration for their car repair services dependent on the number of
insurance policies they sold on the insurers' behalves may be an object infringement of Article 101, in particular where national law requires that intermediaries
and brokers should be independent of insurers.

5. Postal Services

(c) Application of the competition rules

Jurisprudence of the EU Courts and the Commission. Recent developments **12.143**
in the postal sector have also been subject to scrutiny under the merger regime.
In particular, in M.6570 *UPS/TNT Express* (30 January 2013) the Commission

prohibited a proposed acquisition by UPS of TNT Express, which would have reduced the number of companies operating on the markets for international express deliveries of small packages in the EEA from four to three or two. Although the parties offered divestiture commitments, the Commission considered these insufficient in the absence of an upfront buyer commitment: see Press Release IP/13/68 (30 January 2013). On appeal, Case T-194/13 *United Parcel Service v Commission*, not yet decided. In M.6503 *LaPoste/Swiss Post/JV* (4 July 2012) the Commission cleared a joint venture between LaPoste and Swiss Post to carry out their international mail deliveries, subject to divestiture commitments. The Commission considered in particular the 'very strong position' of La Poste, as the incumbent operator on a market which had been liberalised fairly recently, and in which 'no entrants are to be expected in the medium term': para 85. It considered the JV would strengthen that position. The merger was cleared on condition that Swiss Post divest itself of its French subsidiary.

6. Agriculture

(b) Application of the competition rules

12.159 Article 101(3). The ECN has published a report on the activities of competition authorities in the food sector, which summarises the actions taken by the Commission and the Member States' NCAs in this area, '*ECN Report on competition law enforcement and market monitoring activities by European competition authorities in the food sector*', of 24 May 2012: the Report is available on the ECN section of the DG Comp website.

7. Transport

(b) Rail, road and inland waterway transport

(ii) Liberalisation measures in the railway sector

12.171 First railway package.
Fn 590 The Court of Justice has ruled on the proceedings brought by the Commission for failure to implement: see Case C-557/10 *Commission v Portugal*, judgement of 25 October 2012; C-528/10 *Commission v Greece*, judgment of 8 November 2012; and Cases C-473/10, etc, *Commission v Hungary*, judgments of 28 February 2013.

12.172 Second and third railway packages. On 30 January 2013, the Commission published proposals for a Fourth Railway Package. The proposals are available on the DG TRANS website, at http://ec.europa.eu/transport/modes/rail/packages/2013_en.htm.

Single European Railway Area.   On 21 November 2012, Directive 2012/34/   **12.173**
EU establishing a single European railway area (OJ 2012 L343/32), was
adopted. The deadline for transposition is 16 June 2015 (Article 64, Directive
2012/34/EU).

(c) Maritime transport

(i) Application of the competition rules

Application of Regulation 1/2003.   The Commission has announced that   **12.174**
it will not renew the Maritime Transport Guidelines, OJ 2008 C245/2: Vol II,
App E20, which expired on 26 September 2013: see Press Release IP/13/122 (19
February 2013).

(d) Air transport

(iii) Particular issues

Airline alliances.   **12.195**
Fn 662 See also COMP/39595 *Continental/United/Lufthansa/Air Canada*, decision of 23 May 2013, accepting commitments under Article 9 of Regulation 1/2003
in respect of a revenue sharing joint venture between Star Alliance members Air
Canada, United and Lufthansa.

Groundhandling services.   In Case C-288/11P *Mitteldeutsche Flughafen and*   **12.198**
Flughafen Leipzig-Halle v Commission, judgment of 19 December 2012, [2013]
2 CMLR 483, paras 46 et seq, the Court of Justice confirmed that the construction of airport infrastructure is a part of the economic activity of operating an
airport. The construction of an additional runway at an existing airport could not
be divorced from the economic activity of operating a passenger airport, but was to
be treated as part of the costs that an airport operator would normally have to bear
itself for the purpose of carrying out that activity.

13

ENFORCEMENT AND PROCEDURE

2. Fundamental Rights and the Commission's
Powers of Enforcement

Relevant rights.   13.007

Fn 25 The General Court in Case T-135/09 *Nexans France v Commission*, judgment of 14 November 2012, [2013] CMLR 4 195, paras 119 et seq held that the challenge to the Commission's action in copying the whole hard drive of a laptop seized during a dawn raid was inadmissible: see the update to paragraph 13.030, below.

Fn 36 The Court of Justice held in Case C-439/11P *Ziegler v Commission*, judgment of 11 July 2013, para 154, that it is the principle of good administration in Article 41 of the Charter that applies to administrative proceedings before the Commission, rather than Article 47. Article 41 provides for a right to have one's affairs handled impartially by the EU institutions. That requirement of impartiality encompasses subjective impartiality (the member of the institution concerned who is responsible for the matter may not show bias or personal prejudice) and objective impartiality (there must be sufficient guarantees to exclude any legitimate doubt as to bias). In respect of the complaint that the appellant's rights had been breached by the Commission investigating an alleged infringement of competition law where it was also itself a victim of that alleged infringement, the Court held that the Commission's objective impartiality is secured in these circumstances by ensuring that the part of the Commission bringing the infringement action is not the same part as that which suffered the damage, and by the addressees' right to appeal the Commission's decision in the European Courts under Article 263 TFEU, which provides the guarantees required by the Charter (paras 157–160).

Fn 38 The Court of Justice confirmed in Case C-439/11P *Ziegler v Commission*, judgment of 11 July 2013, para 154, that it is the principle of good administration in Article 41 of the Charter that applies to administrative proceedings before the Commission, rather than Article 47. Article 41 provides for a right to have one's affairs handled impartially by the EU institutions. That requirement of impartiality encompasses subjective impartiality (the member of the institution concerned who is responsible for the matter may not show bias or personal prejudice) and objective impartiality (there must be sufficient guarantees to exclude any legitimate doubt as to bias). In respect of the complaint that the appellant's rights had been breached by the Commission investigating an alleged infringement of competition law where it was also itself a victim of that alleged infringement, the Court held that the Commission's objective impartiality is secured in these circumstances by ensuring that the part of the Commission bringing the infringement action is not the same part as that which suffered the damage, and by the addressees' right to appeal the Commission's decision in the European Courts under Article 263 TFEU, which provides the guarantees required by the Charter (paras 157–160).

See also Case C-199/11 *Europese Gemeenschap v Otis*, judgment of 6 November 2012, [2013] 4 CMLR 141, in which the Court of Justice was asked whether it was compatible with Article 47 of the Charter of Fundamental Rights for the Commission to bring a civil action in a Member State to seek to recover the damages it has suffered as a result of an infringement of competition law, where it would be relying on its own infringement decision to establish liability, and Article 16(1) of Regulation 1/2003 would prevent the defendant from contesting the decision. The Court confirmed that the Commission is not precluded from bringing such a civil action in a Member State, and in these circumstances the defendant's rights under Article 47 of the Charter are adequately protected by its right to appeal the Commission's decision in the European Courts under Article 263 TFEU, and its right to contest causation and damage in the Member State court.

13.008 **Right to a fair trial.** The Court of Justice held in Case C-439/11P *Ziegler v Commission*, judgment of 11 July 2013, para 154, that it is the principle of good administration in Article 41 of the Charter that applies to administrative proceedings before the Commission, rather than Article 47.

13.009 **'Criminal charge'.** In Case C-501/11P *Schindler v Commission (Elevators and Escalators)*, judgment of 18 July 2013, paras 33–38, the Court of Justice rejected an argument that the imposition of fines by the Commission, rather than by a court, is contrary to Article 6 ECHR and Article 47 of the Charter of Fundamental Rights. The power of review by the General Court under Article 263 TFEU, together with the unlimited jurisdiction to review the fine under Article 261 TFEU and Article 31 of Regulation 1/2003, is sufficient to comply with the requirements of effective judicial protection.

13.010 **Article 8 of the Convention: respect for private and family life.** The General Court in Joined Cases T-289/11, etc, *Deutsche Bahn and others v Commission*, judgment of 6 September 2013 confirmed that the exercise of the Commission's powers of inspection under Article 20(4) of Regulation 1/2003 is a 'clear interference' with the right to respect for private and family life under Article 8 ECHR/

Article 7 Charter of Fundamental Rights. However, it dismissed a complaint that the absence of a requirement for prior judicial authorisation renders the inspection a disproportionate interference as there are sufficient safeguards in place to ensure that rights are protected: see paras 65 et seq.

3. The Commission's Powers of Investigation

(a) Power to obtain information

Information gathering for sectoral inquiries. On 22 July 2013, the Council **13.021** adopted Regulation 734/2013, amending Regulation 659/99 (the Procedural Regulation), OJ 2013 L204/15, as a result of which the Commission now has power also to conduct general inquiries into any economic sector, or type of aid instrument, to consider their compatibility with the EU rules on State aid, Articles 107 and 108 TFEU: see Article 20a of Regulation 659/99 as amended.

(b) Powers of inspection

Inspection of undertakings pursuant to decision. The General Court in **13.025** Joined Cases T-289/11, etc, *Deutsche Bahn and others v Commission*, judgment of 6 September 2013, rejected a challenge to a Commission inspection decision under Article 20(4) of Regulation 1/2003 based on the absence of a requirement for prior judicial authorisation of the inspection. The General Court accepted that the exercise of the Commission's powers of inspection under Article 20(4) is a 'clear interference' with the right to respect for private and family life under Article 8 ECHR / Article 7 Charter of Fundamental Rights, but held that the absence of a requirement for prior judicial authorisation does not render it a disproportionate interference as there are sufficient safeguards in place to ensure that rights are protected: see paras 65 et seq.

Fn 122 On the Commission's obligation to specify the subject-matter of the inspection, see the General Court's judgments in Case T-135/09 *Nexans and Nexans France v Commission*, judgment of 14 November 2012, [2013] 4 CMLR 195; and Case T-410/09 *Almamet v Commission*, judgment of 12 December 2012, [2013] 4 CMLR 788. In *Nexans*, paras 53 et seq, the General Court held that the Commission complied with its duty to specify the subject-matter of its investigation where its decision was sufficient to enable the undertaking to assess the scope of its duty to cooperate, even though the General Court accepted that the decision 'could have been less ambiguous' (on further appeal in Case C-37/12P, not yet decided). In *Almamet*, paras 34 et seq, the General Court considered a complaint about the Commission having based an infringement decision on evidence that was gathered unlawfully, as it was outside the scope of the inspection decision. The General Court held that any addressee can challenge an infringement decision on the basis that the underlying evidence was gathered without using the procedures laid down for gathering it lawfully, such as those in Article 20; however, where the complaint is about procedural irregularities in how the process was conducted, that complaint can only be made by the party from whom the evidence was gathered. In that case, Almamet challenged COMP/39396 *Calcium carbide and magnesium based reagents*, decision of 22 July 2009, [2010] 5 CMLR 1368, on the basis that the Commission had gathered evidence from the premises of another undertaking, Ecka, that related to subject-matter outside the scope of the inspection decision. The General Court held that:

> 'where, as in this case, a party other than the party that submitted to an inspection conducted by the Commission under Article 20 of Regulation No 1/2003 invokes an infringement, during that inspection, of safeguards designed to ensure respect for fundamental rights, the Court must confine itself to checking that the Commission did in fact use the procedure laid down to that effect, without going into the details of the conduct of that procedure unless the party in question invokes a procedural irregularity likely to concern it directly.'

13.027 Assistance by Member States.
Fn 137 Two of the appeals against COMP/398181 *Candle Waxes*, decision of 1 October 2008, on other grounds, were largely dismissed: Cases T-548/08 *Total v Commission*, judgment of 13 September 2013; and T-566/08 *Total Raffinage Marketing*, judgment of 13 September 2013 (fine reduced on grounds of duration). The other appeals (Cases T-540/08, etc, not yet decided) are still pending.

13.028 Inspections and the right to privacy. The General Court in Joined Cases T-289/11, etc, *Deutsche Bahn and others v Commission*, judgment of 6 September 2013, confirmed that the exercise of the Commission's powers of inspection under Article 20(4) of Regulation 1/2003 is a 'clear interference' with the right to respect for private and family life under Article 8 ECHR/Article 7 Charter of Fundamental Rights. However, it dismissed a complaint that the absence of a requirement for prior judicial authorisation renders the inspection a disproportionate interference, as there are sufficient safeguards in place to ensure that rights are protected: see paras 65 et seq.

13.030 Powers that can be exercised during an inspection. The General Court in Case T-135/09 *Nexans France v Commission*, judgment of 14 November 2012, [2013] CMLR 4 195, paras 119 et seq, held that the challenge to the Commission's action in copying the whole hard drive of a laptop seized during a dawn raid was inadmissible. The General Court considered that the Commission's action was a measure implementing the decision under which the inspection was ordered, and it was not itself a decision that could be annulled by the Court. Its legality could only be examined in the context of an appeal against any infringement decision the Commission may issue under Article 101, or an appeal against a decision imposing a penalty under Article 23 for refusing to cooperate with the inspection. On further appeal, on other grounds, in Case C-37/13P, not yet decided. The General Court has therefore not considered directly the question of whether Article 20(2)(c) includes a power for the Commission to take a copy of the whole of a computer hard drive and review the contents at its premises in Brussels at a later date.

Limits on the Commission's use of information acquired. In respect of **13.033** paragraph 13.033(a) of the main text, the General Court held in Joined Cases T-289/11, etc, *Deutsche Bahn and others v Commission*, judgment of 6 September 2013, paras 124–128, that it is lawful for the Commission to use documents obtained during the course of an inspection as a basis upon which to decide under Article 20(4) of Regulation 1/2003 to conduct further inspections. The General Court rejected an argument that it was disproportionate to conduct further inspections instead of making a request for documents under Article 18 of Regulation 1/2003: see paras 185 et seq.

4. Complaints

Procedure: second stage.   **13.047**
Fn 262 The General Court will only review a refusal to grant an extension of the period for responding to the Article 7(1) letter where there has been a manifest failure to have regard to the circumstances of the case, likely to compromise the applicant's right to be associated closely with the procedure: Joined Cases T-104/07&339/08 *Belgische Vereniging van handelaars in-en uitvoerdersgeslependiamant (BVGD) and Diamanthandel A. Spira v Commission*, judgment of 11 July 2013, [2013] 5 CMLR 1055, para 144.

Fn 266 See also Joined Cases T-104/07&339/08 *Belgische Vereniging van handelaars in-en uitvoerdersgeslependiamant (BVGD) and Diamanthandel A. Spira v Commission*, judgment of 11 July 2013, [2013] 5 CMLR 1055, paras 90 et seq.

Procedure: third stage. For an example of significant new evidence emerging, **13.048** and the Commission re-opening a matter once a decision rejecting a complaint has already been taken, see the Commission's decision in COMP/39221 *De Beers/DTC Supplier of Choice*, decision of 5 June 2008, in which the Commission reconsidered its decision of 26 January 2007 rejecting a complaint, following the General Court judgment in Case T-170/06 *Alrosa v Commission* [2006] ECR II-2601. The Commission's reconsidered decision was upheld in Joined Cases T-104/07&339/08 *Belgische Vereniging van handelaars in-en uitvoerdersgeslependiamant (BVGD) and Diamanthandel A. Spira v Commission*, judgment of 11 July 2013, [2013] 5 CMLR 1055. The General Court confirmed that the Commission's power to reconsider its previous decisions arises under the general principle of the right of an authority to re-examine, amend and withdraw its decisions, rather than under Article 7 of Regulation 773/2004: see paras 58 et seq.

13.050 **Lack of Union interest.** In addition to the criteria outlined in the Complaints Notice, and discussed in the main text, for assessing Union interest the Commission may also have regard to measures taken by national authorities: T-432/10 *Vivendi v Commission (France Télécom)*, judgment of 16 October 2013, paras 26 and 42 et seq.

Fn 284 The Court of Justice dismissed the further appeal in Case C-56/12P *European Federation of Ink and Ink Cartridge Manufacturers (EFIM) v Commission*, judgment of 19 September 2013. The case is discussed in paragraph 4.055 of the main text, and the update thereto above.

Fn 289 See also Joined Cases T-104/07&339/08 *Belgische Vereniging van handelaars in-en uitvoerdersgeslependiamant (BVGD) and Diamanthandel A. Spira v Commission*, judgment of 11 July 2013, [2013] 5 CMLR 1055, paras 189 et seq.

13.051 **Complainant's rights after initiation of procedure.**
Fn 303 See also Joined Cases T-104/07&339/08 *Belgische Vereniging van handelaars in-en uitvoerdersgeslependiamant (BVGD) and Diamanthandel A. Spira v Commission*, judgment of 11 July 2013, [2013] 5 CMLR 1055, para 168.

5. Formal Procedure Prior to an Adverse Decision

(a) The nature of Commission proceedings

13.052 **An 'administrative' procedure.** In Case C-501/11P *Schindler v Commission (Elevators and Escalators)*, judgment of 18 July 2013, the Court of Justice followed the approach of the European Court of Human Rights in App 43509/08 *Menarini Diagnostics v Italy*, judgment of 27 September 2011 (referred to in footnote 319 of the main text), and rejected an argument that the imposition of fines by the Commission, rather than by a court, was contrary to Article 6 ECHR and Article 47 of the Charter of Fundamental Rights. It held that the power of review by the Court under Article 263 TFEU, together with the unlimited jurisdiction to review the fine under Article 261 TFEU and Article 31 of Regulation 1/2003, is sufficient to comply with the requirements of effective judicial protection. In Case C-439/11P *Ziegler v Commission*, judgment of 11 July 2013, para 154, the Court confirmed that it is the principle of good administration in Article 41 of the Charter that applies to administrative proceedings before the Commission, rather than Article 47.

13.053 **Hearing by 'an independent and impartial tribunal'.** In Case C-501/11P *Schindler v Commission (Elevators and Escalators)*, judgment of 18 July 2013, the Court of Justice followed the approach of the European Court of Human Rights in App 43509/08 *Menarini Diagnostics v Italy*, judgment of 27 September 2011 (referred to in footnote 319 of the main text), and rejected an argument that the imposition of fines by the Commission, rather than by a court, was contrary to Article 6 ECHR and Article 47 of the Charter of Fundamental Rights. It held that the power of review by the Court under Article 263 TFEU, together with the unlimited jurisdiction to review the fine under Article 261 TFEU and Article 31 of Regulation 1/2003, is sufficient to comply with the requirements of effective judicial protection. In Case C-439/11P *Ziegler v Commission*, judgment of 11 July 2013, para 154, the Court confirmed that it is the principle of good administration in Article 41 of the Charter that applies to administrative proceedings before the Commission, rather than Article 47.

Presumption of innocence and burden of proof. **13.054**
Fn 327 The Court of Justice dismissed the appeals in Case C-457/10P *AstraZeneca v Commission*, judgment of 6 December 2012, [2013] 4 CMLR 233.

(b) Initiation of proceedings and the statement of objections

Initiation of proceedings. **13.057**
Fn 356 The reference in the footnote should be to Article 10 of Regulation 1/2003, rather than to Article 10 of Regulation 773/2004.

Obligation to supply relevant documents. In Case T-404/08 *Fluorsid and* **13.063**
Minmet v Commission, judgment of 18 June 2013, [2013] 5 CMLR 902, paras 120 et seq; and Case T-406/08 *Industries chimiques du fluor v Commission*, judgment of 18 June 2013, paras 136 et seq, the General Court held that where a statement of objections does not expressly refer to particular documents on which the Commission subsequently relies in an infringement decision, but those documents were included in the administrative file and the statement of objections sets out provisional findings of a single and continuous infringement, based on ongoing bilateral and multilateral contacts, that is sufficient to alert the undertaking to the fact that the Commission could use those documents as incriminating evidence against the undertaking. On further appeal, Case C-467/13P *Industries chimiques du fluor v Commission*, not yet decided.

(c) Access to the file

Effect of lack of access on validity of decision. The failure to provide access to **13.069**
inculpatory documents will also lead to those documents being excluded from the evidence upon which the Commission may rely in its decision: see Joined Cases T-379&381/10 *Keramag Keramische Werke and Others v Commission ('Bathroom Fittings')*, judgment of 16 September 2013, paras 115–116 and 264, in which the General Court held to be inadmissible a document relied on by the Commission in its decision which had not been disclosed to the undertaking concerned, and it reviewed the sufficiency of the Commission's evidence finding an infringement in the absence of that document.

13.070   **Exculpatory and incriminating documents.**
Fn 435 See also Joined Cases T-379&381/10 *Keramag Keramische Werke and Others v Commission ('Bathroom Fittings')*, judgment of 16 September 2013, paras 115–116 and 264. The General Court held to be inadmissible a document relied on by the Commission in its decision which had not been disclosed to the under-taking concerned, when reviewing the sufficiency of the Commission's evidence finding an infringement.

13.071   **When the right of access to the file arises.**
Fn 445 In Case T-343/06 *Shell Petroleum v Commission*, judgment of 27 September 2012, [2012] 5 CMLR 1064, paras 84–94, the General Court held that where other parties' replies contain incriminating or exculpatory material the Commission's obli-gation to grant access to those replies is confined to those passages which contain such incriminating or exculpatory material, placed in context if that is necessary to understand them. It does not extend to the whole document. On further appeal, Case C-585/12P, not yet decided.

13.072   **The documents to which access is granted.**
Fn 449 In Case T-343/06 *Shell Petroleum v Commission*, judgment of 27 September 2012, [2012] 5 CMLR 1064, paras 84–94, the General Court held that the Commission's obligation to grant access to other parties' replies is confined to those passages which contain the incriminating or exculpatory material, placed in context if that is necessary to understand them. It does not extend to the whole document. On further appeal, Case C-585/12P, not yet decided.

13.073   **Internal Commission documents.**
Fn 462 See also Case T-561/12 *Beninca v Commission*, judgment of 25 October 2013, regarding a request under Regulation 1049/2001 for internal Commission documents prepared in the context of the merger control regime. The General Court confirmed that the Commission's internal documents prepared in the course of merger control proceedings may fall within the exception in Article 4(3) of Regulation 1049/2001. That exception will apply where the Commission's decision-making process may be prejudiced by disclosure of the document, and in particular in circumstances where its investigation has closed but its decision is under appeal and the possibility remains that it will be required to re-open its proceedings. The request was for disclosure of an internal Commission memoran-dum which related to M.6166 *NYSE Euronext/Deutsche Börse* (1 February 2012), currently under appeal in Case T-175/12 *Deutsche Börse v Commission*, not yet decided.

13.081   **Provision of documents from the file to third parties.**   See also Joined Cases T-104/07&339/08 *Belgische Vereniging van handelaars in-en uitvoerdersgeslepen-diamant (BVGD) and Diamanthandel A. Spira v Commission*, judgments of 11 July 2013, [2013] 5 CMLR 1055, paras 90 et seq.

(d) The hearing and subsequently

Relationship between the decision and the statement of objections.   **13.092**
Fn 569 See, however, Case T-404/08 *Fluorsid and Minmet v Commission*, judgment of 18 June 2013, [2013] 5 CMLR 902, paras 120 et seq; and Case T-406/08
Industries chimiques du fluor v Commission, judgment of 18 June 2013, paras 136
et seq, in which the General Court held that where a statement of objections does
not expressly refer to particular documents which the Commission subsequently
relies on in an infringement decision, but those documents were included in the
administrative file and the statement of objections sets out provisional findings of
a single and continuous infringement, based on ongoing bilateral and multilateral
contacts, that is sufficient to alert the undertaking to the fact that the Commission
could use those documents as incriminating evidence against the undertaking.
On further appeal, Case C-467/13P *Industries chimiques du fluor v Commission*,
not yet decided.

Legal status of the decision.   On the ability of undertakings that are not   **13.093**
addressees of an infringement decision to bring a challenge, see also the General
Court's judgment in Case T-442/08 *International Confederation of Societies
of Authors and Composers (CISAC) v Commission*, judgment of 12 April 2013,
[2013] 5 CMLR 536, paras 63 et seq, discussed in the update to paragraph
13.132, below.

6. Commitments and Settlement

(b) Commitments

Article 9 of Regulation 1/2003.   **13.100**
Fn 602 The most recent commitments decisions are COMP/39847 *E-Books*,
decisions of 12 December 2012 and 25 July 2013; COMP/39230 *Rio Tinto
Alcan*, decision of 20 December 2012; COMP/39654 *Reuters Instrument Codes
(RICs)*, decision of 20 December 2012; COMP/39727 *ČEZ*, decision of 10 April
2013; and COMP/39595 *Continental/United/Lufthansa/Air Canada*, decision of
23 May 2013.

The appeals, noted in the footnote, by Hynix Semiconductor (now trading as SK
Hynix Inc) in Joined Cases T-148&149/10 against COMP/38636 *Rambus*, decision of 9 December 2009, were withdrawn on 5 July 2013.

Enforcement and withdrawal.   The Commission exercised its power under   **13.103**
Article 23(2)(c) of Regulation 1/2003 for the first time in COMP/39530
Microsoft – Tying, decision of 6 March 2013, for Microsoft's failure to comply with the commitment decision of 16 December 2009. It imposed a fine of
€561 million.

9. Review by the General Court

(a) Review of fines under Article 261 TFEU

13.123 **Article 261 TFEU: unlimited jurisdiction regarding fines.** The Court may also take into account evidence on which the Commission did not rely in its decision, and which is not admissible for the purposes of review under Article 263 TFEU: Case T-462/07 *Galp Energía España v Commission*, judgment of 16 September 2013. The General Court partially annulled a Commission decision because the evidence relied upon for a finding of a single and continuous infringement did not establish that the undertaking was aware of the infringing activities in which it did not participate. Although a subsequent statement from the undertaking confirmed that it had in fact been so aware, that evidence was not admissible on a review under Article 263 TFEU: see paras 288 et seq (see also paragraph 13.153, and the update thereto, below). However, the General Court held that it could take account of that evidence in the exercise of its unlimited jurisdiction regarding fines under Article 261 TFEU, and on that basis it considered that the starting point the Commission had used to determine the undertaking's fine should not be adjusted, notwithstanding that it took into account the infringing behaviours which, on review under Article 263 TFEU, the undertaking could not be held liable for: see paras 615 et seq.

Fn 705 See also Case C-501/11P *Schindler v Commission (Elevators and Escalators)*, judgment of 18 July 2013, paras 33–38.

13.124 **The Commission's discretion and the Fining Guidelines.**

Fn 709 See also Case C-501/11P *Schindler v Commission (Elevators and Escalators)*, judgment of 18 July 2013, paras 33–38 and 155–160. The Court of Justice will consider whether the General Court conducted an in-depth review in substance, even if the judgment states that it is according the Commission a considerable margin of discretion. In Case C-510/11P *Kone v Commission*, judgment of 24 October 2013, the Court of Justice considered whether the General Court conducted an in-depth review in substance, notwithstanding it had stated that the test it was applying was whether the Commission had 'manifestly [gone] beyond the bounds of that margin' of discretion: see paras 40 and 44 et seq.

Fn 713 The Court of Justice dismissed the further appeal in Case C-70/12P *Quinn Barlo v Commission* ('*Methacrylates*'), judgment of 30 May 2013, [2013] 5 CMLR 637.

Fn 715 See also Case C-70/12P *Quinn Barlo v Commission* ('*Methacrylates*'), judgment of 30 May 2013, [2013] 5 CMLR 637, para 46.

13.127 **Adjustment of fines in cases of unequal treatment.** See also Joined Cases T-147&148/09 *Trelleborg v Commission*, judgment of 17 May 2013, [2013] 5

CMLR 754, para 104, in which the General Court dismissed a complaint that the Commission had breached the principle of equal treatment in the manner in which it had applied the limitation period to different undertakings. The General Court held that even if the Commission had erred as respects its conclusion that proceedings against another undertaking were time-barred, it was not open to Trelleborg to rely on that illegality as a basis for claiming that proceedings against it should also have been treated as time-barred.

(b) Review of Commission decisions

(i) Reviewable acts of the Commission and standing to bring appeal

Non-reviewable 'acts' of the Commission.   In addition to the acts which are   **13.131**
listed in the main text as non-reviewable, measures taken by the Commission to implement an inspection decision are not reviewable by the General Court: Case T-135/09 *Nexans France v Commission*, judgment of 14 November 2012, [2013] CMLR 4 195, paras 119 et seq, discussed in the update to paragraph 13.030, above.

Standing to bring appeal.   The General Court in Case T-442/08 *International*   **13.132**
Confederation of Societies of Authors and Composers (CISAC) v Commission, judgment of 12 April 2013, paras 63 et seq, permitted CISAC to challenge the Commission's decision in COMP/38698 *CISAC Agreements*, decision of 16 July 2008, [2009] 4 CMLR 577. CISAC is a non-profit non-governmental organisation whose principal task is representing the entities that were addressed by the Commission decision, and facilitating cooperation between them. It had been an addressee of the statement of objections, but was not an addressee of the final decision. The General Court considered that the decision was of direct and individual concern to it, as its activities would be relevant to assessing whether the addressees were bringing to an end the concerted practice found in the decision, and as the decision affected its role as a facilitator of cooperation (particularly in mediating between the societies on issues relating to the grant of multi-territorial licences).

Fn 762 The Court of Justice in C-452/10P *BNP Paribas v Commission*, judgment of 21 June 2012, [2012] 3 CMLR 723, upheld the appeal against the General Court's judgment, but gave final judgment rather than remit the appeal and dismissed the challenge to the Commission's decision.

(ii) The grounds of annulment

Procedural irregularities.   A further example of a procedural irregular-   **13.134**
ity which was held not to vitiate the Commission's decision was (a) an initial refusal by the Commission to grant access to original recordings of an interview it had conducted with an employee of a leniency applicant; and (b) an incorrect transcription of the interview (which was revealed when the Commission

subsequently granted partial access to the recording), omitting a statement by a Commission official that the witness should not worry about whether the answer to the question he had been asked was 'true or not'. The General Court held that as undertaking had eventually been granted full access to the original recording, and the Commission had not relied on that particular witness' evidence in its statement of objections, the irregularity did not vitiate the Commission's decision: Case T-482/07 *Nynäs v Commission*, judgment of 16 September 2013, paras 104 et seq.

13.135 **Failure to respect the rights of the defence.**
Fn 784 See also T-587/08 *Fresh Del Monte Produce*, judgment of 14 March 2013, paras 704–713. On further appeal, Cases C-293 & 294/13P, not yet decided.

13.137 **Adequacy of reasoning.**
Fn 794 The Court of Justice dismissed the appeals in Case C-457/10P *AstraZeneca v Commission*, judgment of 6 December 2012, [2013] 4 CMLR 233.

Fn 800 A further, recent example is the General Court's judgment in Case T-380/10 *Wabco Europe v Commission (Bathroom Fittings)*, judgment of 16 September 2013, paras 108–112.

(iii) The standard of review

13.143 **Errors of law.**
Fn 822 The Court of Justice in Case C-439/11P *Ziegler v Commission*, judgment of 11 July 2013, held that it is necessary to define the relevant market in order to determine whether there was an appreciable effect on trade between Member States in that market (para 63) but that the Commission had provided a sufficiently detailed description of the services with which its decision was concerned to constitute a definition of the market for these purposes (paras 67–73).

13.147 **Decisions involving complex economic assessment.** In addition to the decisions listed in the main text, in Case C-73/11 *Frucona Košice v Commission*, judgment of 24 January 2013, [2013] 2 CMLR 719, paras 74–75, the Court of Justice held that determining whether a measure amounts to a State aid because the public authority did not act in the same way as a private creditor involves the kind of complex economic assessment which may result in the European courts conducting a more limited review.

Fn 836 A recent example of a judgment in respect of a clearance decision is Case T-405/08 *SPAR Österreische Warenhandel v Commission*, judgment of 7 June 2013.

13.149 **Exercise of the Commission's discretion.** The case law referred to in the main text should be read in the light of the Court of Justice's judgment in Case C-510/11P *Kone v Commission*, judgment of 24 October 2013, at least insofar as the discretion exercised by the Commission pertains to fines. The appellant complained that by considering only whether the Commission had 'manifestly [gone] beyond the bounds of [its] margin' of discretion in assessing the cooperation of an under-taking under the Leniency Notice the General Court had failed to comply with Article 47 of the Charter on Fundamental Rights, and Article 6 ECHR. The Court of Justice accepted that the manifest error test does not meet the requirements of Article 47 Charter/Article 6 ECHR: see para 44. The Court cannot use the Commission's margin of discretion as a basis for dispensing with the conduct of an in-depth review of the law and of the facts: see paragraph 13.124, and the updates thereto, above.

Fn 844 See also Joined Cases T-104/07&339/08 *Belgische Vereniging van han-delaars in-en uitvoerdersgeslependiamant (BVGD) and Diamanthandel A. Spira v Commission*, judgments of 11 July 2013, [2013] 5 CMLR 1055, paras 219 et seq.

(iv) Procedural aspects

Whether decisions can be supported by new material. Although the Commission is not permitted to rely on evidence that is not contained in the decision for the purposes of review under Article 263 TFEU, the General Court may nonethe-less take such evidence into account in the exercise of its unlimited jurisdiction regarding fines under Article 261 TFEU: Case T-462/07 *Galp Energía España v Commission*, judgment of 16 September 2013, discussed in the update to paragraph 13.123, above. **13.153**

Fn 864 See also Case T-380/10 *Wabco Europe v Commission (Bathroom Fittings)*, judgment of 16 September 2013, paras 108–112, in which the General Court rejected the Commission's attempt to provide additional arguments in support of its decision, and partially annulled the decision on grounds of lack of reasons.

Measures of organisation and inquiry. With respect to the General Court hear-ing oral evidence, the Court of Justice observed in Case C-501/11P *Schindler v Commission (Elevators and Escalators)*, judgment of 18 July 2013, para 46, that it is for an applicant to apply for witnesses to be examined. It appears that the General Court cannot be criticised on appeal for not having heard witness evidence of its own motion. **13.154**

Power of partial annulment. In Case C-441/11P *Commission v Verhuizingen Coppens*, judgment of 6 December 2012, [2013] 4 CMLR 312, the Court of Justice held that the General Court erred in annulling COMP/38543 *International Removal Service*, decision of 11 March 2008, entirely rather than partially. The General Court had annulled the decision in relation to Coppens on the basis that it had only engaged in one of the two infringing behaviours found by the Commission (it engaged in cover pricing, but had not entered into compensation agreements). The Court of Justice held that the decision should have been annulled only in respect of the infringing behaviour in which Coppens had not engaged, and in respect of the attribution of a single and **13.156**

continuous infringement. The Court of Justice held that the Commission's decision stood in respect of the infringing behaviour in which Coppens did engage. For an example of the General Court applying this judgment, see Case T-462/07 *Galp Energía España v Commission*, judgment of 16 September 2013, paras 535 et seq.

In Case C-287/11P *Commission v Aalberts (Fittings Cartel)*, judgment of 4 July 2013, [2013] 5 CMLR 867, the Court of Justice held that the General Court was correct to annul COMP/38121 *Fittings* (OJ 2007 L283/63) in its entirety, as the conduct in which the undertaking had engaged was not specified as an infringement in the decision, and as such it could not be severed from the remainder of the decision.

13.157 **Consequences of successful appeal by some addressees of the decision.** The General Court's judgments in the 22 appeals brought against COMP/38698 *CISAC Agreements*, decision of 16 July 2008, [2009] 4 CMLR 577, are a stark illustration of the operation of this principle. The General Court annulled the Commission decision finding an anti-competitive concerted practice, as against 21 of the appellants (Cases T-392, 398, 401, 410, 411, 413–422, 425, 428, 432–434, 442/08, judgments of 12 April 2013). However, it dismissed the appeal against this finding brought on different grounds in Case T-451/08 *Föreningen Svenska Tonsättares Internationella Musikbyrå*, judgment of 12 April 2013, [2013] 5 CMLR 577. This appellant had not pleaded that the Commission had insufficient evidence to establish a concerted practice, which was the ground of appeal that succeeded in the 21 other appeals. The General Court held that its attempt to adopt the other appellants' submissions on this ground was inadmissible, and it therefore went on to consider the grounds of appeal that had been advanced. The appeal on these other grounds was dismissed.

Fn 888 See also Cases T-496/07 *Repsol Lubricantes y Especialidades v Commission*; and T-495/07 *PROAS v Commission*, judgments of 16 September 2013, paras 444 et seq, and paras 456 et seq, respectively. The General Court had partially annulled the Commission's decision as against two of the addressees, on the basis that the evidence of the leniency applicants, on which the Commission had relied, was not sufficient to establish their participation in certain aspects of the infringing conduct. In *Repsol* and *PROAS* the General Court refused the Commission's request that it should increase the fines imposed on the leniency applicants on account of the successful appeal by the other two addressees.

The UK Competition Appeal Tribunal has recently granted applications for permission to appeal out of time, following the successful appeal by other addressees against an OFT decision. In *Somerfield Stores and Cooperative Group Food v OFT, and Gallaher v OFT* [2013] CAT 5, para 93, the Tribunal held that parties entering into an early resolution agreement with a NCA have a legitimate expectation that the NCA will be able to defend its decision, even though they can have no such expectation that it will do so successfully. The Tribunal considered that the progress of the appeals in *Imperial Tobacco Group plc & Ors v Office of Fair Trading* [2011] CAT 41, in which the OFT abandoned the theory of harm set out in its defence and skeleton argument part way through the oral hearing, were sufficient to constitute 'exceptional circumstances' that warranted an extension of time to file an appeal. On appeal to the Court of Appeal, not yet decided.

Fn 889 The Court of Justice dismissed the appeal in Case C-286/11P *Commission v Tomkins*, judgment of 22 January 2013, [2013] 4 CMLR 466. It held, disagreeing with Advocate General Mengozzi, that the General Court did not err in law by giving Tomkins the benefit of its subsidiary's appeal. In circumstances where the liability of a parent company is wholly derived from that of its subsidiary, and where both companies have brought actions before the European Courts seeking a reduction in their fines on the same basis (in this case, on the basis of the duration of the infringement), then it is not necessary for the scope of their actions, or the arguments deployed, to be identical in order for the General Court to recalculate the fine imposed on the parent company on account of the outcome of the appeal by the subsidiary.

See also Case C-679/11P *Alliance One International v Commission*, judgment of 26 September 2013, paras 106–107. The Court of Justice dismissed a cross-appeal by the Commission against the General Court's judgment in Case T-41/05 *Dimons* [2011] ECR II-7101, in which the General Court had reduced the fine imposed on the parent company, Dimon, on account of the reduction of the fine imposed on its subsidiary in Case T-38/05 *Agroexpansion* [2011] ECR II-7005.

Costs and other orders.   **13.160**
Fn 906 See also C-452/10P *BNP Paribas v Commission*, judgment of 21 June 2012, [2012] 3 CMLR 723.

(d) Interim relief from the General Court

Generally.   **13.164**
Fn 931 See also Case T-164/12 *Alstom v Commission*, Order of the President of 29 November 2012, [2013] 4 CMLR 415, allowing an intervention by National Grid. The appeal is against a decision by the Commission to transmit information to the High Court of England & Wales, under Article 15(1) of the National Courts Notice (see paragraph 16.041 of the main text for a discussion of Article 15(1) of the National Courts Notice). National Grid is the claimant in the proceedings before the national court, and the request to the Commission under Article 15(1) was made at its application. It was allowed to intervene in the General Court proceedings, and to make representations on the application for interim measures.

14

FINES FOR SUBSTANTIVE INFRINGEMENTS

1. Introduction

(a) Jurisdiction and the Commission's discretion

The jurisdiction to fine.   14.001
Fn 1 In 2012 the Commission imposed fines totalling €1.88 billion (compared with €614m in 2011, and €2.87 billion in 2010).

Legal certainty.   14.004
Fn 17 See also Case C-501/11P *Schindler v Commission (Elevators and Escalators)*, judgment of 18 July 2013, para 58.

Fines and the European Convention on Human Rights. In Case C-501/11P **14.006**
Schindler v Commission (Elevators and Escalators), judgment of 18 July 2013, the Court of Justice followed the approach of the European Court of Human Rights in App 43509/08 *Menarini Diagnostics v Italy*, judgment of 27 September 2011, and rejected an argument that the imposition of fines by the Commission, rather than by a court, was contrary to Article 6 ECHR and Article 47 of the Charter of Fundamental Rights. It held that the power of review by the Court under Article 263 TFEU, together with the unlimited jurisdiction to review the fine under Article 261 TFEU and Article 31 of Regulation 1/2003, is sufficient to comply with the requirements of effective judicial protection.

(b) Intentional or negligent infringement

Generally. It is not necessary to establish separately intentional or negligent **14.009**
conduct on the part of a parent company, where it is held liable for the conduct of its subsidiary as part of the same undertaking: Case C-501/11P *Schindler v Commission (Elevators and Escalators)*, judgment of 18 July 2013, paras 90 and 101 et seq.

Fn 41 The Court of Justice confirmed in Case C-681/11 *Schenker*, judgment of 18 June 2013, [2013] 5 CMLR 831, that Article 5 of Regulation 1/2003 does not require Member States to establish conditions of intention or negligence for the imposition of a fine, but if they do so then those conditions must be at least as stringent as those in Article 23 of Regulation 1/2003: paras 35–36. Disagreeing with Advocate General Kokott's Opinion of 28 February 2013, the Court held that reliance by an undertaking on legal advice or a previous NCA decision that its conduct was not contrary to EU competition law is not sufficient to show that an infringement was not committed intentionally or negligently. To avoid a finding that an infringement was committed intentionally or negligently, an undertaking must show that it could not have been aware of the anti-competitive nature of its conduct. If an undertaking characterised its conduct wrongly in law, then it cannot show that it could not have been aware of the anti-competitive nature of its conduct: para 38.

14.011 **Knowledge of the law is not a prerequisite to intention.**
Fn 54 The Court of Justice dismissed the appeals in Case C-457/10P *AstraZeneca v Commission*, judgment of 6 December 2012, [2013] 4 CMLR 233, paras 74 et seq.

14.014 **Rebutting intention or negligence.** The Court of Justice confirmed in Case C-681/11 *Schenker*, judgment of 18 June 2013, [2013] 5 CMLR 831, that reliance by an undertaking on legal advice or a previous NCA decision that its conduct was not contrary to EU competition law is not sufficient to show that an infringement was not committed intentionally or negligently. To avoid a finding that an infringement was committed intentionally or negligently, an undertaking must show that it could not have been aware of the anti-competitive nature of its conduct. If an undertaking characterised its conduct wrongly in law, then it cannot show that it could not have been aware of the anti-competitive nature of its conduct: para 38.

2. The Basic Amount of the Fine

14.016 **In general.**
Fn 74 See the update to paragraph 14.027, below on the Court of Justice's judgment in Case C-444/11P *Team Relocations v Commission*, judgment of 11 July 2013.

(a) **Value of sales**

(i) *Applicable turnover*

14.019 **Sales in the relevant market.** The Court of Justice has upheld the General Court's approach of including all sales in the relevant market which could have been affected, rather than only the sales shown to have been affected, by the infringing conduct: Case C-444/11P *Team Relocations v Commission*, judgment of 11 July 2013; see in particular paras 77 et seq.

See also Joined Cases T-379&381/10 *Keramag Keramische Werke and Others (Bathroom Fittings) v Commission*, judgment of 16 September 2013, paras 361–362, where the General Court rejected an argument that an undertaking's sales made in the same market, but through a separate distribution channel and with different rebate structures and prices and list prices, should be excluded from the value of sales for fining purposes as the infringement was likely to relate to these sales indirectly, within the meaning of the Fining Guidelines.

Fn 85 The Court of Justice dismissed the appeal in Case C-444/11P *Team Relocations v Commission*, judgment of 11 July 2013; see in particular paras 77 et seq. It also dismissed the appeal in Case C-276/11P *Viega v Commission*, judgment of 13 March 2013.

Direct and indirect sales.　　　　　　　　　　　　　　　　　　　　　　14.020

Fn 86 The case reference in the footnote to the main text should read Cases T-56/09, etc, not yet decided. In respect of the judgment in Case T-204&212/08 *Team Relocations v Commission (International Removal Services)* [2011] ECR II-3569, [2011] 5 CMLR 889, the Court of Justice dismissed the further appeal, on other grounds, in Case C-444/11P *Team Relocations v Commission*, judgment of 11 July 2013.

Captive sales.　　　　　　　　　　　　　　　　　　　　　　　　　　14.021

Fn 88 The appeals against the Commission's decision in COMP/39180 *Aluminium Fluoride*, decision of 25 June 2008, in Case T-404/08 *Fluorsid and Minmet v Commission*, judgment of 18 June 2013, [2013] 5 CMLR 902; and Case T-406/08 *Industries chimiques du fluor v Commission*, judgment of 18 June 2013 (on further appeal, Case C-467/13P, not yet decided) were dismissed.

In Case T-82/08 *Guardian Industries v Commission*, judgment of 27 September 2012, [2012] 5 CMLR 1234, paras 104–106, the General Court upheld the Commission's decision not to take into account €1 billion of captive sales when it calculated the fines of the other addressees of its decision in COMP/39165 *Flat Glass*, decision of 28 November 2007, as the infringement that the Commission found related to sales to independent customers.

Fn 89 See, however, the General Court judgment in Case T-82/08 *Guardian Industries v Commission* (see the update to footnote 88 above).

Sales outside the EEA.　In order to determine the value of sales of undertakings　14.024
within the EEA, to which their shares of sales in the relevant geographic area (wider than the EEA) should be applied, the Commission may consider the sales invoiced in the EEA by the undertaking, rather than the sales delivered by it in the EEA, provided that using sales invoiced in the EEA 'reflects the reality of the market, that is to say for it to be the best criterion for ascertaining the effects of the cartel on competition in the EEA'. That criterion will be met in circumstances where the end use location of the relevant product is outside Europe but some of the main original

equipment manufacturers are based in the EEA: Case T-146/09 *Parker ITR and Parker-Hannifin v Commission (Marine Hoses)*, judgment of 17 May 2013, [2013] 5 CMLR 712, paras 208 et seq (on further appeal, Case C-434/13P *Commission v Parker Hannifin Manufacturing and Parker-Hannifin*, not yet decided). The decision was partially annulled on other grounds: Cases T-146/09, etc, *Parker ITR and Parker-Hannifin v Commission (Marine Hoses)*, judgments of 17 May 2013.

Fn 94 The General Court upheld the Commission's analysis of the geographic scope of the cartel in COMP/39180 *Aluminium Fluoride*, decision of 25 June 2008, in Case T-404/08 *Fluorsid and Minmet v Commission*, judgment of 18 June 2013, [2013] 5 CMLR 902, paras 158 et seq. The other appeal did not contest the Commission's finding on this point: Case T-406/08 *Industries chimiques du fluor v Commission*, judgment of 18 June 2013, on further appeal, Case C-467/13P, not yet decided.

On the Commission's application of paragraph 18 of the Fining Guidelines in COMP/39406 *Marine Hoses*, decision of 28 January 2009, see Case T-146/09, etc, *Parker ITR and Parker-Hannifin v Commission (Marine Hoses)*, judgment of 17 May 2013, [2013] 5 CMLR 712, discussed in the update to paragraph 14.024, above.

(ii) Year of turnover

14.025 **The last full business year.**
Fn 96 Two of the appeals against COMP/398181 *Candle Waxes*, decision of 1 October 2008, on other grounds, were largely dismissed: Cases T-548/08 *Total v Commission*, judgment of 13 September 2013; and T-566/08 *Total Raffinage Marketing*, judgment of 13 September 2013 (fine reduced on grounds of duration). In *Total Raffinage Marketing* the General Court upheld the Commission's use of the last three years of sales, as the last year of the infringement was 2004 which was an exceptional year for the industry as the EU was enlarged, and in particular Hungary (where one of the participants was based) joined the EU: see paras 415 et seq. The other appeals (Cases T-540/08, etc, not yet decided) are still pending.

14.026 **Use of a different year.**
Fn 104 The Commission's decision in COMP/39406 *Marine Hoses*, decision of 28 January 2009, was partially annulled on other grounds in Cases T-146/09, etc, *Parker ITR and Parker-Hannifin v Commission (Marine Hoses)*, judgments of 17 May 2013, [2013] 5 CMLR 712 (on further appeal, Case C-434/13P *Commission v Parker Hannifin Manufacturing and Parker-Hannifin*, not yet decided).

(b) **Percentage of the value of sales to reflect gravity of infringement**

14.027 **The 1998 and 2006 Fining Guidelines compared.** In Cases C-444/11P *Team Relocations v Commission* and C-439/11P *Ziegler v Commission*, judgments of 11 July 2013, the Commission asked the Court of Justice to substitute different grounds for the General Court's judgment in Case T-204&212/08 *Team Relocations v*

Commission (International Removal Services) [2011] ECR II-3569, [2011] 5 CMLR 889, insofar as the General Court held that the 2006 Guidelines impose a more onerous obligation on the Commission to state reasons for its fining decisions than did the 1998 Guidelines. The Court of Justice held that the General Court had erred in stating that the 2006 Guidelines impose a more onerous obligation on the Commission, but as this was not an error that bore upon its assessments of the merits of the appeal it refused to substitute the grounds requested: see paras 94 and 116–117 in *Team Relocations* and paras 108 and 111–112 in *Ziegler.*

Fn 111 The Court of Justice has dismissed the further appeal in Case C-444/11P *Team Relocations v Commission*, judgment of 11 July 2013. On this point, see paras 124–126, in which the Court confirmed that the appellant had 'no right to receive a specific explanation regarding the choice to apply that percentage' given that the percentage chosen was at the lower end of the range. To the same effect, see Case C-439/11P *Zeigler v Commission*, judgment of 11 July 2013, paras 122–125; and Case C-429/11P *Portielje and Gosselinv Commission*, judgment of 11 July 2013, paras 128–130.

In Case C-440/11P *Commission v Portielje and Gosselin*, judgment of 11 July 2013, the Court of Justice upheld the Commission's appeal and has overturned the General Court judgment in Cases T-208 & 209/08 *Gosselin Group v Commission* [2011] ECR II-03639, [2013] 4 CMLR 671.

Fn 112 The Commission's decision in COMP/39406 *Marine Hoses*, decision of 28 January 2009, was upheld in respect of the gravity of the infringement, the seriousness of which was 'indisputable': see for example Case T-146/09 *Parker ITR and Parker-Hannifin v Commission (Marine Hoses)*, judgment of 17 May 2013, [2013] 5 CMLR 712, para 252 (on further appeal, Case C-434/13P *Commission v Parker Hannifin Manufacturing and Parker-Hannifin*, not yet decided). The decision was partially annulled on other grounds: Cases T-146/09, etc, *Parker ITR and Parker-Hannifin v Commission (Marine Hoses)*, judgments of 17 May 2013, [2013] 5 CMLR 712.

Factors influencing gravity of infringement.   **14.028**
Fn 116 The General Court upheld the Commission's decision in COMP/39188 *Bananas*, decision of 15 October 2008, in Case T-587/08 *Fresh Del Monte Produce v Commission*, judgment of 14 March 2013, [2013] 4 CMLR 1091 (appeal on liability dismissed; fine reduced, on other grounds); and Case T-588/08 *Dole Food Company v Commission*, judgment of 14 March 2013. On further appeal, Cases 293&294/13P *Fresh Del Monte Produce v Commission*, not yet decided; and Case 286/13P *Dole Food Company v Commission*, not yet decided.

Fn 117 The General Court partially annulled the Commission's decision in COMP/39092 *Bathroom Fittings*, decision of 23 June 2010, in Case T-380/10 *Wabco Europe v Commission;* Joined Cases T-378&379/10 *Keramag v Commission;* Joined

Cases T-373/10, etc, *Villeroy & Boch Austria v Commission*; Case T-364/10 *Duravit v Commission*; and Case T-412/10 *Roca v Commission*, judgments of 16 September 2013, and it reduced the fine in Case T-408/10 *Roca Sanitaro v Commission*, judgment of 16 September 2013. The remaining appeals, in Cases T-368/10, etc, *Rubinetteria Ciscal v Commission*, judgments of 16 September 2013, were dismissed.

14.029 **Differing percentages for participants.**   The Court of Justice has approved the Commission's and General Court's approach in Cases C-429/11P *Portielje and Gosselin v Commission*, judgment of 11 July 2013, at paras 91 et seq; and case C-444/11P *Team Relocations v Commission*, judgments of 11 July 2013, at paras 101 et seq.

Fn 121 Two of the appeals against COMP/398181 *Candle Waxes*, decision of 1 October 2008, on other grounds, were largely dismissed: Cases T-548/08 *Total v Commission*, judgment of 13 September 2013; and Case T-566/08 *Total Raffinage Marketing*, judgment of 13 September 2013 (fine reduced on grounds of duration). The other appeals (Cases T-540/08, etc, not yet decided) are still pending.

Fn 122 The Court of Justice dismissed the further appeal in Case C-444/11P *Team Relocations v Commission*, judgments of 11 July 2013, paras 104–106. In addition, in Case T-352/09 *Novácke chemické závody v Commission*, judgment of 12 December 2012, [2013] 4 CMLR 734, para 58, the General Court rejected the argument that the Commission was obliged to consider the relative gravity of the undertakings' involvement when determining the gravity of the infringement. It held that this 'has to be examined in the context of the possible application of aggravating or mitigating circumstances'.

14.030 **Actual effect of infringement.**   In Cases C-509/11P *Eni v Commission*, judgment of 8 May 2013, [2013] 5 CMLR 607, paras 96–98; and C-511/11P *Versalis v Commission*, judgment of 13 June 2013, [2013] 5 CMLR 797, paras 82–84, the Court of Justice held that in the case of a horizontal pricing or market-sharing agreement it would be 'superfluous' to look at the effects of the agreement in order to determine the gravity of the infringement. Also, in Case C-457/10P *AstraZeneca v Commission*, judgment of 6 December 2012, para 165, the Court of Justice held that a lack of anti-competitive effects was not to be taken into account in circumstances where highly anti-competitive conduct, that was likely to have significant effects on competition, did not have the effects expected because of the intervention of a third party.

14.031 **Implementation of the infringement.**
Fn 130 Two of the appeals against COMP/398181 *Candle Waxes*, decision of 1 October 2008, were dismissed: Cases T-548/08 *Total v Commission*, judgment of 13 September 2013, paras 210–214; and T-566/08 *Total Raffinage Marketing*, judgment of 13 September 2013, paras 163 et seq (fine reduced on grounds of duration). The other appeals (Cases T-540/08, etc, not yet decided) are still pending.

(c) Duration of the infringement

Different multipliers.   14.033

Fn 136 Two of the appeals against COMP/398181 *Candle Waxes*, decision of 1 October 2008, on other grounds were dismissed: Cases T-548/08 *Total v Commission*, judgment of 13 September 2013 (fine reduced on grounds of equal treatment as to duration, see update to paragraph 14.035, below); and T-566/08 *Total Raffinage Marketing*, judgment of 13 September 2013. The other appeals (Cases T-540/08, etc, not yet decided) are still pending.

Legal considerations affecting duration.   The Court of Justice in Case C-70/12P   14.035
Quinn Barlo v Commission ('*Methacrylates*'), judgment of 30 May 2013, [2013] 5 CMLR 637, para 40, held that as Article 101 applies to the economic consequences of agreements or any comparable form of concertation or coordination, rather than their legal form, an infringement may be found throughout the period in which unlawful prices were applied by an undertaking, even though the unlawful contacts formally have come to an end.

In Case T-566/08 *Total Raffinage Marketing v Commission (Candle Waxes)*, judgment of 13 September 2013, paras 549 et seq, the General Court held that the Commission must comply with the principle of equal treatment in determining the multiplier, and that a practice of rounding part years to the nearest whole number can breach the principle of equal treatment by treating the different situations of undertakings in the same way. For example, in that case Total had participated for seven months and twenty eight days, ExxonMobile for eleven months and twenty days, and both were held responsible for a whole year of participation.

Fn 138 The further appeal, on other grounds, in Case C-499/11P *Dow Chemical v Commission (Butadiene rubber)*, judgment of 18 July 2013, was dismissed.

Fn 140 See also Case T-147&148/09 *Trelleborg v Commission (Marine Hoses)*, judgment of 17 May 2013, [2013] 5 CMLR 754, considering the distinction between single and continuous, and single repeated, infringements. The Commission cannot rely on an undertaking's failure to distance itself publicly from an infringement as a basis for establishing that undertaking's ongoing participation in it, if the normal functioning of the cartel has been interrupted, there is no evidence of its actual participation in ongoing contacts, and nor is there evidence that it was aware of contacts between other undertakings with a view to re-starting the cartel: paras 68–69. In that case, however, the infringement was to be treated as a single repeated infringement as Trelleborg had rejoined the cartel and accepted that the cartel it rejoined was the same as that which it had left (paras 72 et seq). The duration of the infringement was reduced accordingly.

Fn 142 The Court of Justice dismissed the further appeal in Case C-70/12P *Quinn Barlo v Commission* ('*Methacrylates*'), judgment of 30 May 2013, [2013] 5 CMLR 637.

(d) Additional amount for cartel participants

14.036 Hardcore cartels.
Fn 146 The Court of Justice has dismissed the further appeal in Case C-444/11P *Team Relocations v Commission*, judgment of 11 July 2013. On this point, see paras 124–126 in which the Court confirmed that the appellant had 'no right to receive a specific explanation regarding the choice to apply that percentage' given that the percentage chosen was at the lower end of the range. To the same effect, see Case C-439/11P *Zeigler v Commission*, judgment of 11 July 2013, paras 122–125; and Case C-429/11P *Portielje and Gosselinv Commission*, judgment of 11 July 2013, paras 128–130.

14.037 The additional amount or 'entry fee'.
Fn 147 The Court of Justice has approved the approach of the General Court in Case C-444/11P *Team Relocations v Commission*, judgment of 11 July 2013, paras 139–141.

3. Aggravating and Mitigating Circumstances

(a) Adjustment of the basic amount

14.038 In general.
Fn 152 The Court of Justice dismissed the appeal in C-429/11P *Portielje and Gosselin v Commission*, judgment of 11 July 2013, paras 91 et seq. See also the Court of Justice's judgment in Case C-440/11P *Commission v Portielje and Gosselin*, judgment of 11 July 2013, paras 110 et seq.

(b) Aggravating circumstances

(i) Repeat infringements

14.042 The previous infringer. The Court of Justice in Cases C-508/11P *Eni v Commission*, judgment of 8 May 2013, [2013] 5 CMLR 607, paras 129–133; and C-511/11P *Versalis v Commission*, judgment of 13 June 2013, [2013] 5 CMLR 797, paras 142–146, confirms that the Commission must provide an adequate explanation of the capacity in which, and the extent to which, the allegedly recidivist undertaking is considered to have participated in a previous infringement. The Court of Justice agreed with the General Court that the Commission had failed to provide sufficient explanation in its decision in COMP/38638 *Butadiene Rubber*, decision of 29 November 2006, of why Eni and Versalis, which were not addressees of the decisions in *Polypropylene*, OJ 1986 L230/1; or *PVC II*, OJ 1994 L239/14, were considered to have been involved in those infringements, and in what capacity and to what extent. It upheld the General Court's judgments annulling the uplift for recidivism. The Commission issued a second statement of objections to Eni and Versalis on 1 March 2013, providing the explanation held by the General

Court to have been absent from the decision and reaching the provisional conclusion that an uplift should be imposed for recidivism: COMP/40032 *BR/ESBR Recidivism*, Press Release IP/13/179 (1 March 2013).

(iii) Instigators, 'ring leaders' and retaliatory measures

Generally.   **14.047**
Fn 180 The uplift of 50 per cent of Shell's fine as both an instigator and a leader in COMP/F/38456 *Bitumen (Netherlands)*, OJ 2007 L196/40, was overturned in Case T-343/06 *Shell Petroleum v Commission*, judgment of 27 September 2012, [2012] 5 CMLR 1064. On further appeal, Case C-585/12P, not yet decided.

(c) **Mitigating circumstances**

In general. The General Court upheld the Commission's decision in **14.051**
COMP/39188 *Bananas*, decision of 15 October 2008, in Case T-587/08 *Fresh Del Monte Produce v Commission*, judgment of 14 March 2013, [2013] 4 CMLR 1091 (appeal on liability dismissed; fine reduced, on other grounds); and Case T-588/08 *Dole Food Company v Commission*, judgment of 14 March 2013. On further appeal, Cases 293&294/13P *Fresh Del Monte Produce v Commission*, not yet decided; and Case 286/13P *Dole Food Company v Commission*, not yet decided.

(i) Factors arising from matters following the Commission's investigation

Prompt termination of an infringement.   **14.052**
Fn 206 The Court of Justice dismissed the further appeals, on other grounds, in Case C-444/11P *Zeigler v Commission*, judgment of 11 July 2013.

Introduction of competition compliance programme. The Court of Justice in **14.053**
Case C-501/11P *Schindler v Commission (Elevators and Escalators)*, judgment of 18 July 2013, para 144, dismissed an appeal against the General Court's approach to the relevance of competition compliance programmes, holding that the appellant's compliance programme 'evidently had no positive effect and, on the contrary, made it more difficult to uncover the infringements at issue'.

Fn 210 The Court of Justice dismissed the further appeal in Case C-70/12P *Quinn Barlo v Commission ('Methacrylates')*, judgment of 30 May 2013, [2013] 5 CMLR 637.

'Effective immunity' in respect of matters proved due to cooperation.   **14.055**
Fn 222 See also Case T-380/10 *Wabco Europe v Commission (Bathroom Fittings)*, judgment of 16 September 2013, paras 133 et seq. The Commission had granted partial immunity under para 23(b) of the 2002 Leniency Notice in respect of the infringements in which the undertaking had been involved in Belgium and France, and the General Court held that once it had done so the Commission was required to remove the value of the undertaking's sales in those geographic areas from its calculation of the basic amount of the fine.

14.056 **Non-contestation or admission of facts in the statement of objections.**
Fn 226 The Court of Justice dismissed the further appeal, on other grounds, in Case C-510/11P *Kone v Commission ('Elevators and Escalators')*, judgment of 24 October 2013.

14.061 **Reduction of fine for delay.**
Fn 241 The General Court's judgment in Case T-372/10 *Bolloré v Commission ('Carbonless Paper')*, judgment of 27 June 2012, is on further appeal: Case C-414/12P, not yet decided.

Fn 245 The Court of Justice dismissed the further appeals against the decision in COMP/37766 *Netherlands Beer Market*, decision of 18 April 2007, in Case C-452/11P *Heineken Nederland and Heineken v Commission*, judgment of 19 December 2012; and C-445/11P *Bavaria v Commission*, judgment of 19 December 2012.

(ii) Factors relating to the undertaking's culpability for the infringement

14.063 **'Substantially limited' involvement.** In COMP/31988 *Bananas*, decision of 15 October 2008, the Commission reduced the fine imposed on Weichert by 10 per cent for having only participated in one aspect of the cartel (para 476), which the General Court further reduced to 20 per cent in order to reflect the relative gravity of its participation: see Case T-587/08 *Fresh Del Monte Produce v Commission*, judgment of 14 March 2013, [2013] 4 CMLR 1091, paras 815–817. On further appeal, Cases C-293 & 294/13P, not yet decided.

14.065 **Pressure from others.**
Fn 266 The Court of Justice dismissed the further appeals, on other grounds, in Cases C-439/11P *Zeigler v Commission;* and C-444/11P *Team Relocations v Commission*, judgments of 11 July 2013.

14.066 **Encouragement or authorisation by a public authority.**
Fn 267 The Court of Justice dismissed the further appeal in C-444/11P *Team Relocations v Commission*, judgment of 11 July 2013, paras 148–150.

Fn 273 The Court of Justice dismissed the further appeal in C-444/11P *Team Relocations v Commission*, judgment of 11 July 2013, paras 148–150.

14.069 **Novelty of infringement.**
Fn 289 The Court of Justice upheld the appeal in Case C-652/11P *Mindo v Commission*, judgment of 13 April 2013, [2013] 4 CMLR 1381, and has referred the case back to the General Court (remitted case not yet decided). The further appeal in Case C-654/11P *Transcatab* was dismissed by Order of 13 December 2012.

Fn 291 The Court of Justice dismissed the appeals in Case C-457/10P *AstraZeneca v Commission*, judgment of 6 December 2012, [2013] 4 CMLR 233.

4. Deterrence, Disgorgement of Benefit and Inability to Pay

(a) Deterrence

In general.   In T-352/09 *Nováćke chemické závody v Commission*, judgment of   **14.071**
12 December 2012, [2013] 4 CMLR 734, paras 62–64, the General Court emphasised that while the Commission has a power to increase a fine for deterrence, it has
no obligation to do so.

Deterrence based on total turnover of the undertaking.   The Court of Justice   **14.072**
dismissed an argument that the multiplier applied for deterrence must be in
strict accordance with the ratio of the undertakings' turnovers compared to
each other, as the fines that would be imposed on the largest undertakings
in the cartel might in those circumstances be disproportionate to the gravity
of the infringement: Case C-499/11P *Dow Chemical v Commission (Butadiene
rubber)*, judgment of 18 July 2013, paras 88–92. It also confirmed that the
multiplier applied to the fine imposed on a parent company for deterrence is not
affected by the fact that it is only attributed with liability for the conduct of its
subsidiary for part of the period of the infringement. It is determined according
to the undertaking's size and resources at the time of the Commission's decision: Case C-679/11P *Alliance One International v Commission*, judgments of
26 September, para 75.

Fn 314 The case references in the footnote to the main text should read Cases
T-144/07, etc, *ThyssenKrupp* and on further appeal, Cases C-504/11P, etc, not yet
decided.

(c) Inability to pay

The Fining Guidelines.   The Court of Justice confirmed that the Commission   **14.075**
has no obligation to take an undertaking's financial hardship into account if it does
not receive a request from it, under para 35 of the Fining Guidelines, before it issues
the infringement decision: Case C-444/11P *Team Relocations v Commission*, judgment of 11 July 2013, paras 184 et seq. The Court of Justice rejected a complaint
that the Commission breaches the principle of equal treatment in circumstances
where it refuses to reduce the fine imposed on an undertaking under para 35 of the
Fining Guidelines because that undertaking did not submit a request for such a
reduction prior to the decision being issued. An undertaking that fails to submit a
timely request, as required by para 35 of the Fining Guidelines, is not in a comparable situation with an undertaking that did submit such a request.

The Court of Justice has also confirmed that inability to pay may be taken into
account under para 37 of the Fining Guidelines, as well as under para 35. In its

decision in COMP/38543 *International Removals Services*, decision of 11 March 2008, the Commission had reduced the fine imposed on Interdean under para 37 rather than para 35. The Court of Justice in Case C-439/11P *Ziegler v Commission*, judgment of 11 July 2013, held that an inability or reduced ability to pay under para 35 cannot be sufficient alone to give rise to a reduction in the fine under para 37, but that an inability to pay may be relevant to determining whether to make a reduction under para 37: see paras 171–174.

14.076 **Approach of the EU Courts.**

Fn 328 The Court of Justice confirmed that the Commission has no obligation to take financial hardship into account if it does not receive a request from the undertaking, under para 35 of the Fining Guidelines, before it issues the infringement decision: Case C-444/11P *Team Relocations v Commission*, judgment of 11 July 2013, paras 184 et seq, discussed in the update to paragraph 14.075, above.

Fn 331 The Court of Justice dismissed the further appeal, on other grounds, in C-444/11P *Team Relocations v Commission*, judgment of 11 July 2013. In Case T-352/09 *Novácke chemické závody v Commission*, judgment of 12 December 2012, [2013] 4 CMLR 734, paras 198–199, the General Court held that merely showing that an undertaking would be forced into bankruptcy by the imposition of a fine is not sufficient to meet this condition. The undertaking must also address the consequences of bankruptcy on its ongoing operations, and the possibility of its assets being transferred to another company.

14.077 **The Commission's approach.** The General Court has dismissed three appeals against the Commission's decision in COMP/39396 *Calcium carbide and magnesium based reagents*, decision of 22 July 2009, discussed in the main text. In Case T-410/09 *Almamet v Commission*, judgment of 12 December 2012, [2013] 4 CMLR 788, paras 265–269 the General Court rejected a complaint from the undertaking that had received a reduction under para 35 of the Fining Guidelines that the fine was nonetheless disproportionate. In Case T-392/09 *1. garantovaná v Commission*, judgment of 12 December 2012, paras 144 et seq, the General Court upheld the Commission's decision not to reduce the fine on account of inability to pay where the company had decided to terminate its activities on the relevant market and realise its assets (on further appeal, Case C-90/13P, not yet decided); and in Case T-352/09 *Novácke chemické závody v Commission*, judgment of 12 December 2012, [2013] 4 CMLR 734 the General Court rejected a complaint by one of the other addressees, which had subsequently been declared bankrupt, that it too should have received a reduction in its fine on this basis. At the time of writing, appeals are still pending in Cases T-384/09, 391/09, 395/09, 399/09, and 406/09, not yet decided.

In respect of the Commission's decision in COMP/38543 *International Removals Services*, decision of 11 March 2008, reducing the fine imposed on Interdean under para 37 of the Fining Guidelines, see the Court of Justice in Case C-439/11P

Ziegler v Commission, judgment of 11 July 2013, discussed in the update to paragraph 14.075, above.

(d) Cap on fines

Maximum fine and consequential adjustment.   **14.078**
Fn 338 In contrast with the position under Article 23(2) of Regulation 1/2003, the Bundesgerichtshof (Federal Court of Justice) has held that the 10 per cent limit in German competition law must be interpreted as the upper range of the 'frame' within which a judge can set a sanction for breach of competition law, in order to comply with the principle *nulla poena sin lege*. It cannot be interpreted as a cap to cut the fine imposed at a maximum level: ECN Brief 02/2013, p33.

Year of turnover for application of cap.   **14.079**
Fn 344 The Commission's approach in COMP/39396 *Calcium carbide and magnesium based reagents*, decision of 22 July 2009, was upheld by the General Court in Case T-392/09 *1. garantovaná v Commission*, judgment of 12 December 2012. On further appeal, Case C-90/13P, not yet decided.

5. Ancillary Matters of Law and Practice

(a) Determination of fines for different infringing parties

In general.   **14.080**
Fn 346 In COMP/31988 *Bananas*, decision of 15 October 2008, the Commission reduced the fine imposed on Weichert by 10 per cent for having only participated in one aspect of the cartel (para 476), which the General Court further reduced to 20 per cent, in order properly to reflect the relative gravity of its participation in the cartel: see Case T-587/08 *Fresh Del Monte Produce v Commission*, judgment of 14 March 2013, [2013] 4 CMLR 1091, paras 815–817. On further appeal, Cases C-293 & 294/13P, not yet decided.

Principle of equal treatment.   The principle of equal treatment must also be rec- **14.081**
onciled with the principle of legality. See, for example, Joined Cases T-147&148/09 *Trelleborg v Commission*, judgment of 17 May 2013, [2013] 5 CMLR 754, para 104, in which the General Court dismissed a complaint that the Commission had breached the principle of equal treatment in the manner in which it had applied the limitation period to different undertakings. The General Court held that even if the Commission had erred as respects its conclusion that proceedings against another undertaking were time-barred, it was not open to Trelleborg to rely on that illegality as a basis for claiming that proceedings against it should also have been treated as time-barred. See also Joined Cases T-379&381/10 *Keramag Keramische Werke and Others (Bathroom Fittings) v Commission*, judgment of

16 September 2013, paras 345–347, in which the General Court rejected a complaint that the Commission had breached the principle of equal treatment by not investigating other undertakings which the appellant alleged were also involved in the infringement.

Fn 353 See also Case C-444/11P *Team Relocations v Commission*, judgment of 11 July 2013, paras 66 and 150, in which the Court of Justice dismissed an argument that the General Court was required to explain the reasons for its judgment in the light of a previous judgment it had given in a separate appeal against the same Commission decision.

Fn 358 See also Case C-499/11P *Dow Chemical v Commission (Butadiene rubber)*, judgment of 18 July 2013, paras 88–92, in which the Court of Justice dismissed an argument that the multiplier applied for deterrence must be in strict accordance with the ratio of the undertakings' turnovers compared to each other, as the fines that would be imposed on the largest undertakings in the cartel might in those circumstances be disproportionate to the gravity of the infringement; and Case T-154/09 *Manuli Rubber Industries v Commission*, judgment of May 2013, para 264, in which the General Court observed that there is no requirement for the fines imposed on small or medium-sized undertakings not to be higher, as a percentage of turnover, than the amount of the fines imposed on larger undertakings.

14.082 **Relevance of previous fining decisions.**   On the explanation required where the Commission changes its approach, the Court of Justice's judgment in Case C-521/09P *Elf Aquitaine v Commission* [2011] ECR II-8947, paras 152–170, indicates that a detailed explanation will also be required where the Commission takes an approach to fining a particular undertaking that is different to the approach it has taken in a previous decision addressed to that same undertaking. The Court of Justice held that the Commission had not adequately explained why it had attributed the conduct of a subsidiary company, Atofina, to the parent company Elf Aquitaine in COMP/37773 *MCAA*, decision of 19 January 2005, but not in COMP/37857 *Organic Peroxides*, decision of 10 December 2003.

See also Case C-444/11P *Team Relocations v Commission*, judgment of 11 July 2013, paras 66 and 150, in which the Court of Justice dismissed an argument that the General Court was required to explain the reasons for its judgment in the light of a previous judgment it had given in a separate appeal against the same Commission decision.

(b) **Fines on parent and successor companies**

14.086 **Effect of joint and several liability.**
Fn 383 The Court of Justice dismissed the appeal in Case C-286/11P *Commission v Tomkins*, judgment of 22 January 2013, [2013] 4 CMLR 466. Disagreeing with Advocate General Mengozzi, the Court held that in circumstances where the

liability of a parent company is wholly derived from that of its subsidiary, and where both companies have brought actions before the European Courts seeking a reduction in their fines on the same basis (in this case, on the basis of the duration of the infringement), then it is not necessary for the scope of their actions, or the arguments deployed, to be identical in order for the General Court to recalculate the fine imposed on the parent company on account of the outcome of the appeal by the subsidiary.

See also Case C-679/11P *Alliance One International v Commission*, judgment of 26 September 2013, paras 106–107, in which the Court of Justice dismissed a cross-appeal by the Commission against the General Court's judgment in Case T-41/05 *Dimons* [2011] ECR II-7101, in which the General Court had reduced the fine imposed on the parent company, Dimon, on account of the reduction of the fine imposed on its subsidiary in Case T-38/05 *Agroexpansion* [2011] ECR II-7005.

(i) Parents and subsidiaries

Decisive influence.   **14.089**
Fn 398 The Court of Justice in Case C-440/11P *Commission v Portielje and Gosselin*, judgment of 11 July 2013, upheld the Commission's appeal and has overturned the General Court judgment in Cases T-208&209/08 *Gosselin Group v Commission* [2011] ECR II-03639, [2013] 4 CMLR 671. The Court confirmed that if a company holds all the capital, or almost all the capital, in a subsidiary company that is sufficient basis for the application of the presumption of decisive influence (para 41) and it is not relevant to consider whether the parent company is also itself engaged in an economic activity and individually constitutes an undertaking, if it is part of the same undertaking as the subsidiary (paras 42–46). The Court also overturned the General Court's conclusion that Portielje had rebutted the presumption of decisive influence (paras 65–73). The appeal in Case C-429/11P *Portielje and Gosselin v Commission*, judgment of 11 July 2013, was dismissed.

Presumption when a parent owns all of the shares in a subsidiary.   The General   **14.090**
Court has held in Case C-343/06 *Shell Petroleum v Commission*, judgment of 27 September 2012, [2012] 5 CMLR 1064, paras 45–51, that the Commission is entitled to apply a presumption of decisive influence where two legal entities within the same undertaking together own all of the shares in a subsidiary, and are in a situation that is analogous to a single legal entity owning all those shares. The infringing subsidiary, Shell Nederland Verkoopmaatschappij ('SNV') was owned, indirectly, by Shell Transport and Trading ('STT'), and Koninklijke Nederlandsche Petroleum Maatschappij ('KNPM'), who held 40 per cent and 60 per cent shares respectively in the holding company that owned SNV. The General Court held that in the light of the structure of the Shell group the situation was analogous to SNV being held by a single parent company, and the Commission was entitled to rely on a presumption that the two companies STT and KNPM exercised a decisive influence over SNV's conduct. On further appeal, Case C-585/12P, not yet decided.

Fn 406 The Court of Justice dismissed the appeals in Joined Cases C-628/10P & 14/11P *Alliance One v Commission*, judgment of 19 July 2012, [2012] 5 CMLR 738. In particular, see paras 50 et seq.

The General Court dismissed the appeal against COMP/39181 *Candle Waxes*, decision of 1 October 2008, and the attribution of liability to Total, in the absence of specific indica to corroborate the presumption that it did exercise decisive influence: Case T-548/08 *Total v Commission*, judgment of 13 September 2013, paras 34–37; and Case T-566/08 *Total Raffinage Marketing*, judgment of 13 September 2013, paras 494 et seq (fine reduced on grounds of duration). The other appeals (Cases T-540/08, etc, not yet decided) are still pending.

14.091 **Presumption when a parent owns virtually all of the shares in a subsidiary.** The Court of Justice in Case C-508/11P *Eni v Commission*, judgment of 8 May 2013, [2013] 5 CMLR 607, para 47, confirmed that the presumption of decisive influence arises where a parent company holds 'all or almost all' of the shares in a subsidiary.

Fn 408 The Court of Justice upheld the appeal, on other grounds, in Case 521/09P *Elf Aquitaine v Commission*, judgment of 29 September 2011.

Fn 410 The Court of Justice dismissed the further appeal in Case C-289/11P *Legris Industries v Commission* (*Copper Fittings*), judgment of 3 May 2012.

14.092 **The presumption of decisive influence is rebuttable.**
Fn 411 The further appeal in Case C-494/11P *General Technic-Otis v Commission* was dismissed by Order of 15 June 2012.

14.093 **Evidence rebutting the presumption of decisive influence.** A further factor that has been held to be insufficient to rebut the presumption of decisive influence is the systematic refusal of an individual employee/consultant of the subsidiary to comply with the parent company's instructions and commercial policy, and his ignoring of the parent company's code of ethics: Case T-146/09 *Parker ITR and Parker-Hannifin v Commission* (*Marine Hoses*), judgment of 17 May 2013, [2013] 5 CMLR 712, paras 185 et seq (on further appeal, Case C-434/13P *Commission v Parker Hannifin Manufacturing and Parker-Hannifin*, not yet decided).

In Case C-521/09P *Elf Aquitaine v Commission* [2011] ECR I-8497, the Court of Justice held that although the Commission is not obliged to make the same assessment of whether to impose liability on a parent company as in its previous decisions, it is required to explain its reasons if it makes a different assessment in respect of the same parent company in a subsequent case. The Court of Justice considered that the Commission had not adequately explained why it had attributed the conduct of a subsidiary company, Atofina, to the parent company Elf Aquitaine in COMP/37773 *MCAA*, decision of 19 January 2005, but not in COMP/37857 *Organic Peroxides*, decision of 10 December 2003.

In respect of the appeals against the Commission's decision in COMP/38543 *International Removals Services*, decision of 11 March 2008, referred to in the main text, the Court of Justice in Case C-440/11P *Commission v Portielje and Gosselin*, judgment of 11 July 2013, upheld the Commission's appeal and has overturned the General Court judgment in Cases T-208&209/08 *Gosselin Group v Commission* [2011] ECR II-03639, [2013] 4 CMLR 671. In respect of the points noted in footnote 429 of the main text, the Court confirmed that the mere fact that the holding entity did not adopt any management decisions in a manner consistent with the formal requirements of national company law is not sufficient to rebut the presumption of decisive influence: see paras 66 and 83. The appeal in Case C-429/11P *Portielje and Gosselin v Commission*, judgment of 11 July 2013, was dismissed.

Fn 416 The Court of Justice dismissed the appeals in Joined Cases C-628/10P & 14/11P *Alliance One v Commission*, judgment of 19 July 2012, [2012] 5 CMLR 738. The further appeal in Case C-495/11P *Total and Elf Aquitaine v Commission (Hydrogen Peroxide and Perborate)* was dismissed by Order of 13 September 2012.

Fn 418 The Court of Justice dismissed the further appeal in Case C-289/11P *Legris Industries v Commission (Copper Fittings)*, judgment of 3 May 2012, para 55, as inadmissible.

Fn 420 The Court of Justice dismissed the appeal, and the Commission's cross-appeal, in Case C-508/11P *Eni v Commission*, judgment of 8 May 2013, paras 64–69.

Fn 422 See also Case T-146/09 *Parker ITR and Parker-Hannifin v Commission (Marine Hoses)*, judgment of 17 May 2013, [2013] 5 CMLR 712, para 181 (on further appeal, Case C-434/13P *Commission v Parker Hannifin Manufacturing and Parker-Hannifin*, not yet decided).

Fn 427 See also the General Court judgment in Case T-392/09 *1. garantovaná v Commission*, judgment of 12 December 2012, para 56. On further appeal, Case 90/13P, not yet decided.

Fn 428 The Court of Justice dismissed the further appeal in Case C-499/11P *Dow Chemical v Commission (Butadiene rubber)*, judgment of 18 July 2013. See also the Court of Justice's judgments in Case C-521/09P *Elf Aquitaine v Commission* [2011] ECR II-8947 (discussed in the update to paragraph 14.093, above).

Decisive influence established on the facts. The General Court upheld the **14.095** Commission's decision in COMP/39188 *Bananas*, decision of 15 October 2008, in Case T-587/08 *Fresh Del Monte Produce v Commission*, judgment of 14 March 2013, [2013] 4 CMLR 1091 (appeal on liability dismissed; fine reduced, on other grounds); and Case T-588/08 *Dole Food Company v Commission*, judgment of 14 March 2013. On further appeal, Cases 293&294/13P *Fresh Del Monte Produce v Commission*, not yet decided; and Case 286/13P *Dole Food Company v Commission*, not yet decided.

14.096 **Decisive influence over the conduct of a joint venture.** The Court of Justice has confirmed the Commission's approach to attributing responsibility to parent companies for the conduct of a joint venture, in COMP/38629 *Chloroprene Rubber,* decision of 5 December 2007. In Cases C-179/12P *Dow Chemical Company v Commission;* and C-172/12P *El du Pont de Nemours v Commission*, judgments of 26 September 2013, the Court held that, provided the factual evidence demonstrates the actual exercise of decisive influence, there is no error of law in holding two parent companies and the joint venture in which they each have a 50 per cent shareholding to be a single undertaking for the purposes (and only for the purposes) of establishing liability for participation in an infringement of competition law: see in particular *Dow*, para 58 and *du Pont*, para 47.

Fn 440 On the compatibility of the Commission's approach with the Merger Regulation, see in particular *Dow*, paras 58 and 64–66, and *du Pont*, paras 47 and 51–53.

14.097 **Equal treatment of parent companies.** The principle of equal treatment of parent companies does not require that where a subsidiary is sold the original and new parent companies must both be attributed with responsibility for the subsidiary's conduct: Case C-444/11P *Team Relocations v Commission*, judgment of 11 July 2013, paras 160 et seq.

Fn 441 The Court of Justice dismissed the appeals in Joined Cases C-628/10P & 14/11P *Alliance One v Commission*, judgment of 19 July 2012, [2012] 5 CMLR 738. Agreeing with Advocate General Kokott's Opinion of 12 January 2012, the Court held at paras 53 et seq that there would be a breach of the principle of equal treatment if the Commission relied on evidence of actual exercise of decisive influence in order to attribute responsibility to some parent companies, but sought to rely solely on the presumption of decisive influence as a basis for attribution in respect of others.

Fn 442 The Court of Justice dismissed the appeals in Joined Cases C-628/10P & 14/11P *Alliance One v Commission*, judgment of 19 July 2012, [2012] 5 CMLR 738. Agreeing with Advocate General Kokott's Opinion of 12 January 2012, the Court held at paras 53 et seq that there would be a breach of the principle of equal treatment if the Commission relied on evidence of actual exercise of decisive influence in order to attribute responsibility to some parent companies, but sought to rely solely on the presumption of decisive influence as a basis for attribution in respect of others.

(ii) Successor undertakings

14.101 **Subsidiary is sold by one parent to another and subsidiary continues as a legal entity.** The Court of Justice held in Case C-444/11P *Team Relocations v Commission*, judgment of 11 July 2013, paras 160 et seq, that the Commission has a discretion whether to attribute responsibility to a parent company, and the fact that it attributes responsibility to a company which was the parent of the infringing subsidiary during one period does not require it also to attribute responsibility to another company which was the parent of the infringing subsidiary during a different period.

Fn 451 See also Case T-146/09 *Parker ITR and Parker-Hannifin v Commission (Marine Hoses)*, judgment of 17 May 2013, [2013] 5 CMLR 712, paras 83 et seq (on further appeal, Case C-434/13P *Commission v Parker Hannifin Manufacturing and Parker-Hannifin*, not yet decided).

Responsibility where original and new parents in same undertaking. See also **14.103**
Case C-511/11P *Versalis v Commission*, judgment of 13 June 2013, [2013] 5 CMLR 797, paras 52–58. The strategic chemical business activities of EniChem, which included the activities in respect of which the Commission found an infringement in COMP/38638 *Butadiene Rubber*, decision of 29 November 2006, had been transferred to Versalis, a second subsidiary of the parent company Eni. The proceedings against EniChem were closed, and the Commission decision was addressed to Eni and Versalis. The Court of Justice upheld the attribution of EniChem's conduct to Versalis as both entities were wholly owned subsidiaries of Eni, and part of the same undertaking.

6. The Leniency Notice

(a) The grant of immunity from fines

The 2006 Leniency Notice. **14.109**
Fn 499 The Court of Justice dismissed the further appeal, on other grounds, in Case C-501/11P *Schindler v Commission (Elevators and Escalators)*, judgment of 18 July 2013.

Paragraph 8(b) immunity. **14.112**
Fn 501 The General Court's judgment in Case T-151/07 *Kone Oyj*, judgment of 13 July 2011, [2011] 5 CMLR 1065, was upheld on further appeal: Case C-510/11P *Kone v Commission*, judgment of 24 October 2013. On the standard of review to be applied to the Commission's consideration of the extent of an undertaking's cooperation, see the update to paragraph 14.128, below.

Fn 504 The further appeal in Case C-654/11P *Transcatab* was dismissed by Order of 13 December 2012.

(b) Procedure for applications and securing a marker

Procedure for applications for immunity. The General Court held in Case **14.114**
T-404/08 *Fluorsid and Minmet v Commission*, judgment of 18 June 2013, [2013] 5 CMLR 902, paras 135–136, that if the Commission does not intend to grant

immunity it has no obligation to notify the applicant undertaking at the statement of objections stage.

(c) Partial immunity and reductions

14.120 **Percentage reductions.**
Fn 529 The Court of Justice dismissed the further appeal in Case C-70/12P *Quinn Barlo v Commission* ('*Methacrylates*'), judgment of 30 May 2013, [2013] 5 CMLR 637.

14.121 **Evidence adding significant added value.**
Fn 531 For a further example of the General Court disagreeing with the Commission's exercise of its discretion in determining the reduction in an undertaking's fine, see T-154/09 *Manuli Rubber Industries v Commission*, judgment of May 2013, paras 318 et seq.

Fn 534 The further appeal in Case C-494/11P *Otis v Commission (Elevators and Escalators)* was dismissed by Order of 15 June 2012.

14.122 **Effective immunity.** The General Court dismissed an argument, in Case T-370/06 *Kuwait Petroleum v Commission*, judgment of 27 September 2012, [2012] 5 CMLR 1209, that effective immunity under para 23(b) of the 2002 Leniency Notice should be available not only where the undertaking provides evidence of facts previously unknown to the Commission, but also where the undertaking provides evidence that enables the Commission to prove an infringement that it otherwise would not have had sufficient evidence to prove. The General Court held, at para 33, that the Commission's power under para 23(b) of the 2002 Leniency Notice must be interpreted restrictively. Where an undertaking provides evidence that corroborates facts already known, the Commission is entitled to treat that as cooperation warranting a percentage reduction. On further appeal in Case C-581/12P, not yet decided.

See also Case T-380/10 *Wabco Europe v Commission (Bathroom Fittings)*, judgment of 16 September 2013, paras 133 et seq. The Commission had granted partial immunity under para 23(b) of the 2002 Leniency Notice in respect of the infringements in which the undertaking had been involved in Belgium and France, and the General Court held that once it had done so the Commission was required to remove the value of the undertaking's sales in those geographic areas from its calculation of the basic amount of the fine.

(d) Interaction with national systems

14.125 **ECN Model Leniency Programme.** A revised Model Leniency Programme was issued in November 2012. The main changes are that all undertakings applying to the Commission for leniency in cases concerning more than three Member States will be able to submit a summary application to national competition authorities, where previously only the first applicant, ie the immunity applicant, was entitled to use summary applications under the model leniency programme; and the ECN has agreed on a standard template for summary applications, which can be used in all Member States. The revised Model Programme is available on the DG Comp website.

Protection of corporate statements from disclosure.   See the updates to para-   **14.126** graphs 16.040 et seq, below, regarding the Commission's legislative proposals on access to corporate statements in actions for damages in Member State courts.

(e) Review by the EU Courts of the application of the Leniency Notice

In general.   **14.127**
Fn 551   See also Case T-587/08 *Fresh Del Monte Produce*, judgment of 14 March 2013, [2013] 4 CMLR 1091, paras 885–886, in which the General Court reduced the fine imposed on Weichert because the information it provided had enabled the Commission to establish the existence of the infringement with less difficulty, but refused to reduce it any further than by 10 per cent because the undertaking had nonetheless continued to deny the infringement throughout the administrative procedure. On further appeal in Cases C-293 & 294/13P, not yet decided.

Review of the Commission's discretion.   The case law referred to in the main   **14.128** text should now be read in the light of the Court of Justice's judgment in Case C-510/11P *Kone v Commission*, judgment of 24 October 2013. The appellant complained that by considering only whether the Commission had 'manifestly [gone] beyond the bounds of [its] margin' of discretion in assessing the cooperation of an undertaking under the Leniency Notice the General Court had failed to comply with Article 47 of the Charter on Fundamental Rights, and Article 6 ECHR. The Court of Justice accepted that the manifest error test does not meet the requirements of Article 47 Charter/Article 6 ECHR: see para 44. The Court cannot use the Commission's margin of discretion as a basis for dispensing with the conduct of an in-depth review of the law and of the facts. The Court went on to hold that, notwithstanding the General Court appeared to apply an incorrect legal test, on the facts of the case the General Court had conducted an in-depth review of the fine in substance: see paragraph 13.124, and the updates thereto, above.

Fn 554   See also Case T-347/06 *Nynäs v Commission*, judgment of 27 September 2012, [2012] 5 CMLR 1139, para 62.

15

THE ENFORCEMENT OF THE COMPETITION RULES BY NATIONAL COMPETITION AUTHORITIES

2. The European Competition Network ('ECN')

Generally.   **15.005**
Fn 13 See also the ECN's Report on Investigative Powers and Report on
Decision-Making Powers, both of 31 October 2012, which contain a com-
parative analysis of the enforcement powers conferred on NCAs in different
Member States, and identify areas of divergence; available on the DG Comp
website.

Competence to adopt decisions. The Court of Justice confirmed in Case   **15.010**
C-681/11 *Schenker*, judgment of 18 June 2013, [2013] 5 CMLR 831 that Article 5
of Regulation 1/2003 does not require Member States to establish conditions of
intention or negligence for the imposition of a fine, although if they do so then
those conditions must be at least as stringent as those in Article 23 of Regulation
1/2003: paras 35–36 (ie the undertaking must show that it could not have been
aware of the anti-competitive nature of its conduct). It also confirmed that although
Article 5 does not expressly provide a power for NCAs to declare that an infringement has occurred without imposing a fine, it does not exclude that power and
if the undertaking concerned has participated in a leniency programme then the
NCA may confine its decision to a finding that an infringement occurred, without
imposing a fine.

3. Cooperation between Members of the ECN in the Application of the Competition Rules

(a) Avoidance of multiple proceedings

(i) Principles of case allocation

15.014 Notification of proceedings.
Fn 46 As at 30 September 2013, 1,657 investigations had been notified by NCAs through the ECN. The five leading NCAs in terms of numbers of cases notified remained as stated in the main text.

(iv) Parallel and multiple proceedings

15.022 Coordinated investigations by NCAs and the Commission.
Fn 70 The Commission's decisions in COMP/39847 *E-books*, decisions of 12 December 2012 (OJ 2012 C283/7) and of 25 July 2013 (Press Release IP/13/746 (25 July 2013)) accepting commitments from five publishing companies, and Apple, considered the sale of e-books *inter alia* in the UK.

(e) Ongoing liaison on policy and proceedings

15.041 Subsequent liaison in a case being dealt with by an NCA.
Fn 141 As of 30 September 2013, 690 envisaged NCA decisions had been notified to the ECN. The leading NCAs in terms of numbers of cases dealt with remained as stated in the main text.

4. Cooperation between the Commission and National Courts

15.047 Transmission of information by the Commission. On 22 July 2013, the Council adopted Regulation 734/2013, amending Regulation 659/99 (the Procedural Regulation), OJ 2013 L204/15, as a result of which the Commission may now provide information in its possession, or its opinion, to national courts applying the EU rules on State aid, Articles 107 and 108 TFEU: see Article 23a of Regulation 659/99 as amended.

15.052 Commission as a party to proceedings before a national court. In Case C-199/11 *Europese Gemeenschap v Otis*, judgment of 6 November 2012, [2013] 4 CMLR 141 the Court of Justice confirmed that the Commission can appear as a claimant in proceedings in a Member State court, in order to seek damages for losses the EU institutions have suffered as a result of a breach of competition law. The Court was asked whether it was compatible with Article 47 of the Charter of Fundamental Rights for the Commission to bring an action for damages in the courts of a Member State where it would be relying on its own infringement deci-sion to establish liability, and Article 16(1) of Regulation 1/2003 would prevent the defendant from contesting the decision. It held that the Commission has authority to appear in Member State proceedings in these circumstances, and that the defend-ant's rights under Article 47 of the Charter are adequately protected by its right to appeal the Commission's decision in the European Courts under Article 263 TFEU, and its right to contest causation and damages in the Member State court.

Effect of a Commission investigation on a national court. 15.053
Fn 182 Recent examples of the High Court exercising its discretion whether to allow national proceedings to progress include *Secretary of State for Health v Servier* [2012] EWHC 2761 (Ch) (Henderson J.), staying proceedings until after the oral hearing before the Commission in COMP/39612 *Perindopril (Servier)*, but refusing to extend the stay until a decision was issued following the oral hearing; and *Infederation v Google* [2013] EWHC 2295 (Ch) (Roth J.), refusing a stay other than on one issue, and otherwise ordering staged disclosure while the Commission investigation in COMP/39740 *Google* is ongoing.

5. Convergence and Consistency in the Application of the Competition Rules

(a) Parallel application of EU and national competition law

Generally. The Commission has proposed a Directive on certain rules 15.055 governing actions for damages under national law for infringements of the competition law provisions of the Member States and of the European Union (COM(2013) 404 final, COD 2013/0185) ('Draft Damages Directive'), issued on 16 June 2013, which includes a proposal that where a NCA has taken a decision finding an infringement of either EU or national competition laws, the national courts are also bound not to take a decision running counter to it. If adopted, the proposal will make NCA infringement decisions binding upon national courts in the same way that Commission infringement decisions are binding under Article 16 of Regulation 1/2003. See Article 9 of the Draft Damages Directive.

(b) The convergence rule

The convergence rule and Article 101. 15.058
Fn 195 The Court of Justice in Case C-226/11 *Expedia Inc*, judgment of 13 December 2012, [2013] 4 CMLR 439, para 31, confirmed that although NCAs may take account of the market share thresholds set by the Commission's *De Minimis* Notice when determining whether an agreement has an appreciable effect on competition, they are not required to do so.

(c) **Consistency with decisions of ECN members**

15.064   **The effect of an appeal against a Commission decision.**

Fn 209   Further examples include: *WM Morrison Supermarkets v Mastercard & Ors* [2013] EWHC 1071 (Comm), applying *National Grid Electricity Transmission v ABB and others* [2009] EWHC 1326 and refusing to stay proceedings that were brought in reliance on the Commission decision on multilateral interchange fees (see footnote 68 in the main text); and *CDC Project 14 v Shell & Ors*, judgment of the District Court of the Hague of 1 May 2013, Case No C/09/414499/HA ZA 12-293, refusing to stay proceedings before pleadings had closed in a claim brought in reliance on COMP/39181 *Candle Wax*, decision of 1 October 2008.

16

LITIGATING INFRINGEMENTS IN THE NATIONAL COURTS

2. Effectiveness and Equivalence of National Procedures

Examples of lack of effectiveness of domestic procedures. 16.011
Fn 42 The Court of Justice held in Case C-536/11 *Bundeswettbewerbsbehörde v Donau Chemie*, judgment of 6 June 2013, [2013] 5 CMLR 658 that where a potential damages claimant seeks access to documents which form part of the file in public law proceedings concerning the application of Article 101, it is incompatible with European law (in particular the principle of effectiveness) for such access to be made subject to the consent of the parties to those proceedings. A domestic rule to that effect would be liable to make it impossible or excessively difficult to protect the right to compensation conferred on parties adversely affected by an infringement of Article 101. It must be possible for a national court to balance the competing interests in each individual case, in order to determine whether access should be granted or not, in the same way as in respect of leniency materials following Case C-360/09 *Pfleiderer v Bundeskartellampt* [2011] ECR I-5161. See further paragraph 16.043, and update thereto, below.

3. Forum and Applicable Law

(a) Brussels Regulation and Lugano Convention

Foreign jurisdiction. 16.014
Fn 50 The 15th Edition of Collins (ed), *Dicey, Morris and Collins on The Conflict of Laws* (2012) is now available.

The Brussels I Regulation. A recast 'Brussels II Regulation' (Regulation 16.015
1215/2012 on jurisdiction and the recognition and enforcement of judgments in civil and commercial matters (recast), OJ 2012 L351/1) was adopted on 20 December 2012, in order to develop further the European area of justice by removing the remaining obstacles to the free movement of judicial decisions in line

with the principle of mutual recognition. It currently will apply to all of the EU Member States except for Denmark (Recital (41) Brussels II Regulation: the UK and Ireland have exercised their right to 'opt-in' to the measure, but Denmark has not). The main change from the Brussels I Regulation are:

(a) a provision conferring priority on the courts of a Member State in whose favour the parties to the dispute have concluded a jurisdiction agreement (Articles 31(2) and 31(3) Brussels II Regulation);

(b) the extension of the rules on jurisdiction to disputes involving non-EU defendants, including to situations where the same issue is pending before a court inside and outside the EU (Articles 33 and 34 Brussels II Regulation).

Brussels II will apply from 10 January 2015 (Article 81 Brussels II Regulation). Where judgments are handed down prior to that date, or instruments are drawn up or settlements are approved or concluded prior to that date, they will continue to be governed by Brussels I Regulation (Article 66(2) Brussels II Regulation). The references in the main text to the Brussels I Regulation will not be materially altered by the recast provisions in Brussels II.

16.021   **Matters relating to a contract or tort.**   The Landgericht Dortmund has referred to the Court of Justice a number of questions on the proper interpretation of the Brussels I Regulation in the context of a follow-on damages action involving defendants from several different Member States. It has asked where the 'harmful event' occurred for the purposes of Article 5(3); whether in these circumstances it is 'expedient' to hear the claims against all the defendants together under Article 6 (see paragraphs 16.023 et seq, and the updates thereto, below); and whether a jurisdiction or arbitration clause in a contract for the supply of goods is to be given effect if it excludes the jurisdiction that the court would otherwise have under Article 5(3) and/or Article 6. See Case C-352/13 *Cartel Damage Claims Hydrogen Peroxide (CDC) v Evonik Degussa and others*, not yet decided.

Fn 69 The 15th Edition of Collins (ed), *Dicey, Morris and Collins on The Conflict of Laws* (2012) is now available. The relevant paragraphs are now 11-285 et seq.

Fn 70 In *Bord Na Mona Horticulture v British Industries* [2012] EWHC 3346 (Comm), paras 85–86, the High Court (Flaux J.) considered the case to be one where it was difficult to say where the harmful event occurred, and could not be satisfied that it took place in England. The claimants could proceed only on the basis that they suffered damage in England.

Fn 71 On the application of the principle laid down in Case C-220/88 *Dumez France v Hessiche Landesbank (Helaba)* [1990] ECR I-49, para 22, to competition damages claims, see *Deutsche Bahn v Morgan Crucible* [2013] CAT 18; affirmed on appeal at [2013] EWCA Civ 1484 (permission to appeal refused in a reasoned judgment by two Lords Justices). The UK Competition Appeal Tribunal rejected the non-UK domiciled defendants' contention that, since many of the claimants' purchases from the defendants were allegedly indirect, the damage sustained was incapable of founding jurisdiction under Article 5(3). The Court of Appeal confirmed that that judgment was correct, and held that the defendants' contentions depended on a misreading of *Dumez*. Article 5(3) does not require that, in order to be a relevant connecting factor between a defendant and the putative jurisdiction, the harmful event must be one of which the claimant is an immediate victim. That would involve a search for a connecting factor between the claimant and the putative jurisdiction, rather than between the defendant and the putative jurisdiction, which is what Article 5(3) and the Brussels Regulation more generally is concerned with (para 20). The Court of Appeal referred (para 22) to the articulation of the principle by Advocate General Darmon in *Dumez*, para 52, that:

> 'the place where the damage occurs is, for indirect victims, the place where the initial damage manifested itself, in other words the place where the damage to the direct victim occurred.'

Fn 72 On the application of Case C-364/93 *Marinari v Lloyds Bank* [1995] ECR I-2719, to competition damages claims, see *Deutsche Bahn v Morgan Crucible* [2013] CAT 18, upheld on appeal at [2013] EWCA Civ 1484, discussed in the update to footnote 71 above. The Tribunal considered that in accepting jurisdiction it was not construing Article 5(3) in a manner that encompassed a situation where adverse consequences of a harmful event were felt elsewhere, as on the facts of that case the relevant damage for jurisdictional purposes was all sustained in England.

Fn 73 In *Bord Na Mona Horticulture v British Industries* [2012] EWHC 3346 (Comm), para 91, the High Court considered an argument based on the Court of Justice's judgment in Cases C-509/09 & C-161/10 *E-Date Advertising v X and Martinez v MGM*, judgment of 25 October 2011, [2012] 1 CMLR 163. It observed that, if it were relevant to consider the claimant's 'centre of interest' for the purposes of a claim for damages for breach of competition law, this is the place where the claimant is habitually resident, not the place where it made its purchases.

(b) Jurisdiction over defendants based outside the territory

Co-defendants. The Landgericht Dortmund has referred to the Court of Justice **16.023** a number of questions on the proper interpretation of the Brussels I Regulation in the context of a follow-on damages action involving defendants from several different Member States. It has asked where the 'harmful event' occurred for the purposes of Article 5(3) (see paragraph 16.021 of the main text, and the updates thereto, above); whether in these circumstances it is 'expedient' to hear the claims against all the defendants together under Article 6; and whether a jurisdiction or arbitration clause in a contract for the supply of goods is to be given effect if it excludes the jurisdiction that the court would otherwise have under Article 5(3) and/or Article 6. See Case C-352/13 *Cartel Damage Claims Hydrogen Peroxide (CDC) v Evonik Degussa and others*, not yet decided.

The Commission has observed, in its proposed Directive on certain rules governing actions for damages under national law for infringements of the competition law provisions of the Member States and of the European Union (COM(2013) 404 final, COD 2013/0185) ('Draft Damages Directive'), issued on 16 June 2013, that where actions are brought in different Member States by different claimants, they should also be considered to be 'related' within the meaning of Article 6(1) of the Brussels I Regulation (and Article 30 of the Brussels II Regulation: see the update to paragraph 6.015, above). See Recital (30) to the Draft Damages Directive.

Fn 82 In *Bord Na Mona Horticulture v British Polythene Industries* [2012] EWHC 3346 (Comm), paras 78–83, the High Court (Flaux J.) doubted whether the reasoning in Case C-103/05 *Reisch Montage* [2006] ECR I-6827 applies to cases where the action against the anchor defendant is substantively unsustainable rather than merely precluded as a matter of national procedural law.

16.026 **Declining jurisdiction.**
Fn 100 See also the English Court of Appeal's analysis in *Starlight Shipping Company v Allianz Marine & Aviation Versicherungs & Ors* [2012] EWCA Civ 1714, paras 41–49, where the court considered whether or not two actions were 'mirror images' of each other for the purpose of applying Article 27 of the Brussels I Regulation.

Fn 103 In *CDC Project 14 v Shell & Ors*, judgment of the District Court of the Hague of 1 May 2013, Case No C/09/414499/HA ZA 12-293, the Court refused to stay proceedings in the Netherlands under Article 28 before pleadings had closed, as it was not yet clear whether there was a risk of reaching a judgment that was irreconcilable with the judgment that might be reached in proceedings brought in England and Wales.

(c) **Choice of applicable law**

16.031 **Rome Convention and scope of applicable law.**
Fn 113 The 15th Edition of Collins (ed), *Dicey, Morris and Collins on The Conflict of Laws* (2012) is now available. The relevant part is Chapter 32.

4. Establishing the Existence of an Infringement

16.035 **Nature of the cause of action under Articles 101 and 102.** Although a claim for damages for breach of Article 101 or 102 has traditionally been characterised in English law as a claim in tort for breach of statutory duty, in *W H Newson*

Holding & Ors v IMI and Ors [2012] EWHC 3680 (Ch), the High Court (Roth J.) refused to strike out a claim brought under s 47A of the Competition Act 1998 for the tort unlawful means conspiracy, in circumstances where the follow-on claim (see paragraph 16.038, and the updates thereto, below) was based on a finding that Article 101 is infringed by an agreement that has as its object the prevention, restriction or distortion of competition. The Court of Appeal upheld the High Court's conclusion that such a cause of action is potentially available under s 47A, but considered that the Commission decision relied upon in that case did not contain findings of the requisite subjective intent to injure the particular claimants: *W H Newson Holding & Ors v IMI and Ors* [2013] EWCA Civ 1377.

The claimant's task. The Commission has proposed a Directive on certain **16.036** rules governing actions for damages under national law for infringements of the competition law provisions of the Member States and of the European Union (COM(2013) 404 final, COD 2013/0185) ('Draft Damages Directive'), issued on 16 June 2013, which includes a proposal that Member States shall ensure claimants are able to claim full compensation for harm they suffer as a result of breaches of national competition law as well as EU law: Article 2 of the Draft Damages Directive.

Follow-on actions: binding elements of the decision. The Commission has pro- **16.038** posed a Directive on certain rules governing actions for damages under national law for infringements of the competition law provisions of the Member States and of the European Union (COM(2013) 404 final, COD 2013/0185) ('Draft Damages Directive'), issued on 16 June 2013, which includes a proposal that where a NCA has taken a decision finding an infringement of either EU or national competition laws, the national courts are also bound not to take a decision running counter to it. If adopted, the proposal will make NCA 'infringement decisions' binding upon national courts, in the same way that Commission decisions are binding under Article 16 of Regulation 1/2003. See Articles 4(10) and 9 of the Draft Damages Directive.

Fn 132 See also *Bord Na Mona Horticulture v British Industries* [2012] EWHC 3346 (Comm), paras 42–43.

Fault. The Commission has proposed a Directive on certain rules governing **16.039** actions for damages under national law for infringements of the competition law provisions of the Member States and of the European Union (COM(2013) 404 final, COD 2013/0185) ('Draft Damages Directive'), issued on 16 June 2013. In line with the views it expressed in the White Paper on Damages Acts for Breach of the EU antitrust rules, discussed in the main text, the Commission has not proposed any provision that would relieve infringers from liability on grounds of absence of fault. Departing from its view in the White Paper, there is no proposal to relieve infringers from liability where they made an 'excusable error'.

Fn 138 The Court of Justice confirmed in Case C-681/11 *Schenker*, judgment of 18 June 2013, [2013] 5 CMLR 831 that if Member States do establish conditions of intention or negligence for the imposition of a fine, those conditions must be at least as stringent as those in Article 23 of Regulation 1/2003: paras 35–36. Disagreeing with Advocate General Kokott's Opinion of 28 February 2013, the Court held that reliance by an undertaking on legal advice or a previous NCA decision that its conduct was not contrary to EU competition law is not sufficient to show that an infringement was not committed intentionally or negligently. To avoid a finding that an infringement was committed intentionally or negligently an undertaking must show that it could not have been aware of the anti-competitive nature of its conduct. If an undertaking characterised its conduct wrongly in law, then it cannot show that it could not have been aware of the anti-competitive nature of its conduct: para 38.

16.040 **Access to evidence held by competition authorities.** The Commission has proposed a Directive on certain rules governing actions for damages under national law for infringements of the competition law provisions of the Member States and of the European Union (COM(2013) 404 final, COD 2013/0185) ('Draft Damages Directive'), issued on 16 June 2013, which includes significant proposals in respect of accessing evidence held by competition authorities. The main proposals are:

(a) a complete prohibition on disclosure of leniency corporate statements and settlement submissions: Articles 6(1) and 7(1)of the Draft Damages Directive;

(b) a temporary prohibition on disclosure of other information prepared for the purposes of proceedings before a competition authority, until after the proceedings are closed: Article 6(2) and 7(2) of the Draft Damages Directive.

These prohibitions are proposed to bind competition authorities, undertakings investigated for breach of competition law, and also other undertakings that have documents in their possession through access to the file during the course of the competition authority's investigation. The prohibitions are proposed in respect of documents/information relating to investigations by the Commission, as well as to investigations by national competition authorities.

16.041 **Request from the national court to the Commission.** The Commission has proposed a Directive on certain rules governing actions for damages under national law for infringements of the competition law provisions of the Member States and of the European Union (COM(2013) 404 final, COD 2013/0185) ('Draft Damages Directive'), issued on 16 June 2013, which includes significant proposals in respect of accessing evidence held by competition authorities: see the update to paragraph 16.040, above.

Fn 145 The General Court has suspended the Commission's decision to transmit the information, while the challenge is pending: Order of the President of 29 November 2012.

Material provided to NCAs under national leniency programmes. The **16.043** Court of Justice held in Case C-536/11 *Bundeswettbewerbsbehörde v Donau Chemie*, judgment of 6 June 2013, [2013] 5 CMLR 658 that where a potential damages claimant seeks access to documents which form part of the file in public law proceedings concerning the application of Article 101, it is incompatible with European law (in particular the principle of effectiveness) for such access to be made subject to the consent of the parties to those proceedings. A domestic rule to that effect would be liable to make it impossible or excessively difficult to protect the right to compensation conferred on parties adversely affected by an infringement of Article 101. It must be possible for a national court to balance the competing interests in each individual case, in order to determine whether access should be granted or not, in the same way as in respect of leniency materials following Case C-360/09 *Pfleiderer v Bundeskartellampt* [2011] ECR I-5161.

The Commission has proposed a Directive on certain rules governing actions for damages under national law for infringements of the competition law provisions of the Member States and of the European Union (COM(2013) 404 final, COD 2013/0185) ('Draft Damages Directive'), issued on 16 June 2013, which includes significant proposals in respect of accessing evidence held by competition authorities, and in particular in respect of accessing leniency materials: see the update to paragraph 16.040, above.

Fn 148 The Court of Justice held in Case C-536/11 *Bundeswettbewerbsbehörde v Donau Chemie*, judgment of 6 June 2013, [2013] 5 CMLR 658 that where a potential damages claimant seeks access to documents which form part of the file in public law proceedings concerning the application of Article 101, it is incompatible with European law (in particular the principle of effectiveness) for such access to be made subject to the consent of the parties to those proceedings. A domestic rule to that effect would be liable to make it impossible or excessively difficult to protect the right to compensation conferred on parties adversely affected by an infringement of Article 101. It must be possible for a national court to balance the competing interests in each individual case, in order to determine whether access should be granted or not, in the same way as in respect of leniency materials following Case C-360/09 *Pfleiderer v Bundeskartellampt* [2011] ECR I-5161.

Fn 149 The judgment in Case T-344/08 *EnBW Energie Baden-Württemberg v Commission*, judgment of 22 May 2012, is under appeal in Case C-365/12P, not yet decided.

16.044 **Material provided to the Commission under EU leniency programme.** The Commission has proposed a Directive on certain rules governing actions for damages under national law for infringements of the competition law provisions of the Member States and of the European Union (COM(2013) 404 final, COD 2013/0185) ('Draft Damages Directive'), issued on 16 June 2013, which includes significant proposals in respect of accessing evidence held by competition authorities, and in particular in respect of accessing leniency materials: see the update to paragraph 16.040, above.

16.046 **Regulation 1049/2001: exceptions to the obligation to disclose.** The General Court in Case T-380/08 *Netherlands v Commission*, judgment of 13 September 2013, held that if information was gathered for the purposes of investigating a potential breach of competition law, there is a presumption that that information will be within the exemptions provided in Article 4(2), first indent and third indent, of Regulation 1049/2001, as its disclosure would affect the integrity of the Commission's inspections, investigations and audits, and the undertakings' commercial interests (para 42). That presumption may be rebutted in any individual case, or may be outweighed by the public interest in disclosure (para 45). However, a victim's right to claim compensation for a breach of competition law is a private interest for these purposes, not a public interest. It is a matter for the court seised of a damages claim to decide what evidence is required, under the law applicable to the dispute, and to request the transmission of information by the Commission under Article 15(1) of Regulation 1/2003 if appropriate (paras 79 et seq).

16.047 **Regulation 1049/2001: obligation to examine individual documents requested.** In respect of paragraph 16.047(c) of the main text, the General Court in Case T-380/08 *Netherlands v Commission*, judgment of 13 September 2013, held that if information was gathered for the purposes of investigating a potential breach of competition law, there is a presumption that that information will be within the exemptions provided in Article 4(2), first indent and third indent, of Regulation 1049/2001, as its disclosure would affect the integrity of the Commission's investigations and the undertakings' commercial interests (para 42). That presumption may be rebutted in any individual case, or may be outweighed by the public interest in disclosure (para 45).

Fn 180 See also Case T-561/12 *Beninca v Commission*, judgment of 25 October 2013, in which the General Court confirmed that the Commission's internal documents prepared in the course of merger control proceedings may fall within the exception in Article 4(3) of Regulation 1049/2001. That exception will apply where the Commission's decision-making process may be prejudiced by disclosure of the document, and in particular in circumstances where its investigation has closed but its decision is under appeal and the possibility remains that it will be required to re-open its proceedings. The request was for disclosure of an internal

Commission memorandum which related to M.6166 *NYSE Euronext/Deutsche Börse* (1 February 2012), currently under appeal in Case T-175/12 *Deutsche Börse v Commission*, not yet decided.

5. Declarations of Invalidity

Effect on resulting agreements.   In *Deutsche Bank and others v Unitech Global* **16.054** *and another* [2013] EWHC 2793 (Comm), paras 25–33 the High Court has rejected the contention that the invalidity of a horizontal agreement can affect the validity of vertical, implementing agreements. Teare J. held that even if competition law was breached in the process by which the London Interbank Offered Rate (known as 'LIBOR') was set, and the 'horizontal' LIBOR agreements between the banks were void, that would not affect the validity of the 'vertical' credit and swap agreements which were based upon LIBOR. In particular, in para 30, Teare J. considered this approach to be consistent with the Court of Appeal's judgment in *Courage v Crehan* [1999] ECC 455.

6. Injunctive Relief

Development of English case law.   The Consumer Rights Bill 2013 proposes to **16.060** substitute an amended s 47A in the Competition Act 1998: cl 82 and Sch 7. The proposed amendment will enable the Competition Appeal Tribunal to grant injunctions, as well as the High Court: see para 4 of Sch 7, substituting a new s 47A(3)(c).

Mandatory injunctions.   In *Chemistree Homecare v Abbvie* [2013] EWHC **16.061** 264 (Ch), the High Court (Roth J.) refused an injunction as the claimant had failed to show there was a real prospect of success on either dominance or abuse, or that the balance of convenience supported granting the injunction (upheld in *Chemistree Homecare v Abbvie* [2013] EWCA Civ 1338, where the Court of Appeal agreed that dominance could not be established).

7. Actions for Damages

(a) Introduction

Guidance on quantification of damages.   The Commission has adopted a **16.064** Communication on quantifying harm in actions for damages based on breaches of Article 101 or 102 TFEU (COM(2013) 3440, OJ 2013 C167/19), and an accompanying Practical Guide (SWD(2013) 205) ('Quantification Guide'), alongside its proposal for a Directive on certain rules governing actions for damages under national law for infringements of the competition law provisions of the Member

States and of the European Union (COM(2013) 404 final, COD 2013/0185) ('Draft Damages Directive'), adopted on 16 June 2013 (see the update to paragraph 16.040, above). Updated paragraph references to the Quantification Guide are given in the updates to paragraphs 16.077 et seq, below.

16.065 **Consultation on collective redress.** On 11 June 2013 the Commission adopted a Recommendation on common principles for injunctive and compensatory collective redress mechanisms in the Member States concerning violations of rights granted under Union law, OJ 2013 L201/60. The particular recommendations are discussed in the update to paragraph 16.068, below. In the UK, the Consumer Rights Bill 2013 proposes to amend the Competition Act 1998 to provide for collective redress mechanisms: cl 82 and Sch 7, in particular see paras 5–12 of Sch 7.

(b) The potential parties to the suit

(i) Potential claimants

16.066 **Who can sue?** The Court of Justice confirmed in Case C-199/11 *Europese Gemeenschap v Otis*, judgment of 6 November 2012, [2013] 4 CMLR 141 that the Commission is not precluded from bringing a civil action in a Member State to seek to recover the damages it has suffered as a result of a breach of competition law. The Court was asked whether it was compatible with Article 47 of the Charter of Fundamental Rights for the Commission to bring an action for damages in the courts of a Member State where it would be relying on its own infringement decision to establish liability, and Article 16(1) of Regulation 1/2003 would prevent the defendant from contesting the decision. It held that the Commission has authority to appear in Member State proceedings in these circumstances, and that the defendant's rights under Article 47 of the Charter are adequately protected by its right to appeal the Commission's decision in the European Courts under Article 263 TFEU, and its right to contest causation and damage in the Member State court.

16.067 **Indirect purchasers.** The Commission has proposed a Directive on certain rules governing actions for damages under national law for infringements of the competition law provisions of the Member States and of the European Union (COM(2013) 404 final, COD 2013/0185) ('Draft Damages Directive'), issued on 16 June 2013, which includes a proposal that Member States should recognise a passing-on defence, save where it is legally impossible for the indirect purchasers or purchases further down the supply chain to claim compensation: see Article 12 of the Draft Damages Directive. The Commission's introductory comments on its proposed Article 12 observe that it is framed to address the particular problem of indirect purchasers being unable to claim because of national rules on causation, including rules on foreseeability and remoteness (see p17 of the proposal). The Draft Damages Directive also proposes that where a claim is brought by an indirect purchaser, the claimant should bear the burden of proving the loss was passed on to him: see Article 13 of the Draft Damages Directive.

Collective redress. On 11 June 2013 the Commission adopted a **16.068** Recommendation on common principles for injunctive and compensatory collective redress mechanisms in the Member States concerning violations of rights granted under Union law, OJ 2013 L201/60 ('the Collective Redress Recommendation'). The recommendations include:

(a) representative entities should not be confined to public bodies, but should include designated bodies: para 4;
(b) claimant parties should be constituted on an 'opt-in' basis, and persons should be able to join the claimant at any point prior to judgment on, or settlement of, the claim: paras 21 and 23, respectively;
(c) claimant parties should declare the source of their funding at the start of proceedings, and provision should be made to deal with third party funding: paras 14–16;
(d) collective alternative dispute resolution mechanisms should be available, and use of such mechanisms should be subject to the parties' consent: paras 25–26;
(d) the losing party should pay the legal costs of the winner, and provision should be made to ensure that lawyers' remuneration is not calculated in such a way that it creates incentives to litigate unnecessarily: paras 13 and 29–30.

In the UK, the Consumer Rights Bill 2013 proposes to amend the Competition Act 1998 to provide for collective redress mechanisms: cl 82 and Sch 7, in particular see paras 5–12 of Sch 7.

(c) Causation and quantum of loss

Causation. The Commission has proposed a Directive on certain rules govern- **16.074** ing actions for damages under national law for infringements of the competition law provisions of the Member States and of the European Union (COM(2013) 404 final, COD 2013/0185) ('Draft Damages Directive'), issued on 16 June 2013, which includes a proposal that Member States should apply a rebuttable presumption that an infringement of competition law caused harm: see Article 16(1) of the Draft Damages Directive.

Causation: loss of a chance. In *Albion Water v Dŵr Cymru Cyfyngedig* [2013] **16.075** CAT 6, paras 205–220 the UK Competition Appeal Tribunal awarded damages to Albion Water based on business that it would have tendered for, had Dŵr Cymru supplied it with an input product at a price that was not unfair and did not impose an unlawful margin squeeze. The Tribunal was satisfied in this case that the claimant would have had a substantial chance of winning the contract had it bid for it, and reduced the damages claimed by one third on account of the uncertainty as to whether it would in fact have won or not.

The Commission has proposed a Directive on certain rules governing actions for damages under national law for infringements of the competition law provisions of the Member States and of the European Union (COM(2013) 404 final, COD 2013/0185) ('Draft Damages Directive'), issued on 16 June 2013, which includes a proposal that Member States should ensure that claimants are able to claim 'full compensation' for the harm they have suffered, which includes loss of profits: see Articles 2 and 14 of the Draft Damages Directive.

16.077   **Assessing quantum: the draft Guidance Paper.**   The Commission has proposed a Directive on certain rules governing actions for damages under national law for infringements of the competition law provisions of the Member States and of the European Union (COM(2013) 404 final, COD 2013/0185) ('Draft Damages Directive'), issued on 16 June 2013, which includes a proposal that Member States should ensure that there is a rebuttable presumption that harm was caused by an infringement of competition law, and that the burden and level of proof required for the quantification of harm does not render the exercise of the claimant's right to compensation practically impossible or excessively difficult: see Article 16 of the Draft Damages Directive. It has also published a Communication on quantifying harm in actions for damages based on breaches of Article 101 or 102 TFEU (COM(2013) 3440, OJ 2013 C167/19), and an accompanying Practical Guide (SWD(2013) 205) ('Quantification Guide'). The references given in the main text to the draft Guidance Paper, should now be read as follows:

Fn 294 The reference to para 6 of the draft Guidance Paper should be read as para 6 of the Quantification Guide.

Fn 295 The reference to para 11 of the draft Guidance Paper should be read as paras 11–12 of the Quantification Guide.

Fn 296 The reference to para 17 of the draft Guidance Paper should be read as para 20 of the Quantification Guide.

Fn 297 The reference to para 25 of the draft Guidance Paper should be read as para 29 of the Quantification Guide. The Quantification Guide sets out at Section IV guidance on the choice of method.

16.078   **Comparator-based methods.**   The Commission has proposed a Directive on certain rules governing actions for damages under national law for infringements of the competition law provisions of the Member States and of the European Union (COM(2013) 404 final, COD 2013/0185) ('Draft Damages Directive'), issued on 16 June 2013, which includes a proposal that Member States should ensure that there is a rebuttable presumption that harm was caused by an infringement of competition law, and that the burden and level of proof required for the quantification of harm does not render the exercise of the claimant's right to compensation practically impossible or excessively difficult: see Article 16 of the Draft Damages Directive. It has also published a Communication on quantifying harm in actions for damages based on breaches of Article 101 or 102 TFEU (COM(2013) 3440, OJ 2013 C167/19), and an accompanying Practical Guide (SWD(2013) 205) ('Quantification Guide'). The Quantification Guide sets out comparator-based methods in Section 2(II), and references given in the main text to the draft Guidance Paper, should now be read as follows:

Fn 298 The reference to para 47 of the draft Guidance Paper should be read as para 53 of the Quantification Guide.

Fn 299 The reference to para 61 of the draft Guidance Paper should be read as para 67 of the Quantification Guide.

Fn 300 The discussion of regression analyses is at paras 69 et seq of the Quantification Guide.

Fn 301 The worked example of a comparator model in the hypothetical flour cartel is at paras 32 et seq.

The use of economic models. The Commission has proposed a Directive on cer- **16.079** tain rules governing actions for damages under national law for infringements of the competition law provisions of the Member States and of the European Union (COM(2013) 404 final, COD 2013/0185) ('Draft Damages Directive'), issued on 16 June 2013, which includes a proposal that Member States should ensure that there is a rebuttable presumption that harm was caused by an infringement of competition law, and that the burden and level of proof required for the quantification of harm does not render the exercise of the claimant's right to compensation practically impossible or excessively difficult: see Article 16 of the Draft Damages Directive. It has also published a Communication on quantifying harm in actions for damages based on breaches of Article 101 or 102 TFEU (COM(2013) 3440, OJ 2013 C167/19), and an accompanying Practical Guide (SWD(2013) 205) ('Quantification Guide'). The Quantification Guide sets out simulation modeling methods in Section 2(III)(A), and references given in the main text to the draft Guidance Paper, should now be read as follows:

Fn 302 The reference to para 88 of the draft Guidance Paper should be read as para 100 of the Quantification Guide.

Fn 303 The reference to para 92 of the draft Guidance Paper should be read as para 104 of the Quantification Guide.

Cost-based methods. The Commission has adopted a proposal for a Directive **16.080** on certain rules governing actions for damages under national law for infringements of the competition law provisions of the Member States and of the European Union (COM(2013) 404 final, COD 2013/0185) ('Draft Damages Directive'), adopted on 16 June 2013, which includes a proposal that Member States should ensure that there is a rebuttable presumption that harm was caused by an infringement of competition law, and that the burden and level of proof required for the quantification of harm does not render the exercise of the claimant's right to compensation practically impossible or excessively difficult: see Article 16 of the Draft Damages Directive. It has also published a Communication on quantifying harm in actions for damages based on breaches of Article 101 or 102 TFEU (COM(2013) 3440, OJ 2013 C167/19), and an accompanying Practical Guide (SWD(2013) 205) ('Quantification Guide'). The Quantification Guide sets out cost-based and finance-based modeling methods in Section 2(III)(B), and references given in the main text to the draft Guidance Paper, should now be read as follows:

Fn 304 The reference to para 94 of the draft Guidance Paper should be read as para 107 of the Quantification Guide.

16.081 **Prices inflated by cartel: examples in national courts.**
Fn 306 The UK Government has not pursued its suggestion that there should be a rebuttable presumption that loss has been suffered: paras 4.36–4.37 of the Government's Response to the consultation paper *Private Actions in Competition Law: A Consultation on Options for Reform* (January 2013). However, the Commission has proposed a Directive on certain rules governing actions for damages under national law for infringements of the competition law provisions of the Member States and of the European Union (COM(2013) 404 final, COD 2013/0185) ('Draft Damages Directive'), issued on 16 June 2013, which includes a proposal that Member States should ensure that there is a rebuttable presumption that harm was caused by an infringement of competition law: see Article 16(1) of the Draft Damages Directive.

16.082 **Prices inflated by cartels: the draft Guidance Paper.** The Commission has proposed a Directive on certain rules governing actions for damages under national law for infringements of the competition law provisions of the Member States and of the European Union (COM(2013) 404 final, COD 2013/0185) ('Draft Damages Directive'), issued on 16 June 2013, which includes a proposal that Member States should ensure that there is a rebuttable presumption that harm was caused by an infringement of competition law, and that the burden and level of proof required for the quantification of harm does not render the exercise of the claimant's right to compensation practically impossible or excessively difficult: see Article 16 of the Draft Damages Directive. It has also published a Communication on quantifying harm in actions for damages based on breaches of Article 101 or 102 TFEU (COM(2013) 3440, OJ 2013 C167/19), and an accompanying Practical Guide (SWD(2013) 205) ('Quantification Guide'). The Quantification Guide sets out guidance on quantifying the harm caused by cartels in Section 3, and references given in the main text to the draft Guidance Paper, should now be read as follows:

Fn 307 The reference to paras 120 et seq of the draft Guidance Paper should be read as paras 141 et seq of the Quantification Guide.

Fn 308 The reference to para 125 of the draft Guidance Paper should be read as para 145 of the Quantification Guide.

Losses arising from exclusionary conduct. The Commission has adopted pro-   **16.083**
posed a Directive on certain rules governing actions for damages under national law
for infringements of the competition law provisions of the Member States and of
the European Union (COM(2013) 404 final, COD 2013/0185) ('Draft Damages
Directive'), issued on 16 June 2013, which includes a proposal that Member States
should ensure that there is a rebuttable presumption that harm was caused by an
infringement of competition law, and that the burden and level of proof required
for the quantification of harm does not render the exercise of the claimant's right
to compensation practically impossible or excessively difficult: see Article 16 of the
Draft Damages Directive. It has also published a Communication on quantifying harm in actions for damages based on breaches of Article 101 or 102 TFEU
(COM(2013) 3440, OJ 2013 C167/19), and an accompanying Practical Guide
(SWD(2013) 205) ('Quantification Guide'). The Quantification Guide sets out
guidance on quantifying the harm caused by exclusionary conduct in Section 4,
and references given in the main text to the draft Guidance Paper, should now be
read as follows:

Fn 309 The reference to para 168 of the draft Guidance Paper should be read as para 188 of the Quantification Guide.

Losses arising from exclusionary conduct.   **16.083**
Fn 309 In *Albion Water v Dŵr Cymru Cyfyngedig* [2013] CAT 6 the UK
Competition Appeal Tribunal awarded damages for an unlawful margin squeeze
and unfair pricing based on a detailed calculation of what the claimant's costs of
supplying its product would have been, if it had been offered the input products
it needed at a non-abusive price, and what price it would have been able to sell its
product for. In particular, the Tribunal held that where a dominant undertaking
could have charged a range of prices, absent its unlawful conduct, the counterfactual should be constructed using a figure in the middle of the range of lawful
prices, not the highest that could lawfully have been charged: paras 69–71. The
Tribunal also used this counterfactual to work out what profits Albion had lost as
a result of having lost the chance to tender for additional customers (see the update
to paragraph 16.075, above).

Exemplary damages. In *Albion Water v Dŵr Cymru Cyfyngedig* [2013] CAT 6,   **16.085**
paras 286–355, the Tribunal declined to award exemplary damages, notwithstanding 'a conspicuous and reprehensible failure of corporate governance' (para 286).

'Passing-on' defence. The Commission has proposed a Directive on certain   **16.087**
rules governing actions for damages under national law for infringements of the
competition law provisions of the Member States and of the European Union
(COM(2013) 404 final, COD 2013/0185) ('Draft Damages Directive'), issued on

16 June 2013, which includes a proposal that Member States should recognise a passing-on defence, save where it is legally impossible for the indirect purchasers, or purchasers further down the supply chain, to claim compensation: see Article 12 of the Draft Damages Directive. The Commission has also proposed that Member States should ensure that their courts have the power to estimate which share of an overcharge was passed on, and that the burden and level of proof required for the quantification of harm does not render the exercise of the claimant's right to compensation practically impossible or excessively difficult: see Articles 13 and 16 of the Draft Damages Directive.

16.088 **Treatment of the passing-on defence in the Member States.** In the UK, the issues associated with the existence of a passing-on defence have also been noted by the Competition Appeal Tribunal in the context of a jurisdictional challenge under Article 5(3) of the Brussels I Regulation: see *Deutsche Bahn v Morgan Crucible* [2013] CAT 18, discussed in the update to paragraph 16.021, above.

16.089 **Passing on defence: the draft Guidance Paper.** The Commission has proposed a Directive on certain rules governing actions for damages under national law for infringements of the competition law provisions of the Member States and of the European Union (COM(2013) 404 final, COD 2013/0185) ('Draft Damages Directive'), issued on 16 June 2013, which includes a proposal that Member States should recognise a passing-on defence, save where it is legally impossible for the indirect purchasers, or purchasers further down the supply chain, to claim compensation: see Article 12 of the Draft Damages Directive. The Commission has also proposed that Member States should ensure that their courts have the power to estimate which share of an overcharge was passed on, and that the burden and level of proof required for the quantification of harm does not render the exercise of the claimant's right to compensation practically impossible or excessively difficult: see Articles 13 and 16 of the Draft Damages Directive. It has also published a Communication on quantifying harm in actions for damages based on breaches of Article 101 or 102 TFEU (COM(2013) 3440, OJ 2013 C167/19), and an accompanying Practical Guide (SWD(2013) 205) ('Quantification Guide'). The Quantification Guide sets out guidance on assessing the impact of pass-on in Section 3(II)(A)(3), and references given in the main text to the draft Guidance Paper, should now be read as follows:

Fn 347 The reference to para 143 of the draft Guidance Paper should be read as para 162 of the Quantification Guide.

Fn 348 The reference to paras 149 et seq of the draft Guidance Paper should be read as paras 168 et seq of the Quantification Guide.

Fn 349 The reference to para 155 of the draft Guidance Paper should be read as paras 175 et seq of the Quantification Guide.

(d) Limitation periods

Limitation period for bringing claims. The Commission has proposed a **16.090**
Directive on certain rules governing actions for damages under national law for
infringements of the competition law provisions of the Member States and of the
European Union (COM(2013) 404 final, COD 2013/0185) ('Draft Damages
Directive'), adopted on 16 June 2013, which includes a proposal that Member
States should ensure that their limitation periods for bringing private damages
actions should be at least five years, and that time should not begin to run until a
claimant has knowledge of, or can reasonably be expected to have knowledge of: the
infringing behaviour; its qualification as an infringement of Union or national
competition law; the harm caused to him; and the identity of the infringer: Article
10 of the Draft Damages Directive.

Limitation periods in follow-on actions. The Commission has proposed a **16.091**
Directive on certain rules governing actions for damages under national law for
infringements of the competition law provisions of the Member States and of the
European Union (COM(2013) 404 final, COD 2013/0185) ('Draft Damages
Directive'), adopted on 16 June 2013, which includes a proposal that Member
States shall ensure that their limitation periods for bringing private damages actions
should be at least five years, and that time should not begin to run until a claimant
has knowledge of, or can reasonably be expected to have knowledge of: the infringing behaviour; its qualification as an infringement of Union or national competition law; the harm caused to him; and the identity of the infringer: Article 10 of
the Draft Damages Directive. In addition, the Commission proposes that where a
competition authority investigates the behaviour in question, the limitation period
should be suspended until at least one year after the infringement decision has
become final or the proceedings are otherwise terminated: Article 10(5) of the
Draft Damages Directive.

In the UK, the Consumer Rights Bill 2013 proposes to amend the Competition
Act 1998 to provide for the essentially same limitation period to apply in the
Competition Appeal Tribunal as in the High Court, subject to any provision in the
Tribunal rules which defers the date on which time begins to run: cl 82 and Sch 7,
para 8, and in particular the proposed s 47E(7) which provides for the continued
application of the Tribunal rules.

17

STATE AIDS

1. Introduction

Legislative developments. In July 2013, the Council adopted Regulation **17.003** 733/2013, amending Regulation 994/98 (the Enabling Regulation) and increasing the categories of aid in respect of which the Commission is able to adopt block exemption regulations: OJ 2013 L217/28; see the update to paragraph 17.070, below. On the same day it adopted Regulation 734/2013, amending Regulation 659/99 (the Procedural Regulation), in particular increasing the Commission's powers to gather information in State aid cases: OJ 2013 L204/15; see the update to paragraph 17.075, below.

2. The Concept of an Aid

(a) An advantage

The test to be applied. In order to assess whether or not an undertaking has **17.010** received an advantage by reason of a State measure, the Commission is required to make a complete analysis of all the relevant elements of the State intervention and its context. In Case T-525/08 *Poste Italiane v Commission*, judgment of 13 September 2013, the General Court annulled a Commission decision finding that Poste Italiane had received an economic advantage from the interest rates that the Italian Treasury paid for funds deposited with it, which the Commission found were higher than the interest rate that a private borrower would be prepared to pay. The General Court held that for the purposes of determining whether the market economy investor principle was satisfied in relation to the interest payments received, the Commission should not have focused exclusively on the higher interest rate that Poste Italiane received, but should have looked at the State intervention as a whole, particularly at the fact that Poste Italiane was legally obliged to place the funds with the Treasury. The Commission had failed to consider the alternative rate of return that would have been available to Poste Italiane, had it been it free to pursue alternative investment strategies in the absence of that legal obligation to place the funds with the Treasury. Provided that the Treasury's interest rate did not exceed the rate of return available under such alternative investment strategies, no advantage would be conferred: see paras 66–68. It followed that the Commission had not established to the requisite legal standard that Poste Italiane had received an economic advantage.

An advantage does not arise where the State merely compensates an undertaking for the expropriation of its property, doing so at rates that do not exceed the market value of the property expropriated: SA/32225 *Expropriation compensation of Nedalco*, decision of 2 October 2013.

17.012 **The 'market economy investor' principle.**   In Case C-73/11P *Frucona Košice v Commission*, judgment of 24 January 2013, [2013] 2 CMLR 719, the Court of Justice held that the market economy investor principle can be relied on by the State to demonstrate that it is not conferring an advantage on an undertaking in financial difficulties where it allows the undertaking to enter arrangements for partial payment of its tax debts, rather than resorting to bankruptcy procedures.

Fn 69 In Case C-73/11P *Frucona Košice v Commission*, judgment of 24 January 2013, [2013] 2 CMLR 719, the Court of Justice overturned the General Court's judgment, and remitted the case, as the General Court had failed to consider what impact the duration of bankruptcy proceedings (and consequent delay in recovery) would have on a private creditor. Remitted case not yet decided. The Court of Justice dismissed the appeal in Case C-405/11P *Buczek Automotive v Commission*, judgment of 21 March 2013.

In SA/35131 *Intervention de la Wallonie en faveur de la Sonaca*, decision of 5 June 2013, the Commission accepted that the debt to equity conversion of a debt owed to the Walloon Region by a Belgian aeronautics company would not constitute State aid because a private investor would have been prepared to do likewise in the same circumstances.

Fn 72 See also SA/35378 *Financing of Berlin Brandenburg Airport*, decision of 19 December 2012, in which a capital injection of €1.2 billion by the State to enable the construction of an airport to be finalised would be made on terms that would be acceptable to a private investor operating under normal market conditions.

(b) Granted by a Member State or through State resources

17.018 **Imputability of the measure to the State.**
Fn 100 A further example is Case T-387/11 *Nitrogénművek Vegyipari Zrt (Hungarian Development Bank) v Commission*, judgment of 27 February 2013, paras 58–66.

State resources. In the *French vegetables* cases (Cases T-139/09 *France v* **17.019**
Commission, T-243/09 *Fédération de l'organisation économique fruits et légumes
(Fedecom) v Commission*, and T-328/09 *Producteurs de légumes de France v
Commission*, judgments of 27 September 2012), measures that were financed by
a combination of funds provided by a particular industrial institution, and funds
provided by way of voluntary contributions from farmers' organisations, still
involved the use of State resources in circumstances where the State was represented on the committees that decided how the money should be spent, such that
it was able to guide the use of the resources.

For an example of the application of Case C-345/02 *Pearle and Others* [2004]
ECR I-7139, discussed in the main text, see Case C-677/11 *Doux Élevage v
Ministère de l'Agriculture*, judgment of 30 May 2013. The Court of Justice considered a decision of the French Agriculture Ministry by which it extended, to
all traders in a particular economic sector, an agreement that required traders
to pay a compulsory levy to a trade organisation. The trade organisation was
neither part of, nor controlled by, the State, and carried out various represen-
tational and promotional activities to advance the interests of the sector. The
Court noted that the funds received by the organisation by way of the levy were
not State resources because they did not go through the State budget or any
other State body, and the State did not relinquish any of its own resources. It
held that as the State had no power to use the funds, or control how the organisation spent them, they could not be considered State resources: see paras 32
and 36 et seq.

'Granted directly or indirectly through State resources'. As to what is required **17.021**
to constitute 'a sufficiently direct connection between the measure in question and
the [State's] loss of revenue', in Joined Cases C-399/10P & C-401/10P *Bouygues
Télécom v Commission*, judgment of 19 March 2013, [2013] 3 CMLR 127, the
Court of Justice held that the State's offer of a shareholder loan could itself constitute State aid, at least where that offer and its public announcement advantaged the
recipient in terms of its economic position, even if the loan agreement was never
signed and the loan was never actually provided.

(e) **Affecting inter-State trade**

De minimis: **block exemption.** In March 2013 the Commission published for **17.027**
consultation a draft of a new general *de minimis* Regulation. The Commission is
not proposing any increase in the current *de minimis* ceiling of €200,000 over a
three year period. However, the draft proposes a new safe harbour provision for
loans below €1 million repayable within five years. It also proposes to strengthen
Member States' monitoring and reporting obligations in respect of *de minimis* aid.
The draft Regulation is available in the consultations section of the DG Comp
website.

(f) Particular applications

17.030 **Tax measures and levies.**
Fn 201 See also Case T-275/11 *TF1 v Commission*, judgment of 16 October 2013, in which the General Court held that, although there was a relationship between the State aid provided to a public service broadcaster by way of budgetary grants, and the introduction of two new taxes on advertising and electronic communications respectively, those taxes could not be regarded as an integral part of the aid measure because the revenue from the taxes was not hypothecated to the aid, and it did not impact directly on the amount of aid provided: see paras 65 and 81.

17.031 **Tax measures: differential taxation.** On the cancellation, or special rescheduling, of tax debt, see Case C-73/11 P *Frucona Košice v Commission*, judgment of 24 January 2013, [2013] 2 CMLR 719. Although the Court of Justice overturned the General Court's judgment and remitted the case, it accepted that in principle entering such an arrangement rather than invoking bankruptcy procedures could constitute a State aid, unless the State can demonstrate that a hypothetical 'market economy investor', if owed the same amount of money by that undertaking, would be prepared to do the same in pursuing his own commercial interests. Remitted case not yet decided.

Fn 205 In SA/25338 *Corporate tax exemption of Dutch public enterprises*, decision of 2 May 2013, the Commission formally asked the Netherlands under Article 108(1) to abolish its long-standing exemption of public undertakings from corporation tax, at least insofar as those undertakings engage in economic activities, as defined by EU law (such as publicly owned ports and airports). The Member State has accepted the Commission's request: OJ 2013 C204/11.

Fn 210 In SA/33726*Deferral of payment of the milk levy in Italy*, decision of 17 July 2013, OJ 2013 L309/40, the Commission found that Italy granted an unlawful State aid by adopting a law that granted milk producers a six-month deferral of the date on which they were due to pay to the Italian Government an instalment in respect of a levy that the State had paid to the EU budget on their behalf. The Commission concluded that the deferment was an unlawful aid, equivalent to an interest-free loan: paras 13, second indent, and 28.

17.033 **Tax measures: objective justification by the logic of the tax system.** In Case T-379/09 *Italy v Commission*, judgment of 13 September 2012, the General Court dismissed an argument by Italy that the 'logic of the system' of excise duties on diesel justified the laying down of a rate for diesel used for heating glasshouses that was lower than the rate provided for other users of diesel for agricultural purposes. The fact that diesel duties fell more heavily on glasshouse operators, ie high users of diesel, was a natural consequence of applying a tax to that commodity. To the extent that the lower rate was intended to 'level the playing field' between glasshouse growers and outdoor growers, this did not show that the lower rate was not a selective advantage, but was an argument that was relevant (if at all) to whether or not the lower rate was justified such that it might be authorised under Article 107(3).

If a State grants a tax exemption, the fact that there is a system of authorisation in place by which undertakings obtain the benefit of the exemption does not in itself make the tax exemption selective. However, in order to be justified, the degree of latitude granted to the authorities in deciding whether to grant the exemption or not must be limited to verifying whether the undertaking meets the conditions laid down in order to pursue an identifiable tax objective, and the criteria to be applied by those authorities must be inherent in the nature of the tax regime: Case C-6/12 *P Oy*, judgment of 18 July 2013, paras 23–24. The Court did not have sufficient information available to it to assess whether the Finnish tax rules at issue in that case (under which the tax authorities could grant individual authorisations for tax losses to be carried forwards into future tax years, in cases where companies had changed ownership, if special reasons were shown) were justified by the logic of the Finnish taxation scheme.

The provision of infrastructure. The Court of Justice in Case C-288/11P **17.037** *Mitteldeutsche Flughafen and Flughafen Leipzig-Halle v Commission*, judgment of 19 December 2012, [2013] 2 CMLR 483, paras 46 et seq, confirmed that an airport operator's construction of an additional runway at an existing airport could not be divorced from its economic activity of operating a passenger airport, but was to be treated as part of the costs that an airport operator would normally have to bear itself for the purpose of carrying out that activity. The UK Department for Communities and Local Government issued guidance following this judgment (document ERDF-GN-1-010), which is available on the 'ERDF: national guidance' section of the gov.uk website. The provision of public funds for infrastructure projects may, however, avoid constituting State aid if it can be structured in such a way as to exclude the possibility of any net advantage to the recipient: see, for example, the Commission decision in the *German incubators* case, OJ 2005 L295/44.

In July 2013 the Commission published for consultation a draft of revised guidelines on State aid to airports and airlines. The revised draft sets out the conditions for the compatibility of investment aid and operating aid to airports and for start-up aid to airlines. It also explains the application of the market economy operator principle to the public funding of airports, and the Commission's approach to assessing financial relationships between airports and airlines. The draft would provide, for the first time, for the grant of investment aid for airports (with fewer than 5 million passengers per year), and the grant of operating aid to small airports (with fewer than 3 million passengers) for a transitional period of up to 10 years. The new guidelines are expected to be adopted at the beginning of 2014. The draft is available on the consultations section of the DG COMP website; see also Press Release IP/13/644 (3 July 2013).

3. Aids that are Compatible with the Internal Market

17.041 **Article 107(2)(b)—Disasters and exceptional occurrences.**
Fn 267 See also Case SA/35482 *Actions urgentes en faveur des populations tou-chées par les séismes* (19 December 2012), in which the Commission relied on Article 107(2)(b) to authorise an aid scheme worth €2.66 billion to support the recovery of the Italian agricultural sector from the damage caused by the earthquakes of May 2012.

4. Aids that may be Compatible with the Internal Market

(a) Generally

17.044 **The exercise of the Commission's discretion.**
Fn 289 See also SA/28599 *Aid for the deployment of digital terrestrial television – Spain* (19 June 2013).

Fn 294 The appeal against the General Court's judgment in Cases T-394/08, etc, *Regione autonomadella Sardegna v Commission* [2011] ECR II-6255 was dismissed by the Court of Justice in C-630/11P *HGA v Commission*, judgment of 13 June 2013.

See also Case SA/33984 *Green Investment Bank* (17 October 2012), in which the Commission was asked to approve the provision of State resources to establish a bank that would make available sources of credit or investment finance that the market has so far failed to make available for particular categories of projects or borrowers. The Commission authorised the aid to the bank, but did not, at the same time, authorise aids to any of the downstream recipients of the loans and investments that the bank will make, requiring instead that the State aid compatibility of those loans be assessed on a case-by-case basis. In addition, it considered that the arrangements must not be indefinite, but must lapse once a market in the relevant form of loans or investments has been created.

(b) Article 107(3)(a)

17.048 **Guidelines on national regional aid: Article 107(3)(a) and (c).** On 19 June 2013 the Commission adopted new Guidelines on regional State aid for 2014–2020, OJ 2013 C209/1 ('the 2014–2020 Guidelines'). These prolong the existing Guidelines on National Regional Aid for 2007–2013 until 30 June 2014, after which the new Guidelines will come into effect: paras 186 et seq of the 2014–2020 Guidelines. In broad terms, the 2012–2020 Guidelines will focus the Commission's resources on the larger regional aid measures, and on aid for investments by larger enterprises in the more developed of the assisted areas.

Areas eligible for regional aid.   On 19 June 2013 the Commission adopted new   **17.050**
Guidelines on regional State aid for 2014–2020, OJ 2013 C209/1 ('the 2014–2020
Guidelines'). These prolong the existing Guidelines on National Regional Aid
for 2007–2013 until 30 June 2014, after which the new Guidelines will come into
effect: paras 186 et seq of the 2014–2020 Guidelines. The 2014–2020 Guidelines will
increase the proportion of the EU population living in areas eligible for regional aid, to
47.2 per cent: para 148 and footnote 52 of the 2014–2020 Guidelines. A safety net is
also provided, to ensure that no Member State loses more than 50 per cent of its entitlement under the 2007–2013 Guidelines: paras 163–166 of the 2014–2020 Guidelines.

Disadvantaged regions.   On 19 June 2013 the Commission adopted new   **17.051**
Guidelines on regional State aid for 2014–2020, OJ 2013 C209/1 ('the 2014–2020
Guidelines'). These prolong the existing Guidelines on National Regional Aid for
2007–2013 until 30 June 2014, after which the new Guidelines will come into
effect: paras 186 et seq of the 2014–2020 Guidelines.

Areas entitled to aid at lower rates under Article 103(3)(c).   On 19 June 2013   **17.052**
the Commission adopted new Guidelines on regional State aid for 2014–2020, OJ
2013 C209/1 ('the 2014–2020 Guidelines'). These prolong the existing Guidelines
on National Regional Aid for 2007–2013 until 30 June 2014, after which the new
Guidelines will come into effect: paras 186 et seq of the 2014–2020 Guidelines.

Other aspects of entitlement to regional aid.   On 19 June 2013 the Commission   **17.053**
adopted new Guidelines on regional State aid for 2014–2020, OJ 2013 C209/1
('the 2014–2020 Guidelines'). These prolong the existing Guidelines on National
Regional Aid for 2007–2013 until 30 June 2014, after which the new Guidelines
will come into effect: paras 186 et seq of the 2014–2020 Guidelines.

(c) Article 107(3)(b)

Temporary measures following the 2008 financial crisis.   **17.057**
Fn 325 The most recent overview of national State aid measures adopted in
response to the financial and economic crisis is Commission MEMO/13/337 (16
April 2013).

(d) Article 107(3)(c)

Guidelines and rules on sectoral aid.   **17.062**
Fn 348 Following the expiry of the Commission Communication on certain legal
aspects relating to cinematographic and other audiovisual works, OJ 2002 C43/6,
on 13 November 2013 the Commission adopted a new Communication on State
aid for films and other audiovisual works: OJ 2013 C332/1.

Fn 349 On 26 January 2013 the Commission published new EU Guidelines for
the application of State aid rules in relation to the rapid deployment of broadband

networks: OJ 2013 C25/1. The new guidelines came into force from 27 January 2013, and will be applied to all decisions taken after that date in respect of notified aid, including aids granted and notified prior to that date (para 87 of the Guidelines), and in respect of unlawful aid granted after that date (para 88 of the Guidelines). The 2009 guidelines will still apply to unlawful aid granted while they were in force.

Fn 350 For an example of a case in which the Protocol was considered by the General Court, see Case T-520/09 *TF1 v Commission*, judgment of 10 July 2012.

Fn 358 In July 2013 the Commission published for consultation a draft of new guidelines on State aid to airports and airlines. The draft guidelines set out the principles by reference to which the Commission may authorise the provision of public financing to airlines for launching a new route, or a new schedule involving more frequent services, which increases the connectivity of an airport with fewer than 3 million passengers per year and serving a relatively less well connected region of the EU. The draft guidelines are available on the consultations section of the DG Comp website; see also Press Release IP/13/644 (3 July 2013).

Fn 369 In December 2012 the Commission published a new Communication on Short-term Export-credit Insurance: OJ 2012 C392/1. This Communication replaces the previous Communication and applies from 1 January 2013 until 31 December 2018.

17.064 **Aid for rescuing and restructuring firms in difficulty.**
Fn 370 On 5 November 2013 the Commission published for consultation a draft of new Guidelines on State aid for rescuing and restructuring non-financial undertakings in difficulty. The draft guidelines are available on the consultations section of the DG Comp website; see also Press Release IP/13/1037 (5 November 2013). In the meantime, the Commission has prolonged the Guidelines on State aid for rescuing and restructuring firms in difficulty, OJ 2004 C244/2, while it continues to develop the revised guidelines: Press Release IP/12/1042 (28 September 2012).

Fn 372 For an example of the application of this provision, see Case T-209/11 *MB System v Commission*, judgment of 3 July 2013.

(f) **Aid authorised by the Council**

Authorisation by the Council: Article 107(3)(e).
17.068 **Fn 394** The appeal in Case C-167/11P *Cantierenavale De Poli v Commission*, was dismissed by Order of 22 March 2012. The appeal in Case C-200/11P *Italy v Commission*, was also dismissed by Order of 22 March 2012.

17.070 **The Enabling Regulation, and the General Block Exemption Regulation.** On 22 July 2013, the Council adopted Regulation 733/2013, amending Regulation 994/98 (the Enabling Regulation): OJ 2013 L217/28. The amended Regulation increases the Commission's power to adopt block exemption regulations, so as to cover additional categories of aid including:

(a) culture and heritage conservation;
(b) making good the damage caused by natural disasters;
(c) making good the damage caused by certain adverse weather conditions in fisheries;
(d) forestry;
(e) the promotion of certain food products;
(f) conservation of marine and freshwater biological resources;
(g) sports;
(h) residents of remote regions for transport, when such aid has a social character and does not discriminate as to the identity of the carrier;
(i) certain broadband infrastructure;
(j) infrastructure in support of the objectives listed in the amended Regulation and in support of other objectives of common interest, in particular the Europe 2020 objectives.

These new categories of aid are areas where the Commission has acquired solid case experience and where there is limited potential distortion of competition: see Press Release IP/13/728 (23 July 2013).

Fn 404 In September 2012 the Commission published detailed guidance on the practical application of the General Block Exemption Regulation, in the form of answers to 'frequently asked questions', which is available in the State Aid section of the DG Comp website.

(g) Article 106(2)

Exemptions for services of general economic interest: Article 106(2). Although **17.071** Member States have a broad discretion as to which services they recognise as services of general economic interest (SGEI), the General Court held in T-79/10 *Colt Télécommunications France v Commission*, judgment of 16 September 2013 that they must nonetheless be able to demonstrate the justification for considering the service in question a SGEI, and that there is a market failure justifying State intervention (ie that the service would otherwise either not be provided at all, or would not be provided under the same conditions as respects price or quality): paras 119–120 & 149 et seq.

For a further example of a case in which the General Court found that the Commission did not have sufficient information to approve aid under Article 106(2) without opening a formal investigation, see Case T-137/10 *Coordination bruxelloise d'Institutions sociales et de santé ('CBI') v Commission*, judgment of 7 November 2012, in which the General Court annulled the Commission decision in Case NN54/2009 approving aid to public hospitals in Belgium.

17.073 **SGEI Communication, Article 106(2) Framework and Article 106(2) Decision.** In respect of the note in the main text that the EU Framework for State aid in the form of public service compensation (the Article 106(2) Framework) and Decision 2012/21 (the Article 106(2) Decision) require that there must be mechanisms for ensuring that the undertaking is not over-compensated, see for example SA/33037 *Retroactive compensation of SIMET SpA for public transport services provided between 1987 and 2003* (2 October 2013), in which the Commission found the provision of monetary compensation to a bus service operator could not be regarded as permissible compensation for carrying out an SGEI as (a) the parameters for calculating the amount of the compensation were not established in advance; and (b) the possibility of over-compensation could not be ruled out, as it was not possible to establish the net costs of providing the services because the operator was not implementing a separate accounting method capable of identifying those costs (final decision not yet published, but see paras 40–41 of the Commission's letter opening an investigation under Article 108(2), OJ 2013 C216/45).

Fn 417 The Commission has issued a new Staff Working Document, in April 2013 (SWD(2013) 53/final 2, '*Guide to the application of the European Union rules on state aid, public procurement and the internal market to services of general economic interest, and in particular to social services of general interest*', which is available on the State aid section of the DG Comp website.

Fn 421 See also Case SA/33989 *Poste Italiane*, decision of 21 November 2012.

5. Supervision under Article 108

17.075 **Procedures under Article 108 and Regulation 659/1999.** On 22 July 2013, the Council adopted Regulation 734/2013, amending Regulation 659/99 (the Procedural Regulation): OJ 2013 L204/15. The main amendments include:

(a) Powers for the Commission to request information from Member States other than the notifying Member State, or from an undertaking or association of undertakings, in circumstances where the information provided to it by the notifying Member State is not sufficient: Article 6a of Regulation 659/99 as amended.

(b) Where the Commission requests information from an undertaking or association of undertakings, the power to impose fines and periodic penalty payments for the provision of incorrect or misleading information: Article 6b of Regulation 659/99 as amended.

(c) Clarification of the process for submitting a complaint to the Commission, in particular to provide that the Commission shall notify a complainant if it reaches the view that the facts and law put forward do not provide sufficient grounds to show, on the basis of a *prima facie* examination, the existence of unlawful aid or misuse of aid. The complainant is then to be provided with a period in which it may provide further comments. If it does not receive further comments, the Commission may treat the complaint as withdrawn: Article 20(2) of Regulation 659/99 as amended.

(d) Power for the Commission to conduct sector inquiries in the same way as in Article 101/102 cases: Article 20a of Regulation 659/99 as amended (see paragraph 13.021 and the update thereto on sector inquiries).

(e) Power for the Commission to transmit information in its possession, or opinions, to national courts in the same way as it does under Article 15 of Regulation 1/2003 in Article 101/102 cases: Article 23a of Regulation 659/99 as amended (see paragraph 15.047, and the update thereto on Article 15 of Regulation 1/2003).

The references in the main text to the Regulation 659/99 (the Procedural Regulation) will not be altered by the amendments, save where otherwise indicated in the update to the relevant paragraph.

(b) Notification of new aids

Time limit for review of new aid. **17.084**
Fn 475 The General Court judgment in Case T-79/10 *Colt Télécommunications France v Commission*, judgment of 16 September 2013, illustrates that the time taken by a Member State to submit a complete notification can impact significantly on the time taken by the Commission to review a new aid. In that case, France had notified the proposed aid measure in June 2008, but subsequently the Commission sent further information requests and it was not until France provided supplementary information in August 2009 that the Commission considered the notification to be complete. The Commission reached its decision within two months of that date. On appeal, the General Court held that the Commission's preliminary examination only commenced once it received the completed notification in August 2009 (para 50), and that it had therefore been completed within the required timeframe. The General Court also rejected a complaint that the length of the discussions between the Commission and France meant that the Commission should have opened a formal investigation under Article 108(2). The Commission enjoys a certain margin of discretion in determining whether or not a case presents 'serious difficulties' for the purposes of Article 108(2), and the mere fact that the Commission had initiated a dialogue with the French State does not in itself indicate there are such difficulties, nor did the number of requests sent by the Commission: paras 55–56 and 59. The Court did note that the content of discussions between the Commission and the notifying Member State during this phase of the proceedings may, in certain circumstances, reveal such difficulties: para 58. It found, however, that the content of the discussions in this case did not do so.

17.086 Preliminary examination of a notification.   In Case C-646/11P *Falles Fagligt Forbund (3F) v Commission*, judgment of 24 January 2013, para 32, the Court of Justice held that the fact that the Commission's preliminary examination has been of longer duration than two months is an indicator that the Commission may have had serious doubts as to the compatibility of the aid, but is not, of itself, sufficient to lead to a conclusion that the Commission was required to open the formal investigation procedure.

Fn 482 See also Case T-79/10 *Colt Télécommunications France v Commission*, judgment of 16 September 2013, discussed in the update to paragraph 17.085 and footnote 475, above.

(c) **The formal investigation procedure under Article 108(2)**

17.091 Final decision under Article 108(2).
Fn 510 The Court of Justice in Case C-288/11 *Mitteldeutsche Flughafen and Flughafen Leipzig-Halle v Commission*, judgment of 19 December 2012, [2013] 2 CMLR 483, dismissed the appeal against the General Court's judgment in Cases T-443&455/08 *Freistaat Sachsen and Land Sachsen-Anhalt v Commission*, judgment of 24 March 2011.

17.092 Conditional positive decisions.
Fn 511 The Court of Justice dismissed the appeal in Case C-287/12P *Ryanair v Commission*, judgment of 13 June 2013, against the General Court's judgment in Case T-123/09 *Ryanair v Commission*, judgment of 28 March 2012 (upholding the General Court's conclusion that the Commission had not given a condition clearance decision: see paras 67 et seq).

7. Unlawful Aid and Misuse of Aid

17.104 Recovery decision.
Fn 558 The appeal, on other grounds, against the General Court's judgment in Cases T-394/08, etc, *Regione autonomadella Sardegna v Commission* [2011] ECR II-6255 was dismissed by the Court of Justice in C-630/11P *HGA v Commission*, judgment of 13 June 2013.

17.109 Defences open to the Member State: absolute impossibility.   In Case SA/20829 *Scheme concerning the municipal real estate tax exemption granted to real estate used by non commercial entities for specific purposes*, decision of 19 December 2012, OJ 2013 L166/24, at paras 191 et seq, the Commission accepted that recovery may be impossible where there are significant difficulties in quantifying how much aid has been paid. It accepted that it would be impossible to recover aid granted by way of exemptions from municipal real estate taxes, where those exemptions had been found to be incompatible with State aid rules but only insofar as the relevant land/building was used for economic activities, because of the difficulties in assessing retrospectively the proportion of each property that was used for economic activities.

Fn 582 See also Case C-263/12 *Commission v Greece*, judgment of 17 October 2013, paras 34 et seq.

Request for information and information injunction. On 22 July 2013, the **17.100** Council adopted Regulation 734/2013, amending Regulation 659/99 (the Procedural Regulation): OJ 2013 L204/15. The amendments include, in particular, an expansion of the Commission's power to request information from other sources: see the update to paragraph 17.075, above.

8. Judicial Remedies

(a) National Courts

New aids (including alterations to existing aids). Advocate General Mengozzi **17.115** has suggested in his Opinion of 27 June 2013, in Case C-284/12 *Deutsche Lufthansa v Flughafen Frankfurt-Hahn*, not yet decided, that the national court of a Member State is bound to order the suspension of payments of aid in circumstances where the Commission has issued a decision under Article 108(2) formally to investigate that aid (para 32). He suggests also that the national court cannot refuse to order the recovery of payments already made, without having first referred to the Court of Justice of the European Union the question of whether the aid is lawful; however, the payments can be made into a blocked account, pending the resolution of the Commission's investigation, if national law permits such arrangements (para 44).

Enforcement of Commission decisions. In respect of Commission deci- **17.116** sions formally to investigate under Article 108(2), see the Opinion of Advocate General Mengozzi of 27 June 2013, in Case C-284/12 *Deutsche Lufthansa v Flughafen Frankfurt-Hahn*, not yet decided, discussed in the update to paragraph 17.115, above.

(b) The EU courts

(ii) Applicants before the EU Courts

Actions by the Commission. Where a Member State fails to take the neces- **17.119** sary action to recover unlawful State aid, the Commission may ultimately ask the Court of Justice to impose a fine. In Case C-610/10 *Commission v Spain*, judgment of 11 December 2012, the Court of Justice fined Spain €20 million for its long-standing failure to recover aid which had been granted to certain producers of stainless steel products and electrical appliances for use in the home. In addition, Spain was required to pay a daily fine of €50,000 for each further day for which it failed to comply with the Court's previous judgment ordering recovery of the aid. Spain's failure to fulfil its obligations had persisted for more than 10 years since the date of delivery of that judgment, and for more than 22 years since the date on which the relevant Commission decision was adopted.

17.122 **Challenge by complainants to refusal to open formal procedure.** For an example of the General Court conducting a review of a Commission decision not to open the formal procedure, see Case T-304/08 *Smurfit Kappa Group v Commission*, judgment of 10 July 2012. The General Court annulled a decision not to open the formal procedure, where that decision was based on a misapprehension that the Regional Aid Guidelines precluded the Commission from doing so in circumstances where the thresholds relating to market share and increase in production capacity were not exceeded.

Fn 681 The Court of Justice dismissed the appeal in Case C-615/11P *Commission v Ryanair*, judgment of 16 May 2013, against the General Court's judgment in Case T-442/07 *Ryanair v Commission* [2011] ECR II-333.

Fn 682 See also Case T-304/08 *Smurfit Kappa Group v Commission*, judgment of 10 July 2012.

Fn 686 The Court of Justice dismissed the appeal in Case C-646/11P *Falles Fagligt Forbund (3F) v Commission*, judgment of 24 January 2013; see in particular paras 32–36.

Challenge by complainants to decision following formal investigation.
17.123 **Fn 692** See also Case T-182/10 *AISCAT v Commission*, judgment of 15 January 2013.

17.126 **Lack of reasoning.**
Fn 707 The Court of Justice dismissed the appeal in Case C-405/11P *Buczek Automotive v Commission*, judgment of 21 March 2013.

(iii) The grounds of annulment

17.128 **Review of the exercise of the Commission's discretion.**
Fn 722 See also Case T-387/11 *Nitrogénművek Vegyipari Zrt (Hungarian Development Bank) v Commission*, judgment of 27 February 2013, para 25, where the General Court held that 'in order to establish that the Commission committed a manifest error in assessing the facts such as to justify the annulment of the contested decision, the evidence adduced by the applicant must be sufficient to make the factual assessments used in the decision at issue implausible'.

Fn 725 The Court of Justice upheld the appeal on other grounds in Case C-73/11P *Frucona Košice v Commission*, judgment of 24 January 2013, [2013] 2 CMLR 719.

(iv) Interim relief

Member States.   **17.132**

Fn 738 See also Case T-366/13R *France v Commission*, Order of 29 August 2013, in which the General Court refused France's application for interim measures, seeking to suspend the effect of the Commission's order requiring the recovery of unlawful aid from the shipping company SNCM. France had argued that implementation of the recovery order would entail the liquidation of SNCM. The General Court considered, however, that France's interest as a Member State was in protecting general interests at a national level (para 25), whereas SNCM was able to protect its own interests by bringing proceedings in the national courts for the suspension of its obligation to repay the aid, on the ground that repayment would be likely to cause it to suffer serious irreparable harm (paras 44 et seq).

Lightning Source UK Ltd.
Milton Keynes UK
UKOW06f1206080414

229592UK00001B/1/P